SUCCESSFUL INVESTING IN AN AGE OF ENVY

Other books by Gary North—

Marx's Religion of Revolution, 1968
An Introduction to Christian Economics, 1973
None Dare Call It Witchcraft, 1976
How You Can Profit from the Coming Price Controls, 1977
Unconditional Surrender—God's Program for Victory, 1981
The Dominion Covenant: Genesis, 1982

SUCCESSFUL INVESTING IN AN AGE OF ENVY

Gary North

Steadman Press
1982

Published by
Steadman Press
P.O. Box 8204
Ft. Worth TX 76112

This book is dedicated to the economist whose writings:
1. Deserve a Nobel Prize for clarity
2. Convinced me to buy silver coins in 1963
3. Introduced me to the critique of envy

Murray N. Rothbard

TABLE OF CONTENTS

INTRODUCTION

Over the past few years, I have written numerous articles for my bi-weekly newsletter, *Remnant Review*. Because many of these have dealt with basic economic theory, and strategies for investing and personal survival that grow out of economic theory, I have decided to rewrite them, update them, and republish them. This book is therefore a compilation of older essays, but I find that they are still as relevant as when I wrote them. In some cases, they are more relevant.

By putting them into a book format, I make available the information in a more digestable form. Also, the index offers readers more rapid access to the specifics. The cost of getting this information to readers is also much less, given the efficiencies of modern book production.

There is some repetition in the book because certain ideas appeared in my newsletter on several occasions over a period of seven years. Nevertheless, some repetition is desirable if it drives home an important point into the memory of readers. I have always tried to keep from repeating myself too often, which is another reason for reprinting these essays. Subscribers to *Remnant Review* who have come on board recently probably don't understand fully what my economic presuppositions are, and what strategies I have recommended in the past. The book will give new subscribers this perspective, and I will spare old-time subscribers the misery of going over familiar ground.

Unlike so many "How to Profit" books, this one focuses on underlying trends in the modern economy that tend to be ignored by more conventional economists and even newsletter writers. I am convinced that these contemporary presuppositions concerning the nature of government, the economy, and the legitimacy of wealth are crucially important. They are important for a proper understanding of the drift which has overtaken us politically and economically. But they are also important in providing us with confidence in what we are doing with our capital. I cannot stress this too much. We are taking steps in our personal and business lives that will be resented by others in the future, should others find out what we have done. It is imperative that every success-oriented investor have complete confidence in what he is doing, and this includes moral confidence. If you know what has to be done, but you neglect doing it because you think it's somehow immoral, or mean, or hard-hearted toward others, then you might as well never have known what to do. If anything, it will be worse, since you will be second guessing yourself once these crises hit the economy. "Why didn't I do that?" you'll say to yourself a hundred times. This book will make it easier for you psychologically to pursue a course of action that will help you to survive a whole series of economic and social disruptions.

This book is a complement to my earlier compilation, *How You Can Profit from the Coming Price Controls.* There is some overlap, but not too much. The survival strategies I present in the price controls book are very specific. This book also has some specific recommendations—investment *tactics,* as I call them—but I am concentrating on investment *strategies* here. I focus on an *approach* to investing, a kind of world-and-life view that rests on certain assumptions about the modern economy, including modern voters and politicians. What I want my readers to have after finishing this book is a *comprehensive understanding* of where this economy is going and what can be done to hedge themselves against it. Too many investors are going about their program in an ad hoc, haphazard manner. Their investments are not integrated into a well-thought-out framework. In short, *too many investors have inconsistent investment portfolios.* If you read and understand this book, you should be able to know where the weaknesses are in your present investment program.

Each chapter is a self-contained unit, but each fits into a integrated whole. Step by step, you will be given the fundamentals of economic analysis, as these fundamentals apply to the real world. I really believe that a thorough reading of this book will make it possible for readers to make investment decisions confidently, knowing that they are following the basic rules of successful investing in an age of envy. You will become your own economic advisor, in effect. If the book increases your own personal confidence as you make key investment decisions, then it will have been worth the money, time, and effort spent in mastering these principles. Some of you will find that you have already taken the proper steps financially, but this book will give you better a understanding of what you have done, why it was right that you did it, and why you should not feel guilty when your decisions enable you to command resources in the future.

Guilt is a mental crippler, a source of emotional paralysis. This book is designed not only to provide you with accurate information concerning investing, but also the *proper attitude* toward financial success. If you do well, but needless guilt leads you to throw away your advantage, then your techinical expertise in the investment world will have profited you little. This book is a handbook of guilt-avoidance. It is a complement to David Chilton's important book, *Productive Christians in an Age of Guilt-Manipulators* (Box 8000, Tyler, TX: Institute for Christian Economics, 1981; $4.95). There are a lot of envious people in the world, and far too many religious specialists in guilt manipulation. You had better know how to defend yourself.

The Institute for Christian Economics is a tax-exempt, non-profit research organization. I'm the president. At the end of this book, there is an essay, "What is the ICE?" This explains the economic education program we have designed to help counter the effects of the religion of envy in our day. We publish several newsletters, books, position papers, tapes, and other materials. If you would like a free, six-month subscription to any (or all) of them, just write to the ICE and say that you bought and read *Successful Investing in an Age of Envy*.

Institute for Christian Economics
P. O. Box 8000
Tyler, TX 75711

For a free, two-month subscription to *Remnant Review*, see page 308.

Chapter 1

THE ECONOMICS OF ENVY

We are all the direct beneficiaries of the free market system. We have instant access to the largest, most developed wealth-delivery system in the history of man. This system offers us so many choices that we have all learned to screen out new information concerning our opportunities. How many television ads do we pay attention to, compared to those we ignore or instantly forget? How many pieces of "junk mail" do we receive daily? Probably the greatest proportion of our information-gathering efforts is spent in filtering out the bulk of the opportunities available.

The problem we are facing today is that millions of Americans are completely unaware of the way this market system works. They don't appreciate it, they don't understand what principles support it, and they are steadily adopting attitudes that, if expressed in human actions, will unquestionably compromise the ability of the market to continue its delivery of the goods.

Years ago, the economist Joseph Schumpeter wrote that capitalism will not fail because the system has failed to deliver the goods. On the contrary, it will be overthrown because it has *succeeded* so magnificently. As he wrote, "its very success undermines the social institutions which protect it..." (*Capitalism, Socialism, and Democracy*, p. 61). This is our problem today, and future disruptions in the world economy will bring these problems to the forefront.

Where is capitalism's constituency? The businessmen? Few of them really understand the system. Look how fast the executives in Detroit called for a Chrysler bail-out. I watched an interview of Henry Ford by Barbara Walters in 1980. Here was Ford, on prime time T. V., with a large audience, giving his criticism of our times. He complained that too many people hate capitalism. Hardly any of them understand it, he said. Barbara really isn't as silly as she sounds. She asked him if he thought a bail-out of Chrysler was legitimate. Well, he said, he didn't like Federal intervention, but maybe under some circumstances he might approve of it. Well, then, what should be done about the auto industry? she asked. Ford came up with a typical answer. The Federal government should pass a law requiring all foreign manufacturers of automobiles to set up plants in the U. S. They should be required by

1

law to build in the U. S. at least 75% of all cars they sell in the U. S. This, I suppose we are to conclude, is capitalist competition: requiring the Japanese to put up with the arrogance, incompetence, and coercion of the United Auto Workers. This also means that American consumers would have to buy higher priced cars made by American labor. This is Ford's version of the free market: the legislated restriction of consumer choice.

So what help can we expect from businessmen? When they get on national T. V., they come out for some Federal boondoggle that will benefit their industry. It's like the U. S. bicycle industry, which calls for restrictions on the imports of foreign bicycles, but no restrictions on foreign-made parts (which the American firms import). I think Leonard Read is correct: *they don't know the difference between freedom and coercion.* They really think it doesn't make that much difference.

I spoke at a meeting of the Young Presidents Organization back in 1972. This group is made up of men who have created multi-million dollar businesses before age 40. When I explained very carefully the difference between the market's production system and the government's bureaucratic system, and why the latter system infringes on human freedom, one of the listeners replied as follows: "Well, you're making it all a black-and-white question. It's really a lot of gray. We businessmen can make the government system just as productive as the free market, and we can make money while we're doing it!" That was the last time I bothered to speak to YPO. It was the second time I had had this same experience. In fact, I decided to go into business at that point, to get off the sawdust trail for non-profit organizations defending the market. It was too dangerous to invest 100% of my time on such a dead-end trail. Some time, yes, but not 100%. I remember my reply to him when he said, "It's not all black and white; it's really a lot of gray." I was my usual gentle self: "Yes, and I'll bet you've lost your children with that philosophy." He never replied. I guess he really had.

Then what about the children of the rich? Will they defend the market? Hardly. They are guilt-ridden. Their parents have taught them the logic of modern philosophical relativism, as that rich YPO operator had, when they have taught them anything. The kids are smart. They see self-interest masquerading as a social policy. Their teachers in the public schools, or the prestigious schools for the children of the rich, have given them the Marxist line about vested self-interest and social philosophy. They know what their parents are doing. So they come out feeling guilty about their own wealth. The kids became the "Mustang Maoists" of the late-1960's, or at best, the corporate socialists of the 1970's. Their parents send them to Harvard, or even worse, to Stanford. Or to State U. It doesn't make much difference. They send their children into the classrooms of the philosophical enemies of freedom, and they are so very surprised when their children become radicals after three semesters. That eternal line, which goes back to Aristophanes' play, *The Clouds*, is heard in household after household every Easter vacation: "Well, if that's what they're teaching you in college, you'd be better off going to work right now." That's quite true, but then the parents get out their checkbooks and send them right back. It would be too embarrassing at the club to admit that their child quit Stanford to become an auto mechanic. So the folks down at the club sit around and bemoan what's happening on campus—the campus that they're financing, and will continue to finance, until the system topples.

What we find, therefore, is that the free market, in and of itself, is incapable of creating its own intellectual defenders. Worse than this, the market subsidizes its enemies: the intellectuals, the professors, the publishers. Then the children of the capitalists join the army of capitalism's enemies. The defenders of capitalism cannot gain support from the Henry Fords of the world, who wind up financing the Ford Foundations of the world. And they seem so shocked when they find out that their beloved family foundation has been taken over by anti-market intellectuals. Surprise, surprise! *The businessmen prefer it this way*. Never forget this. That's what they created. If it's a question of financing a socialist who is an outspoken foe of the market, or a free market economist who points the finger at the businessman's sell-out of his own principles in calling for Federal intervention, the corporate leaders of today will put up with the socialists.

You think I'm exaggerating? Consider this. When Leonard Read established the Foundation for Economic Education in 1946, he had a rule: never take over $10,000 from any corporation in one year. Don't become known as the arm of a corporation. There were several firms that gave $10,000 back then. Today, there is not a single American corporation, other than private, one-man corporations, that pays FEE 10,000-1980's-purchasing-power dollars per year. The corporate committees have screened out the donations. They look at the Establishment's various foundation rating services, see that FEE is not highly rated (ideology at work), and they don't send in the money. The economic socialists and Keynesians have taken over the rating services, and in this way have screened the giving of corporations. They wouldn't think of censoring anyone; they just give ratings!

We are at a crossroads today. The 1980's will be the decade of the great transformation of American thought. The Keynesians are at the end of the road. The economy is coming unglued. Keynesianism promised permanent glue, even epoxy cement, for the economy. When the system begins to crumble, a lot of groups are going to scramble to pick up the pieces and reshape them according to some very strange economic blueprints. *Our task is to get our blueprint on the table first.* It won't be easy.

Envy

This is perhaps the least understood concept in modern social thought. Practically nothing has been written about it, yet it is at the very heart of modern political economy. That's why you had better understand it and begin to restructure your life style in terms of it.

We normally think of envy as jealousy. But I'm not talking about jealousy, which is related to envy. Jealousy is the same as covetousness. Someone looks at what you own and says to himself, "I wish I had that. If I could get my hands on it, I'd be happy. Maybe I can steal it. Maybe I can get someone to loan me the money to buy it. Maybe I can get Congress to confiscate it and give it to me."

Jealousy is a commonly understood phenomenon. But it's not nearly so insidious as envy. Envy is different. It runs along these lines: "He's got that. I don't have it. I'd like it, but I know I can never get it. Nobody ought to be allowed to have it if everyone can't have one just like it. I'll destroy it. I'll have the government make it illegal to own one. I'll make sure nobody ever has one like it again."

The ugly girl cannot legislate good looks in her favor. She may resent the good looking girl, but nothing she can do will ever get those good looks transferred to her. Jealousy is not applicable in this case. Envy is the problem. How does the ugly girl vent her wrath? By throwing acid in the face of the better looking girl. By hacking her to pieces. This is exactly what happened to a girl at Warren Wilson College in North Carolina in 1959. Her unattractive ex-roommate literally hacked her face up with a hatchet. Why? At the first hearing, she claimed it was envy that drove her to do it. There's even a book about this sort of envy: *Facial Justice*, published in Britain in 1960. It's a *1984*-type book about a future society in which beauty is made illegal, and good looking people are required by law to get face lifts (face drops?) to make them appear average.

Here's another crime that is almost always associated with envy: *arson*. The arsonist resents the prosperity of others. He gets joy from the fire, true enough. But the old question is "Why?" He likes pretty lights? He likes to see flames? He can see flames in his fireplace. Yet how many times have you ever heard anyone refer to the arsonist as envy-dominated? The arsonist gets joy from seeing other people's property, hopes, and visible signs of success being consumed by the flames.

Here's another envy-created phenomenon: *terrorism*. Do you really believe that the professional terrorist thinks that any given act of terror will alter the features of the society, bringing in peace on earth? Of course not. The terrorist uses terror to create a loss of faith in the existing order, or to strike out at the leaders of a political order. The act of terrorism is useful only if your political philosophy makes the destruction of society a blessing in itself. If you resent signs of other men's economic superiority, or social superiority, then terrorism is one way of striking out at what you resent. It's not that the terrorist believes that his acts of violence are furthering a better society as such; it's that he sees a burnt-down society, a blown-up society, and a leveled society as a legitimate goal. Terrorism is made legitimate as a means because only terror and destruction can possibly bring such a burning society into being.

Now consider some of the implications of this. As envy is loosed on the land, we have to devise policies to combat it. How? Can we legislate new wealth-distribution programs? The guilt-ridden capitalists have believed they could buy off the jealousy-dominated socialists with such programs. You know the slogans: "FDR saved capitalism from itself." "We need a government-business partnership." "Every society needs an economic safety net." But these slogans are meaningless to the envious man. It's not redistribution that he wants. He knows that we cannot redistribute the wealth so that the rich man's luxuries are made available to the masses. Even if he didn't know, he wouldn't care. What he wants to see is a society in which *nobody* has access to the luxuries. He's not trying to "get his" at your expense. He's trying to "smash yours" at your expense. His motivation is utterly perverse: it's the act of taking away yours, destroying yours, which gives him his kicks.

In August of 1959, Stephen Nash was executed. Nash was a convicted murderer who boasted about having murdered 11 people, some of them young boys. He spent the last two years of his life in solitary confinement. He had boasted so often in front of the San Quentin inmates about his exploits that they tried to kill him. Why had he killed these people? He gave a reason: "I never got more than the leavings of life, and when I couldn't even get those any more, I started taking something out of other people's lives."

It is my contention that envy is loose in the land. I am convinced that the politics of envy has become the national pastime, and from the local elections to the Federal elections, and beyond: to the Weathermen and the other *presently* underground terrorist factions. I am convinced that the coming economic disruptions will remove whatever traditional restraints there are on rampant envy in this country. When this happens, if it happens, the escalation of violence, both private and public (legislation), will begin to threaten everyone's capital.

The awful truth about envy is that *it cannot be placated*. If you try to buy off the envious man, your very ability to buy him off—the existence of excess capital for you to buy him off, to delay your day of judgment—repulses him. Who was it that Italy's terrorists, the Red Brigades, shot? Aldo Moro, a long-time socialist. Every public official becomes a target, not because of his ideology, but because of his high position as an official. *Every sign of success makes you a potential target*.

Henry Fairlie, writing in *The New Republic* (Sept. 17, 1977), made some incisive comments about the nature of envy. He stressed the fact that men refuse to admit that they are envious, even to themselves. He quotes La Rochefoucald: "Few are able to suppress in themselves a secret satisfaction at the misfortune of their friends."

Although all the deadly sins are morbid and self-destroying, Angus Wilson has said, most of the others provide at least some gratification in their early stages. But there is no gratification for Envy, nothing it can ever enjoy. Its appetite never ceases, yet its only satisfaction is endless self-torment. "It has the ugliness of a trapped rat that has gnawed its own feet in its effort to escape." One thinks of Envy as being a drag on someone, holding him back, as being of no help or reward or pleasure to him. It gnaws, as Angus Wilson says, and it rankles. The endless self-torment is an endless self-mortification. Each of the other sins may bring what seems to be moments of elevation, when they appear to set one above other people. But the slit eyes of Envy are always turned up to what it thinks is superior. However high Envy may seem to aspire, it is in fact always servile. It never straightens its back. . . .

Envy grows most naturally, said Aristotle, in relationships between equals. . . . The United States and other Western societies are not pitting equals against equals, *but unequals against unequals as if they are equals*. This is a distortion of the idea of equality, and it is this distortion, as much as anything else, that has enabled the enemies of equality to move to the offensive. To pit unequals against unequals as if they are equals is to make a breeding ground for Envy. The idea that we are equal has been perverted into the idea that we are identical; and when we then find that we cannot all do and experience and enjoy the things that others do and experience and enjoy, we take our revenge and deny that they were worth doing and experiencing and enjoying in the first place. What we are unable to achieve, we will bring low. What requires talent and training and hard work, we will show can be accomplished without them. We are scarcely able to admire any longer, respect or be grateful for, what is better or lovelier or greater than ourselves. What is exceptional must be pulled down or put down.

Fairlie's conclusion is interesting. It comes from a British social thinker who is basically an economic interventionist. "While the spirit of Envy is loose in our societies, it can reduce our ambitions only to meanness and pettiness. This malice and evil-mindedness are in ourselves, a habitual sin, but never have our societies so conspired to inflame them in us." How dreadfully correct he is. Fearfully correct.

Gossip is one outworking of envy, perhaps the most common. It may be the one form of envy that does give people temporary enjoyment. The other crimes I covered earlier. But there is another outworking of envy that most of the scholars have chosen to ignore: *socialism*. The modern socialist cannot possibly hope that wealth redistribution will appeal to the masses merely as a scheme of getting the other man's goods. Everyone knows who gets the goods in socialism: the bureaucracy. They get the jobs. They get the power. The people who are supposed to be aided get little. Prof. Walter Williams, an economist at George Mason University in Virginia, has calculated that if you divide the budget of the Bureau of Indian Affairs by the number of Indians in the country, the average Indian family would receive over $30,000 a year. You could cut the budget in half, fire all the bureaucrats, and still give each Indian family $15,000 + . But, he says, there are certain individuals who have a vested interest in ridiculing this idea: employees of the Bureau of Indian Affairs.

Why, then, does the appeal of socialism as an idea prosper? Why do voters keep voting for it? There are several good explanations. First, guilt on the part of middle-class and wealthy voters. Second, the attempt to buy off the rioters. Third, poorer and envious voters.

The intellectuals have created modern socialism. They, like Dr. Marx and his patron, Frederick Engels (the son of a wealthy textiles manufacturer), have written up the arguments. Their motives should be obvious: the destruction of the present social order, and the substitution of . . . what? They never said. They never do. Their goal is simply the destruction of the present social order. Their motive: envy.

It is absolutely imperative that you understand this. You've got capital to defend. There are legions of envy-dominated, guilt-ridden people today whose goal in life is to see to it that you do not maintain possession of your capital. They have marked your social class for full destruction, even if it costs them their positions. If the middle class is wiped out financially, how will the university professors who have taught socialism for so long ever survive? They won't. But if they understood this, if they looked that far ahead, they wouldn't care. It's their envy against the rich and successful that motivates them, even if the advent of socialism would spell the economic doom of the middle classes, to which they now belong.

Helmut Schoeck, the German sociologist, has written the finest analysis of envy presently available, *Envy: A Theory of Social Behaviour* (Harcourt, Brace & World, 1970). Until we consider exactly what Schoeck is warning us against, we will be unarmed in our attempts to roll back socialism, or even to arm our children against the nonsense in today's classrooms.

> The various forms of socialism have always recruited a large proportion, if not the majority, of their important supporters and theoreticians from among those people who were deeply troubled by the problem of envy in society. These were mostly people in good, if not excellent, circumstances, who suffered from the idea that they gave cause for envy. Their concern was directed equally towards those who were envied like themselves and toward those who were envious.... The impulse given to socialism by this viewpoint is primarily towards a form of society in which there will be neither envied nor envious. In socialist economists such as Abba P. Lerner, we find the envy-motive used indirectly, appearing now as a social virtue. Thus, a progressively rising income tax is proposed on the grounds that, for the psychological good of the collective, the appeasement of envy in the normal wage-earner— on witnessing the penalties of the highly paid—was quantitatively more important and beneficial than the discomfiture of the few, despoiled by the state for the benefit of the envious [A. P. Lerner, *The Economics of Control*, 1944, p. 37]. This thesis overlooks the fact that there are countless, and often far more painful, occasions for envy than those few really large incomes or inheritances which can be mulcted; it also overlooks the fact that by raising envy to the status of virtue in the interests of the state one only intensifies the suffering of those with a truly envious disposition because politicians feel compelled continually to reveal new 'inequalities' in the society (pp. 249-51).

We are in serious trouble. The problem isn't going to go away. It's going to get a lot worse when the economy starts to slide. The grim fact is that the majority of those who defend the free market haven't come to grips with the reality of envy. They argue that the free market will make most men wealthier, which is accurate. But this carries no weight with the socialists. We can't logically argue that market freedom will make all men economically equal. We can't demonstrate that the market will overcome the problem of envy. The socialists are not interested in raising everyone's standard of living *unless* they can simultaneously abolish economic inequality. *It isn't the rising income of the masses that interests them; it's wiping out the signs of success.*

Implications

When price inflation hits in force, the middle class will finally start paying for its two generations of envy-dominated and guilt-manipulated voting. All those built-in wealth redistribution programs will finally begin to pinch. The middle class will at last discover who always has to finance these massive wealth transfer programs. Since there aren't enough rich people to finance them, only the middle class is left. They are now trapped. There is no escape.

The unemployed poor are finally going to put their envy into action. You can expect waves of sporadic, "senseless" terrorism. But it isn't senseless, in the sense that it makes no sense. It makes very good sense, once you understand envy.

What we are facing is, on one hand, the *Age of the Caesars*. This is the economy of bread and circuses, of government controls, of universal clemency, of State-operated agriculture, of massive taxation, of centralization of political power in the executive. But we are also going to see the *Age of the Vandals*. Have you ever wondered what the motivation of the vandal is? The Vandals at the end of the Roman Empire were tribes of looters. Today's vandal is far more sinister. He's not a looter so much as a destroyer, an arsonist, a bomber. He tears down, not to take, but merely for the sake of ruining other people's capital.

The July, 1980 violence in Liberty City (ah, don't you love government classification categories), the Negro district of Miami, was centered in two public housing projects. Here's the *New York Times'* version of their plight: "Fewer than 20 percent of the apartments have air conditioning, in a city where air conditioning is as important year round as heat is in northern cities in winter" (July 20, 1980). Sure it is! You try living in New York City for a winter without heat, and you'll die. But people in Miami have lived without air conditioning for a summer without dying. Think of the plight of these people. As the *Times* says, "They are desperate and angry people." Here they are in a government-subsidized housing project, with 3,100 people in one project, and 1/3 of them actually earning wages. Why, about 432 of the 762 families live on less than $4,000 a year, the *Times* says. And only 20% of them have air conditioning!

> The mood in and around the public housing complexes is tense. Many residents are afraid to talk and others say the time for talk is past. "It's like, hey, we are tired of talking," one young woman said. "Talk ain't got us nowhere. Right now we just want to express our frustration and don't want to talk to anybody."

A young man in his early 20's, a pistol stuffed in the top of his pants and showing through his shirt, said the community was 'at war.'

"If you don't live here you better stay out," he said. "That goes for the police, the press, and especially the crackers." Other youths who had begun to gather and listen said they had plenty of weapons that they would use "every time the police come in and start some mess."

In the May riots, the Negro rioters attacked only white-owned businesses. The July riots drew no color bar. Negro-owned businesses were looted and vandalized. What is really ominous is this: the local residents admitted that the May violence was organized by armed and trained Vietnam vets who had planned for an excuse. Not this time, however; it was the kids. But the community activist who told this to the *Times*' reporter warned that the Vietnam vets were waiting to see if the community makes good on its promises.

Give them free housing. Give them food stamps. Give them free schooling. But you had better give them working air conditioners too, and "and none of them @#%¢&* window air conditioners, neither, or else there be trouble, whitey." (My summation.)

It's coming, and we can't buy them off. Envy is loose in the land.

As you might imagine, the problem of *terrorism* is closely linked to the problem of envy. The terrorist is ready to smash "the Establishment." Like the arsonist, he finds pleasure in seeing the deprivation of others. He may also be seeking personal "salvation" by his participation in an ideological movement—Marxist, anarchist, or whatever—but his terrorist acts are clearly not positive. Nothing is replaced by terrorism; it is a totally destructive impulse. With economic turmoil, especially when the government (through the central bank) starts inflating the currency on a massive scale, we should expect an increase in terrorist acts. What Europe has come to expect as normal, we will begin to see, too. (See Chapter 26.)

What happens to overstrained police departments if we start getting riots? If the alienated Vietnam veterans of the inner city start going into action, how do law-abiding people protect themselves, in the inner city or in the suburbs? People have got to start thinking about the purchase of burgular alarms, special locks on their doors, fire extinguishers, and weapons: shotguns, handguns, and ammunition. Such fears may seem hypothetical, until the day the riots begin. Then the sporting goods shops are empty, or padlocked. It's too late to take action then.

What we're seeing is the advent of a new set of problems for

American law enforcement officers. We have never had well-trained, well-armed domestic guerillas in this nation. We are going to have them. We have them now. They're waiting, that's all. From what I gather from professional intelligence experts, the American law enforcement establishment has been crippled by the Freedom of Information Act. They can't infiltrate these organizations with informants, since the informants' information can be smoked out by FOI. The informant system, which is the heart of successful crime fighting, has virtually disintegrated in the area of revolutionary organizations.

The fabric of civilization rests on some things we take for granted: honest money, honoring of contracts, freedom of expression, social peace, a minimum of envy, political restraint. All of these things are fading fast. We take for granted those things that are obviously disappearing. We invest in terms of their existence, yet we can see that such things are growing scarce.

There are newsletter writers who tell us that things are bad, but they're going to get a lot better. We won't go over the edge. There are also newsletter writers who tell us that we've gone over the edge, and that nothing will reverse the trend. I am convinced that you're never over the edge until the ground gives way. But I'm also convinced that the ground is visibly slipping. I wouldn't have gone climbing on Mt. St. Helens when the reports started coming in, and I am doing my very best to get away from the edge. I think it's going to go. I think it's going to go within a few years. I really think parts of the edge will start going before the end of 1983, even if the USSR doesn't try to blackmail us, which I think they will.

The envy phenomenon is incredibly potent. It rules most of the world. Men are not safe when they get rich in most parts of the underdeveloped world. That's one of the main reasons they're still underdeveloped nations. We have reduced envy in the West by 1800 years of preaching against the sin of envy, the sin of gossip, the sin of covetousness. The Jews preached the same message (or at least the prophets did) for 1500 years before Christ. It took that kind of systematic, continual leadership to minimize envy and encourage responsible self-interest among members of the West's society. Schoeck is correct: the West's religious commitment against the sin of envy made the West the wealthiest culture in man's history.

For the last century, and especially for the last two generations, the ideology of envy has been loose in the land. We are about to reap the consequences. You had better restructure your investments accordingly.

Keep your assets concealed. If you live in a visibly wealthy section of town, move. I'm dead serious. I can afford to live in the nicest section of my town, but I don't. I live in a home that I bought for $15 a square foot—not ten years ago, but in 1980. Inside, it's nice. Outside, it's average. I do the same with my cars. Being the target of the envious may be literally true. I don't choose to become a target unnecessarily.

We've all been the beneficiaries of religious principles handed down to us as our inheritance—a very ancient inheritance. The socialists have challenged this inheritance. We had better understand the enormous consequences of their success.

"It's People Like You!"

Several years ago I spoke at a meeting of assembled businessmen, students, and assorted free market advocates in Wisconsin. I remember getting into a discussion of the problems facing those of us who believe in free market economics in an era of increasing State intervention. I said that I thought the problem is really more a moral issue than educational, and therefore the mere presentation of economic logic or facts would ultimately fail in our attempts to turn the country around. The problem is envy, not lack of data.

This brought a heated response from one man, who turned out to be an economics professor. Nonsense, he said, it's a question of insufficient data. We know, for example, that people have no comprehension of cause and effect relationships in economic affairs, that they will answer yes to both the following questions on a test: 1) do you think the government should print more money to get us out of a recession; and 2) do you think that inflation is a problem that must be solved? Therefore, he said, they vote incorrectly because they simply don't understand cause and effect.

This brings us to a very important problem. It's not just an issue of pure speculation. It's not merely something that economists debate over. Your future and mine will be influenced greatly by the political decisions of elected officials, and they, in turn, will make these decisions on the basis of ideas. Or self-interest. (Which? Both?)

My economist critic has a vested interest in ideas. His self-interest, even his very self-justification, rests on the idea that neutral, empirical scholarship is valid, and that it can produce effective results. If we abandon this, then why employ economists? He taught, predictably, in a government-financed university. Just a neutral observer, plying his trade, untouched by considerations of morality: he wanted to fight the battle against the State with its money, on its hypothetically neutral ground, free from restraints of moral judgment. And he is not alone in his conviction that the battle we face is a battle of ideas alone. The best of the free market economists of our day agree with him.

That is the main reason we have lost the case.

The socialists, interventionists, and Marxists come before intellectuals and call them to serve in a moral cause which has the added benefit of being part of "the wave of the future," or "the inevitable forces of history." Their economic analysis is so flawed as to be pathetic. Generation after generation of economists have refuted Karl Marx, line by unreadable line. What good does it do? Few of Marx's followers have ever read volume I of *Das Kapital*, let alone volumes two and three. They don't follow Marx because of his economic analysis; they follow him because of his passion, his critique of capitalist culture, his total envy. They follow him because his version of the ancient religion of revolution is presented in the magical name of "science." Having chased God out of their mental universe, they open the door wide to the demons of bureaucracy, blood, and endless purges. What do they care? They have sometimes achieved their fundamental goal: the destruction of civilization (Nazi Germany, the U.S.S.R.). They destroy whenever they come to power.

Schoeck makes a number of exceedingly illuminating observations about envy and its effects. Where it exists, economic growth will be far more difficult, since everyone is afraid to display talents or wealth in front of his neighbors. The hostility toward differentiations of wealth is just too great. Envy, he says, cannot be placated. You cannot redistribute wealth and stamp it out, because it will then be aimed at something else: good looks, fame, or whatever. It takes a huge bureaucracy wielding enormous centralized power even to attempt to placate envy by imposing economic equality. And envy has been growing in the West since 1945. Most interesting of all:

> Sociological research has shown the extent to which this demand for levelling originates with certain groups of intellectuals, the average voter feeling hardly any definite envy towards those with really high incomes, for the objects of our envy are generally those who are almost our equals (p. 195).

In other words, the systematic proclamation of *envy*, coupled with *guilt*, has come from the modern intellectual Left. It has used State-supported educational institutions to achieve its political goal: the creation of an envious voting population. And in our day, the Left has very nearly achieved its goal.

It is too much to expect economists to figure this out. Schoeck isn't an economist. The economist wants to leave morality out of his equations, graphs, and charts. He wants to win the case for freedom by means of overpowering logic or a mountain of statistical correlations. He wants the public to listen to him, read his books, decipher his higher mathematics, and then vote the right way forever.

What he needs to do is to explain to them that this is a moral universe, and that theft is immoral, destructive, and corrupting. He *wants* to tell them that envy is not in their own self-interest, rationally conceived; he *needs* to tell them about the immorality of envy. Even Schoeck, a true German professor, won't go *that* far.

People don't normally accept a philosophy on the basis of logic, graphs, or calculus. They may try to defend their philosophy in terms of these tools later on, if they're academically inclined, but they don't accept or reject a philosophy or a religion on the basis of such mental tools—not often, anyway.

Public Resentment

Envy makes our personal economic planning vastly more difficult. Schoeck is absolutely correct: envy makes men secretive, less able to talk openly about all their plans for the future and their personal economic projects. They are fearful of being regarded as a threat to the peace of mind of others, especially neighbors and close friends.

There is also the education factor. Nobody wants to be thought of as a complete nut, or at least most people don't. Oh, it's not so bad to be a bit eccentric, especially if you can make money at it. But to be eccentric in a time of true social breakdown is exceedingly dangerous. If we are truly playing for the high stakes, then we have to keep envy in mind as we make plans.

Jealousy is one thing. If someone thinks I have a food storage program, he may try to steal it in a time of crisis. But at least I can bargain with him. I can offer to share, or swap, or simply give him a portion of the food. But the envious man is not satisfied with any of this. He wants everyone to starve, since he faces starvation.

Bureaucrats and planners are not jealous. They are agents of *institutionalized envy*. They want to ration food, control lives, gain power—all in the name of envy. They want everyone to have equal shares of a small pie rather than see a huge pie created, but with unequal pieces.

When a major crisis finally arrives, we must be prepared to face a totally fallacious accusation: *"It's people like you who made this mess!"* Not the government, not the interventionists, not the voters who were willing to allow Congress to vote them benefits, or vote other benefits, that could only be paid off with inflated, depreciating money. No, it is *our* fault, for we did not believe the lies. We didn't have confidence. And in a confidence game, that's the worst sin of all.

When you try to show a person that he is participating in some sort of wealth transfer scheme, he resents it. If you show him that the continuation of the scheme, and others like it, will destroy the foundations of modern civilization, he regards you as a threat. When it happens, he will blame you. After all, to blame anyone else would be an admission of his guilt, or his stubbornness in not facing the truth beforehand, or his stupidity, or his lack of foresight, or his unwillingness to change his ways, or his short-run perspective. In short, *your success in the face of predictable disaster will enrage the envious*, especially those who were warned in advance by you. Schoeck is correct: envy is usually directed at those who are close to us, close to our station in life. *We* will be the targets of rage.

This is why I have always advocated a *low profile*. It's very hard for me to achieve it, but you can. And even I intend to keep my neighbors generally ignorant about my personal success. Share ideas, but keep your assets concealed. I can afford a newer model car than my 1972 car and my 1978 VW van. In the short run, I can afford one. Maybe not in the longer run.

I share these thoughts with you because you're probably wondering how you will find kindred spirits in a time of trouble. More important, how can you find each other today, while planning is less expensive? If we must preserve some semblance of the division of labor in a crisis, we will need kindred spirits who have foresight and capital to invest today.

A Shared Moral Framework

The importance of finding out how your potential future partners view the success of others is very important. Be very careful of those who gossip about their economic superiors, or show signs of wanting to get even, not for some real or imagined slight, but simply because the other fellow has more. Envy is a true corruptor. Avoid cooperating with envious people.

It is a good idea to seek out those within a church or somewhat ideological group, but most members will probably not go along with you. Maybe common interests in other areas might suffice, like hunting, or some similar outdoor sport. But on the whole, it's tough to find people who share your concern, share your assessment of the future, and are willing to sacrifice in the present in order to prepare for the future.

I suggest that people start making associations for more practical, short-run goals, but gently press their associates into new avenues of thought. For example, people in an urban neighborhood may be worried about crime. Fine, hit this issue. Get an engraving tool (under $20), or call the local police and find out if some local insurance agency or other outfit loans them. Have "operation watch" meetings. Get people to keep an eye out for each other's property when the other fellow is away from his home. There is a common neighborhood interest in self-defense. Use that as an opening. Get everyone to mark his valuables with a driver's license ID number.

Maybe some people on the block are shop nuts. They have tools. They like to work on projects. If you share their interests, or even if you think you will need their services, get to know them. Talk shop. Find out about tools. Find out what tools are missing in the neighborhood. Offer to pick up whatever is missing. Encourage a "tool swap" among the local shop addicts. Find out what resources are available, and start encouraging friendly barter today. You don't have to press a panic button. You don't have to show your hand in advance. But you know where you're going, and if you don't come on too strong, you may be able to push a few along with you, once they see you as a "regular Joe." Remember, everyone is at least a little worried about the economy. You don't have to tell them what you know is coming. You can ask: "I wonder what's coming? What do you think?" And when he tells you, then ask: "If you're right, what should we be doing now to hedge against that?" Maybe you'll pick him off.

Neighborhood co-operation is crucial. Be helpful. Not too helpful, of course. Being too helpful creates suspicion, resentment, and even a sense of guilt. Ask for favors occasionally. But demonstrate that you're "part of the neighborhood team." And if your neighborhood is like mine, you know there isn't any team. If you plan to stay where you are, you had better form one.

Chapter 2

WHERE THE VOTERS ARE

There are two groups of people, H. L. Mencken once remarked: those who *work* for a living, and those who *vote* for a living.

Mencken had a good point. It was not really as relevant as he thought, but there is a ring of truth about it. Actually, those who are exclusively dependent on welfare payments seldom vote. Children supported by aid to dependent children, people in mental institutions, the hard-core unemployed, and those in the inner cities are not usually voters. Those who are legally eligible to vote among these groups are seldom proficient readers, and they take little or no interest in political affairs, since they have little knowledge of them, interest in them, or confidence concerning them.

Then where do the votes come from? Where do the welfare supporters come from? To some extent, from the elderly. The Gray Panthers are only the most vocal of the retirees. But generally the votes for more welfare programs come from those who are only partially dependent on government intervention, or in some cases not dependent at all. Obviously, there are more middle-class, middle-aged voters than anyone else. They finance the welfare budgets, and they vote for them. But they vote for the programs on a piecemeal basis. If you asked them if they were in favor of a welfare State, they would deny it. If you asked them if they think the welfare system today is beneficial, they would deny it. But they elect representatives who vote for welfare on a massive basis.

Why? Why should people support a system that they have to finance through taxes and which they do not have confidence in? There are several very good reasons, but I think you can summarize them in a few words: *guilt, greed, fear,* and *confusion.* And, of course, *envy.* Always there is envy.

Guilt

This guilt stems from many sources. One is simply religious. Rebellious men sense their own inadequacy in the face of ultimate moral standards. They're absolutely correct. But they seek relief from these guilt feelings though strange means: political action, charity, "good works," masochism, sublimation (I don't know what this is,

17

but Freudian psychologists are always talking about it), and so forth. Remember the commercial that made Zest famous? "For the first time in your life, feel *really* clean!" Some Madison Avenue psychology major knew exactly what he was doing when he wrote that jingle. It sold a lot of Zest.

Modern politics is based on the systematic manipulation of guilt. In fact, without guilt feelings, the whole modern political structure would collapse. If the State passes enough laws, so that everyone has to break many of them daily—sometimes competing Federal bureaucracies mandate mutually contradictory requirements—then the bureaucrats can make people feel guilty constantly. They feel guilty, and they fear exposure. This makes even more manipulation necessary, for people seek salvation through political action. Rushdoony has called this the *Politics of Guilt and Pity* (Thoburn Press, 11121 Pope's Head Rd., Fairfax, VA 22030: $5.00).

Are you better off than your neighbor? If we assume that there is a fixed quantity of resources, then your "large piece of the pie" is the cause of his smaller one. President Nyerere of Tanzania, whose socialistic policies of forced agricultural collectivization and State monopoly over agriculture have crippled that little nation, has put it this way:

> I am going to argue that the whole concept of aid is wrong. I am saying it is not right that the vast majority of the world's people should be forced into the position of beggars, without dignity. In one world, as in one state, when I am rich because you are poor, and I am poor because you are rich, the transfer of wealth from the rich to the poor is a matter of right; it is not an appropriate matter for charity. . . . If the rich nations go on getting richer and richer at the expense of the poor, the poor of the world must demand a change, in the same way that the proletariat in the rich countries demanded change in the past.

Yet if the West had really kept the African tribes in poverty, Nyerere would not have received his education in Marxist and socialist-dominated Western universities. But in any case, his party line is echoed daily in the speeches of United Nations representatives, not to mention California farm union organizers' speeches. The world has bought the "fixed pie" line, in the face of the greatest economic growth in history. If you have wealth, then you are a thief, obviously. And you must be expropriated for your theft. You can't even give it away. As one socialistic fellow student in the university (a middle-ranking Naval Reserve officer, by the way) remarked to me: "I would abolish private charity, make it illegal. It lets a lot of rich thieves assuage their guilt." The State, through taxation, is to be the agency of charity.

We teach this theology in our universities. We preach it in our mainline religious denominations. We fill the high school social studies textbooks with such reasoning. And, having made two generations of potential taxpayers feel guilty—not guilty before God, but guilty before The Masses and their incarnation, the State—we find that social programs of compulsory wealth redistribution are the law of the land.

The tax revolt will not work. You cannot wipe away two generations of bad theology with a few years of political hoopla. If we see a few taxes cut, or the budget balanced (officially), then the off-budget Federal agencies will multiply like flies—like flies on welfare, even—and the Federal Reserve System will buy up private debt (laundered through some modern version of the Reconstruction Finance Corporation) with fiat money. *The modern theology of guilt-atoning taxation will destroy the dollar.* You must not put your hope in the tax revolt. Maybe you can personally escape some taxes by joining the tax revolt, but you will not bring down the modern Welfare State. *The tax revolt will only hasten the demise of the dollar*, and every other fiat currency in the West. To have a successful tax revolt, we have to find a way to deal with the problem of real guilt, and the State (as well as the anti-State) cannot rectify the problem of guilt. Howard Jarvis is not Jesus Christ, after all.

Conclusion? Don't expect miracles from earthly political movements. The very heart of modern politics' problem is the existence of too much faith in political miracles. On the other hand, don't be sucked in by professional guilt-manipulators. Know what you're up against. That's why I recommend the *tithe*. The man who tithes 10% of his income to charitable causes is no easy mark for the guilt-pitchmen. He has done his duty. He has not "saved himself" by tithing, but he has saved himself from the need of paying attention to the guilt-pitchmen.

Greed

Greed is a killer. Greed tells men that they are entitled to more than the free market offers to them for their efforts. Greed tells men that they're worth more, always more. So they start looking for ways to "beat the market," with its limits of open competition. They start looking for aid from the State.

The politician is in the business of getting re-elected. He must go into the market for votes and buy them. He sells the public what it wants in exchange for votes. If the public wants economic favors, then that's what the politician will sell him. (And when the bill comes due—higher taxes—the politician will then start pitching guilt back at the voter—or paper money.) The public establishes the political currency of its realm; the politician responds accordingly, in order to buy the currency of his realm, votes.

Once this process begins, it is almost impossible to reverse it. One of the few cases in history when it was reversed was in England, from 1845-75, only for a single generation. They tore down the trade barriers, strengthened the gold standard, and allowed capital free flow. The result was an outpouring of productivity. But it didn't last long. Remember: that is the only major exception that a nation has voluntarily accepted without suffering a military defeat (like Germany did after World War II, when Erhard could "throw the foreign socialist rascals out"—meaning us—and return to free enterprise with the public's support).

This leads me to a slogan for all successful conventional investing:

"There are more voters who *consume* your product than *produce* your product."

Let me show you some applications. Are you considering making an investment in some apartment houses? You think you can get renters to pay you for your risk and effort. Warning: "There are more renters who vote than owners who vote." You can expect rent controls. You had better plan on rent controls. That's why you had better buy single-family dwellings that at least can be sold to renters, allowing you to pull your capital out in a hurry. A rent-controlled apartment house is a turkey. (A non-rent-controlled apartment house is a sitting duck.) Only if you can convert rental units to condominiums can you get your money out, and there is growing political pressure to make such conversions illegal. *Before you invest, find out where the voters are.*

You see, it's not that some people vote for a living. It's the fact that they vote for subsidies to their living expenses. They work, earn, and pay taxes. But they expect you, as a capitalist investor, to finance their life style, if their life style cannot be covered by their present income level. *And their own voting behavior guarantees higher taxes and more inflation*, which in turn assures you that you will be continually called upon to support their life style. We are talking about a lot of people. Over 40% of American families received Federal money in 1977, *not* counting Federal salaries (*Review of the News* [June 27, 1979], p. 59, citing the *Wall Street Journal*).

Here's another example. What about farming? Should a wise farmer buy more farm land? He must face the grim reality: *There are more voters who eat than voters who farm.*

Do you know what this implies for the future of farming? *Price controls on agricultural produce.* They did it in France during the French Revolution. They did it in Europe in the fascist era. They do it in most of the Third World socialist tribal aggregates (sometimes called nations). When food gets scarce, the voters will see to it that someone else supports their life style. I don't mean the ghetto. I mean middle-class America. You know, the folks who are apt to remark: "Well, I'm glad to know you're storing food. If times get tough, I'll stop in to see you. Ha ha ha." They will, too.

So here's Joe Fertilizer, the American farmer, up to his ears in debt. He buys more land. Its price keeps going up. Of course, the money he earns for the land's output can't pay the interest costs, let alone a profit, but he buys more. He knows food prices will be going up. He will pay off the lender (bank, Federal government, or his elderly next-door neighbor who sold the land on contract) with depreciated dollars. He thinks.

Then comes the price freeze. He sells a standard crop, like wheat or soybeans. It's a crop that is sold on the commodity exchanges. It is easily policed. And the Federal government sends out bureaucrats to see that he sells at the legal price—a loss-producing price. Or, if necessary, the Federal government sends out trucks to pick up the crop, and the Federal official hands Joe a nice check, and thanks him. "See you next year, sucker!"

He has a big farm. It's heavily mortgaged. He can't sell it. He can't make a decent income with it. But he's stuck with the debt. And if he sells his crop in the black market, gets paper money, and tries to pay off his mortgage, what will he tell the tax collector when the latter enquires as to the source of all that fiat money?

Sure, if we have straight-line mass inflation, and if crop prices don't sag, and if the weather holds up, and nobody else has a good year, then Joe will indeed beat the system. Every Joe in America expects this. Every Joe since the beginning of time has expected this. And it never happens. He works his whole life in the fields, and his banker just smiles. For as long as they both shall live.

What's the answer, long-term? Simple: *a debt-free small family farm* which produces *produce*—fruits, vegetables, organic foods that get high prices—that is sold in local markets. The farm that is *small enought not to be visible, small enough not to be worth policing* by the price controllers, *small enough to be owned debt-free*, and not involved in commodity exchange commodities, is the farm that will survive. *All other farming is highly risky*. All other farming is highly illiquid. All other farming will eventually go bankrupt. No debt pyramid goes on forever, and almost no farmer who plays the debt game ever knows when to quit. And even if he did, price controls may not allow him to quit. *The voters who eat need him to support their life styles*. There are a lot of voters who eat.

Fear

When true panic hits—I mean real, unadulterated panic—two generations of guilt-manipulated, greed-manipulated voters are going to start looking for scapegoats. They are going to look for potential victims. And the law courts are going to extend that system of jurisprudence which one friend of mine has labeled "the deeper-pocket jurisprudence." *If you are richer, you are guilty.* Now, let's hear the witnesses.

The rise of Hitler cannot be separated from the rise of Communism and the rise of fear. Men of Europe in the early 1930's were afraid. They had seen a terrible war. They had seen mass inflation. They had seen the expropriation of the middle class. They had seen the abolition of the traditional monarchical political order. They faced grinding depression and the collapse of the world economy by 1932. The whole nineteenth-century world of optimism had disappeared. What would replace it? Not anarchy. People will not live with anarchy. Der Führer. Il Duce. *They* would restore the former glory. *They* would get the trains to run on time. (By the way, Italian trains *didn't* run on time. It's a myth of fascism.) *They* would take care of the Jews, Commies, bankers, Poles, etc. *They would bust a few heads.* Ah, what a pleasant sight, even when you're hungry. *Especially* when you're hungry. It takes your mind off of your growling stomach.

We have not seen real fear in this nation in four decades. We have not seen a major military defeat. We have not seen mass inflation, price controls, shortages, rioting in middle-class areas, and massive, continual strikes. But will we? And can anyone guarantee that we won't?

There is the scent of Weimar Germany in the air—all over the West. There is *the gay abandon of the Roaring Twenties* in the discos. And there is the same nagging feeling that it cannot last, so let us eat, drink, and be merry, for tomorrow we die.

We are about to enter the era of fear. All it will take is a shattering of confidence in our ability to withstand a major threat to our social or political order. And as I intend to demonstrate in subsequent chapters, we are very, very close to that shattering realization.

This is why *you must get out of the major cities.* If you are dependent on municipal services, then you are dependent on municipal labor unions. The story of Germany in the 1920's is a story of grinding, continual strikes and interruptions of basic supplies. The independent trucking slowdown is only a small down payment on what we can expect. New York City should be our model for the future. You must not put yourself at the mercy of municipal unions, blockades, energy black-outs, and other products of an overexpanded "public sector" economy. If you are dependent on most municipal services in a major metropolitan area, then you are only marginally less vulnerable than a Social Security recipient.

If the unions try to tie up this country—a most optimistic word, "if"—then the voters will ultimately rebel. Again, you have to figure out, in advance, where the voters will be. What will they be doing? What kind of response will they demand? I think it's obvious: a man with a cure-all. A man with leadership abilities. He will be dynamic. He will thrive in a climate of fear. So that climate will be made available, even if it weren't built into today's system, which it is.

But fear isn't enough. Fear, plus confidence, produces solutions. It might even produce a traditional free market solution. Therefore, we first need *confusion*.

Confusion

Here is the strategy. Most important, you need universal *moral* confusion. The voters must be confused about life's first principles. To achieve this, you create a compulsory system of tax-supported schools. Tax support is then used to justify the neutralization of moral instruction ("religion") in these schools. The final step is to introduce into the curriculum a programmed instructional package called "values education"—a cover for *total moral relativism leading to nihilism*. To pull this off, you need to create another parallel institution to drain off any protests from morally outraged parents. This can be called the PTA. Eventually, you create a generation of voters who are incapable of *independent* moral outrage. You can then orchestrate their moral outrage for your own political goals. In 1984.

What economic system works? No one seems to know. What legal system works? Again, it's up for debate. What is to be done? Pass another law. What if nothing makes things work? Hire two more bureaucrats to make it work. What if the whole system is disintegrating? Find a *hero of the people* to make it work by busting a few heads.

The public doesn't know what it wants. The special interest groups want to chip away at the overall market system in order to get legislative goodies, and piece by piece the market crumbles. Then we vote for more protection from a crumbling system. State protection.

If the voters knew what they wanted, and if they understood what they were asking for, they would not be clamoring for tax cuts and subsidies at the same time. Congress is politically short-circuited on national issues, because the folks back home can agree only on pork barrel projects and other varieties of "down-home socialism." The result is political drift. The current is flowing toward the "strong man."

The elite rulers need a confused voting public. They have produced a confused voting public. Now they need a major, easily recognized *national emergency* to mobilize the last remaining bit of moral outrage left in the confused voting public.

We have arrived at the *politics of confusion*. It will soon be the *politics of despair*. And when it is, watch out. We will then be set up for the *politics of salvation*. Also known as hell on earth.

Chapter 3

UPPER-CLASS INVESTING

The concept of class position has been a dominant theme among scholars since the 19th century. Karl Marx founded Communism in terms of a theory of history which asserted that class struggles underlie *all* historical development. But what, precisely, is a class? Marx never really said. In the third paragraph from the end of his posthumously published third volume of *Das Kapital*—which he never completed, although the main draft was completed about 15 years before he died— he wrote: "The first question to be answered is this: What constitutes a class?" Quite so; unfortunately for theoretical Marxism, he never was able to figure out an answer. But that hasn't stopped his followers from trying to take over the world in the name of the class struggle.

A decade ago, Prof. Edward Banfield, the Harvard political scientist, offered a new definition of class. So unpopular was the book in which he offered his thesis that the students harassed him out of his job. He went to the University of Pennsylvania for a few years until things cooled off at Harvard. Then he went back. (It had been almost as bad at Pennsylvania. He actually required police protection at one stage.)

Banfield's thesis makes a great deal of sense. He defines class position in terms of *time perspective*, not income.

> In the analysis to come, the individual's orientation toward the future will be regarded as a function of two factors: (1) ability to imagine a future, and (2) ability to discipline oneself to sacrifice present for future satisfaction. The more distant the future the individual can imagine and can discipline himself to make sacrifices for, the "higher" his class. The criterion, it should be noted, is ability, not performance. . . . It must again be strongly emphasized that this use of the term *class* is different from the ordinary one. As the term is used here, a person who is poor, unschooled, and of low status may be upper class; indeed he *is* upper class if he is psychologically capable of providing for a distant future. By the same token, one who is rich and a member of "the 400" may be lower class; he *is* lower class if he is incapable of conceptualizing the future or of controlling his impulses and is therefore obliged to live from moment to moment. (*The Unheavenly City* [Boston: Little, Brown, 1970], pp. 47-48.)

When we consider the ramifications of this definition of class for contemporary attitudes, the implications are grim. What we are seeing in the United States today is the steady increase of lower-class citizens. As men's time perspectives shift to the short run, their class position drops.

What made Banfield's detractors so furious was his argument that since class is a product of time perspective, the government is unlikely to be able to raise people in the ghetto to middle-class status. The government can pour billions of dollars into the ghettos, but the results will be very different from what the bureaucrats have promised. Without a lengthening of time perspective, without an increased commitment to deferred gratification, without an increase of self-discipline for future gains, the ghetto will remain pretty much what it is today.

> *The Lower Class.* At the present-oriented end of the scale, the lower-class individual lives from moment to moment. If he has any awareness of the future, it is of something fixed, fated, beyond his control: things happen *to* him, he does not *make* them happen. Impulse governs his behavior, either because he cannot discipline himself to sacrifice a present for a future satisfaction or because he has no sense of the future. He is therefore radically improvident: whatever he cannot consume immediately he considers valueless. His bodily needs (especially for sex) and his taste for "action" take precedence over everything else—and certainly over any work routine. He works only as he must to stay alive, and drifts from one unskilled job to another, taking no interest in the work (p. 53).

One of the finest examples in history of the difference between the two perspectives—long run vs. short run—is the exchange that took place between Jacob and Esau, the sons of Isaac. The Bible records that exchange. Esau came to Jacob claiming to be on the verge of starvation—a lie, by the way, since as soon as he was fed, he got up and walked away. Jacob demanded for a bowl of pottage something Esau possessed by law as the elder twin: the birthright. The birthright involved a double portion of the father's inheritance, but it also involved increased responsibility on the part of the oldest son for the care of the parents in their old age. Esau willingly traded his birthright for the immediate gratification of eating some stew (Genesis 25:29-34). Esau received exactly what he wanted: stew. Jacob received what he wanted: the birthright. Easu was intensely present-oriented. He put such a low value on the future, that he was willing to forego the special blessing of the birthright in order to fill up his stomach. Esau, the action-oriented hunter, was no match for Jacob, the drab fellow with a vision of the future.

Interest Rates

The existence of positive rates of interest stems from the distinction in the minds of men between *now* and *later*. Men make decisions constantly, choosing to do one thing and not another at any point in time. With the economists' assumption of "other things being equal," men would rather enjoy the use of a good or service in the present than in the future. Give a man the opportunity to choose between a free Rolls Royce today or a year from now, and he will select today's Rolls. Therefore, men discount the value of future goods. They want to be compensated for their forfeiting the use of money now. This *discount* of *future goods* against *present goods* is the pure rate of interest, or *originary* rate of interest. The higher men value the present in comparison to future goods, the higher the rate of interest they will pay to buy today's goods (and the higher the rate of interest they will demand in order to get them to part with their money now).

This provides us with important information concerning economic underdevelopment. If a large number of citizens are present-oriented, there will not be much economic growth in the society. After all, men get what they pay for. They want instant gratification, so they forfeit higher productivity (and higher income) in the future. They buy what they want. A present-oriented society will be marked by high rates of interest, and therefore lower rates of investment. Only very high profit opportunities will lure entrepreneurs into investment avenues. If you have to pay, say, 50% per annum interest or more, then you have to expect better than a 50% return on your money in order to get you to pull your money out of new cars, or out of money-lending, and into the creation of new businesses. In effect, the present-oriented society is buying its higher level of present consumption by sacrificing economic growth in the future.

Conversely, *societies that have a commitment to the future also tend to have low rates of interest*. People don't charge a high premium in order to get them to part with their present capital. They want economic growth, and by forfeiting present consumption in order to buy economic growth, they attain their objectives.

The transformation of modern American culture into a *present-oriented society* has been going on for two generations or more—possibly since the Roaring Twenties. What we have seen is an increasing unwillingness of Americans to lend money, invest, and build for the future. Our savings rate today is under 4%, the lowest in American history and either the lowest or second lowest among Western industrial states. The present-orientation of all classes of society is pronounced. Men want instant gratification. Of course, prices being the same, future vs. present goods, we all want instant gratification. But prices are not the same. There *is* an interest rate, and it is predictable that it will get higher in the long run if this present-orientation continues to spread throughout the society.

The rise of the drug culture, the advent of marijuana as a middle-money ("class") and even upper-money ("class") drug, the emphasis on leisure, and the youth culture all emphasize the value of present experiences over future experiences. The philosophy of "eat, drink, and be merry, for tomorrow we die" is calculated to raise interest rates and reduce investment, thereby stifling future economic growth.

Consider the implications of such a scenario for long-term bonds and mortgages. Rising rates will begin to squeeze out the poorer and middle-money ("class") purchasers of homes. Without bond financing, new uncertainties will be placed on economic development. The pay-off period for investments will get shorter, which means that long-term investing will become more difficult, more costly. The availability of lendable funds at anything like historic rates of interest will dry up. Entrepreneurs will be forced to go with higher risk investments, in order to get the necessary pay-off fast enough to repay the loans.

This will mean disaster for real estate development, *unless* the Federal government steps in to make below-market loans available. But if the government does this—and it's almost a sure thing—then the Federal deficit will get larger, and more fiat money will have to be injected into the system. But fiat money raises prices, and rising prices raises long-term interest rates, since lenders tack on an "inflation premium" to loans, in order to compensate themselves for the fall in the dollar's purchasing power. To keep the real estate markets alive, and to keep savings & loan associations solvent, the government will have to continue the *mad race between fiat money and long-term interest rates*, with the dollar-denominated price of housing continuing to soar, right alongside of mortgage rates.

Keynes' Legacy

John Maynard Keynes defended the short-run applications of his inflationary economic policies by remarking, "In the long run, we are all dead." So are paper currencies. Keynes' remark typifies twentieth-century interventionist economics: a short-run perspective that justifies the hampering of the market—the source of long-run growth in output and wealth.

Obviously, there are exceptions to the spread of short-run thinking. But on the whole, it does describe what's happening to America. Inflation is making people think in short-run terms. Men face increasingly erratic markets, wider swings in the boom-bust cycles, and the threat of monetary breakdown. They shift their focus from 20-year projects to 5-year projects. They have to. Nobody can calculate the economic future 20 years down the road. The best of guesses becomes an amusing intellectual exercise. *The next wave of inflation will wipe out holders of long-term, dollar-denominated assets.* Already, they are being hurt badly. The long-term capital markets are being threatened by a combination of inflation and present-oriented consumers. This is Keynes' legacy: more aggregate demand, more consumer spending, more personal and government debt, less savings. This was Keynes' program for economic reconstruction. The bills are coming due.

A friend of mine visited Argentina in 1979. He reported that there was a lot of economic activity, but that the capital base shows the effects of decades of price inflation. Homes of the rich are stately, but they are running down. Plumbing is old, sometimes half a century out of date. The rich are consuming the capital of their parents and grandparents. The replacement costs of capital have soared, as a result of unanticipated price inflation.

We can expect to face serious inflation over the next decade. The government will continue to make available below-market loans to favored industries and voting groups. We should therefore begin taking seriously Keynes' dictum that in the long run, we are all dead. But in the intermediate run, we are mostly alive, but without capital. The inflation wipes out our capital base before many of us reach retirement age. And for those who have reached retirement age, the government is about to produce a nightmare. This is why sensible investors are rethinking all the traditional avenues of investment. They have to hedge against the coming inflation.

The Grandfather Factor

The President of Grove City College, a 4-year liberal arts college in Northwest Pennsylvania, remarked to me that his college decided several years ago to make large investments in plant facilities. Grove City College is that rarity, a debt-free private college. Instead of building new athletic facilities, or using the money to expand student enrollment, the trustees decided to upgrade the school's physical plant. "In the future," he told me, "we know we may be caught in a financial squeeze because of the inflation. We want to be able to coast later on, without bleeding the college dry by having to make expensive capital repairs."

This is a very sensible philosophy today. In fact, I cannot recommend it highly enough. If you are satisfied with your geographical location—safety, future potential, etc.—then I would strongly recommend *upgrading your home*. I would recommend that real estate speculators now start putting more money into improving the value of their property, rather than continuing to pyramid them. If the experience of Argentina's rich is any guide, we can expect to face a *lengthy period of capital erosion.* We can also expect to experience the "invisible inflation" of *reduced quality.* Manufacturers will adjust their perspective to meet the time demands of the public. If the public is buying instant, cost-effective gratification, then quality considerations will begin to fall by the wayside.

This reduction in product quality is not universal. Some products maintain their markets by means of a reputation for quality. But these products are generally aimed at the upper classes: the rich, or more precisely, those who can afford and who understand the value of durable goods. The "eat, drink, and be merry" outlook is inimical to upper-class time perspectives. The "throw-away society" is not the product of long-term perspectives.

The perspective of the *grandfather* is at the heart of this investment strategy. If a man's philosophy is that of the Schlitz commercial, "You only go around once in life, so grab all the gusto you can," then his attitude toward his grandchildren will be very different from that most familiar in Europe, where the preservation of family capital and the family name is basic to economic decisions, or was a generation ago. The story of Johnny Appleseed is representative of men's long-term planning. We have to look beyond our own lifespans.

Again, this is another area in which the Federal government's policies are wiping out this nation. *There is no worse tax than the inheritance tax.* It tells men, "Use up your capital today. Don't look ahead beyond the grave. You can't control what your kids do. Forget about leaving them a pile of capital. Just live it up now, and to encourage you in this, the Federal government and state governments will see to it that you can't leave that much." *This shortens the time perspective of men.*

For example, men set up trusts for children at early ages because of the gift tax consequences of delaying this decision. But sometimes they wind up with too much money at an early age. So we look for ways to train them. *One of the best ways is to use trust assets to buy income-producing real estate.* The child is told from an early age that this will be his asset, that he must make the best of it that he can. He has to manage it, fix it up, hire the repairmen, keep the books, pay the taxes, and generally get himself involved in entrepreneurship, or at least basic management. But how many trustees ever think of such a strategy? Not many.

The idea that capital can be built up and passed down, generation after generation, with the potential always present of expanding it, and expanding the influence of those who bear the *family name,* has been seriously compromised by modern estate tax laws. We have substituted the State as the eldest son. It gets the double portion, and it becomes legally responsible for the care of the parents. But this child is a parasite. It never grows up. It never learns to be productive. It absorbs, steals, and redistributes. The result: the creation of a pseudo-family, a true monster. *We have sold our children's birthright to the State* for a mess of pottage (or, more to the point, a socialistic pot of message).

Our proper goal is to *train up children who are truly upper class*. They have a commitment to the future. They have an understanding that their efforts have long-term consequences. *We must strive to create a moral perspective in our children's minds that offsets the siren call of the short run in our day*. Ultimately, I know of no capital investment more important than this—not gold, not diamonds, not AAA bonds.

This having been done to the best of our ability, then we must adopt a strategy of wealth-transfer. We have to be realistic about the future. We are going to see the shaking of the economic foundations in the West over the next decade. I think we may see the destruction of the dollar. This being a distinct possibility, we then face some sort of revolutionary transformation: the coming of socialism, or fascism, or a major economic depression, or perhaps a return to the free market. What you must do is to transfer wealth, or claims to wealth, to the next generation in ways not easy to trace. Also, we need to put their visible assets in forms that will probably withstand the ravages of inflation, price controls, and even a full-scale redistributionist State.

Records

My continual suggestion to people who are trying to make long-run investments is this: with the exception of real estate (where the voters are on your side), *don't leave a trail of paper*. Train up children in the knowledge of alternative markets. If a child has a hobby, encourage it. After all, if your parents had encouraged you to collect electric trains as a kid, you would be worth a bundle today. The point I'm trying to make is simple enough: educate your children for the world which is probably coming, and coming very soon. I like *family businesses* for this reason. But the more the business is capable of operating underground, if not now then in the future, the better it is for training purposes. The training will survive, even if the capital does get confiscated at some point.

Over and over, I stress the importance of *goods, not paper*. Put your capital in durable goods, especially productive tools. Services are easier to swap without leaving a trail of paper. Get the tools now, so that you will be ready for swapping later. The investment should be regarded as a means of *purchasing future invisibility*.

The long-run perspective takes discipline. People want a fast pay-off. They want visible confirmation of their genius, measurable in dollars and cents, and easily displayed to the brother-in-law. This is what keeps so many people in the conventional markets. They are not after long-run gains, meaning lifetime gains. They are after brilliant tips that will reflect their own genius.

It is a lot more difficult than you think to break the habits of short-run, or lower-class investing. The guy who buys a gold coin, watches its dollar-denominated price rise, and then brags to his friends about his success, hasn't understood the nature of the economic and political problem. While most gold coin investors are less likely to play this game, I know South African gold share people who are caught up in this "displayable genius" approach.

The longer term you're considering, the *quieter* the investment should be. The fewer records it should leave, because the political transformations of the next decade will shock millions of those who have invested in terms of "business as usual."

I am partial to numismatic (rare) coins because of their long-term potential. The longer you wait to sell, the more you have time on your side. Coins get rarer, and their prices climb. I think that they are very good in trust funds for younger children—matched by real estate as they grow more responsible. I think they are right for personal and professional corporation retirement funds. But remember, these are paper money investments, ultimately. You will trade them in for paper eventually. The idea is to structure your "hard goods" investments to get time working for you, and rare items have this advantage. In a major collapse, they are not the best asset, but on the far side of a collapse, they should perform very well. They are also easier to move rapidly in a crisis.

I think the tax laws will be changed several times over the next decade or two. I think there is a reason why the Federal government has encouraged the proliferation of retirement programs for little people and directors of professional (one-man) corporations. I think the reason has something to do with getting people's assets far more visible. *Visible assets* are the best kind from the perspective of the *tax collector*.

What you need is a sizable proportion of your assets held in forms that can withstand sharp discontinuities, especially of tax laws. You don't need to see your capital go up with every inflationary boom. It may even sometimes sag with the temporary drops in the economy. What you need to do is to *concentrate on those assets that hold up well over long periods of time*. The simplest is the small gold coin. Close behind is silver. You can "buy and forget," which is what you need if you're to devote the bulk of your time to your profession.

The longer your time frame, the better off you will be. The short run must be dealt with on a regular basis, but decisions concerning the long run can be made now with the lowest cost.

What whipsaws out well-meaning investors is the action of the markets, the 6-month movements that seem to indicate that the basic direction of the economy is not toward mass inflation, higher taxes, and controls. But we live in an age of short-term perspectives, both economic and political. For survival, we have to aim beyond the targets announced in *Newsweek*. For survival, we need to discipline ourselves to become upper-class investors.

Chapter 4

THE ERA OF REPUDIATION

> As the perils loom closer, and as men come to apprehend their increasing vulnerability, the instinctive desire for self-preservation —found in organized societies as well as individuals—will prompt them to cede to governments far greater powers of surveillance, control and repression than are compatible with contemporary notions of personal liberty.
>
> Prof. E. J. Mishan
> *The Economic Growth Debate: An Assessment* (1977)

E. J. Mishan is perhaps the most eloquent scholar of the "zero economic growth" school of economists, precisely because he does not see zero economic growth as a pain-free solution to modern economic crises. He believes in the free market, unlike most of the ZEG proponents, but he is convinced that the market cannot deal with the problem of depleted resources. I think he is incorrect, but those who agree with him concerning the need to stop economic growth should ponder the pessimism implicit in that position, which Mishan never tries to conceal.

As I have predicted in the past, the politicians will eventually present us with some form of price controls. This will create the zero-growth situation which Mishan thinks is preferable. In fact, it will create a *shrinking economy*, since men will be required by law to invest time, effort, and capital in the new, less efficient, controlled economy. It is not the free market which cannot deal successfully with problems of irreplaceable resources; it is government planning which fails to solve the problem adequately. We will witness a *rapid escalation of Federal power*, and the *crises will multiply* in response to this expansion. But the public will not demand that the government pull out of the economy. The public will, as now, gripe about government inefficiency, but when this inefficiency leads to bankruptcies and problems in each individual's life, he will call for more subsidies, more intervention, more of the same to "cure" *his* problem. We are trapped.

The New York Times Magazine (Jan. 29, 1978) contained an essay on space exploration by John Noble Wilford, the *Times'* director of science. It contained this comment on our times. It focused on the almost universal confusion and ambivalence of our era. It is this

34

ambivalence, this lack of direction, which plays into the hands of the Caesars and potential Caesars:

> Everywhere we look there is tension between the past and the future, between a pessimism we cannot shake and an optimism we cannot quite believe in. The present is thus a turmoil of understandable nostalgia, crippling indecision and bewildering prospect. The immediate consequence is too often malaise and negativism, a general disorientation. Too much is happening too fast, and the only way out seems to be to retreat into ourselves here and now. We dig in at our individual Maginot Lines against the complexities of life, usually identified with the government, any established order, and science and technology, and seek surcease in new religions and cults, astrology, sports, self-indulgent consumerism and the "mellowing" effects of drugs.

Consider the source, as they say. Here is the chief science writer for the most prestigious newspaper in the country, and he is writing to good, upper-middle-class Liberals. He is concerned about the "individual Maginot Lines" people are constructing around their lives, a most memorable phrase. For those of you who missed the fun of World War II, the Maginot Line was the answer of French generals to the military tactics of World War I, an impregnable line of artillery buried in a huge concrete bunker stretching across France's eastern front. Unfortunately, the guns pointed only east and couldn't be moved, so Hitler's forces swept through Belgium and ignored the Maginot Line. Then they could wipe it out at their leisure, from behind. That, indeed, is what too many of us are doing today: setting up seemingly impregnable defenses against dangers that can smile with impunity at our feeble efforts.

Wilford is not exaggerating about the drift into occultism. "Adam Smith," the author of the immensely successful book, *The Money Game*, the royalties of which were lost when Paul Erdman's Swiss bank went under, was deeply involved in "higher consciousness" activities long before he wrote his first best seller, and his book, on the consciousness cults, *Powers of Mind*, is an excellent introduction to the whole scene. Though it is not always visible, some of the most popular newsletter writers in the hard-money camp are drifting close to astrological techniques of forecasting. At least one newsletter openly uses astrology as its basis of prognosticating the future movement of markets. Max Gunther wrote a book about some of the people involved in such affairs, *Wall Street and Witchcraft* (1971). When Wilford speaks of the rise of the astrological cults, he is not using hyperbolic language; he means it.

The significance of these developments should not be missed. The traditional American values of thrift, self-reliance, planning for one's future, confidence in men's ability to deal with problems, and similar positive characteristics of the American outlook are steadily eroding. Faith in the system of freedom which made possible the development of modern capitalism, with its high production and specialization, is also eroding. *Faith in almost everything is eroding among the most educated segments of the population*—a fitting testimony to the efficiency of government-financed, government-controlled education, with its phony neutrality. It is at least worth commenting that a similar series of crises hit the Roman Empire after the first century A. D. One of the most profound, though difficult, books on the history of late Roman culture and philosophy is Charles Cochrane's *Christianity and Classical Culture* (Oxford University Press, 1940). The same loss of faith in traditional values characterized the latter centuries of Rome. The gamblers and the astrologers, the eastern mystics and the retreatists, vied for public acceptance, while the Emperors centralized power with a vengeance, and then perished in a series of army revolts in the third century. A kind of *social atomism* made possible *political centralization*: the end was the disintegration of the whole Empire. Cochrane's words seem to apply only too well to post-1965 America:

> The *debacle*, however, was not merely economic or social or political, or rather it was all of these because it was something more. For what here confronts us is, in the last analysis, a moral and intellectual failure, a failure of the Graeco-Roman mind.... Accordingly, the doom which awaited *Romanitas* was that of a civilization which failed to understand itself and was, in consequence, dominated by a haunting fear of the unknown. The fear in question could by no possibility be exorcized; since it was a consequence of weaknesses which were, so to speak, built into the very foundations of the system.... In this fear we may see an explanation of many of the most characteristic phenomena of classical and post-classical times. To begin with, it serves to account for the steady and persistent growth of a belief in 'luck'. 'Throughout the whole world', declares Pliny, 'in every place, at all times, Fortune alone is named and invoked by the voices of all; she alone is accused and put in the dock, she is the sole object of our thought, our praise, and our abuse.'...A still more sinister development if possible, was that of a belief in astrological and solar determinism, a faith which invaded the empire with the Chaldeans or *mathematici*....The evil of this superstition was, of course, that it utterly denied the reality of human freedom and responsibility, reducing men to the status of mere automata.... The acceptance of such beliefs involved a picture of nature in terms either of sheer fortuity or (alternatively) of inexorable fate. By so doing, it helped to provoke an increasingly frantic passion

for some means of escape. This passion was to find expression in various types of supernaturalism, in which East and West joined hands to produce the most grotesque cosmologies as a basis for ethical systems not less grotesque (pp. 157-59).

Does any of this sound familiar? Can you recognize signs around us that seem to recall the last days of the Roman Empire? It doesn't take a great deal of imagination to make the connections. What political forms paralleled these philosophical and religious developments? Cochrane spells it out in his description of the rise of Augustus Caesar in the years just prior to the birth of Christ:

> It is significant, also, that the imperial prerogative should have developed as an accumulation of extraordinary rights and duties in the main detached from public office; so that the form and appearance of the republic was preserved and, in some respects, the powers of magistrates and senate substantially increased. For this meant that, behind the facade of traditional republicanism, the scattered elements of executive authority were drawn together. On the one hand, the prince was clothed with rights of initiative, control, and revision, sufficient to ensure to him the effective direction of public policy. On the other, he himself assumed responsibility for the conduct of certain departments, the most important of which was that of foreign affairs and imperial defense, involving command of the fighting forces by land and sea, as well as the administration of unsettled frontier provinces. The powers and duties thus assigned to the emperor were broad and comprehensive. They were, moreover, rapidly enlarged as functions traditionally attached to republican magistracies were transferred one after the other to the new executive, and executive action invaded fields which, under the former system, had been consecrated to senatorial or popular control (p. 20).

The expansion of executive orders in the United States, such as E. O. #11921 (June 15, 1976), which I have analyzed in *How You Can Profit from the Coming Price Controls*: "Blueprint for Tyranny," gives us a most enlightening parallel. The executive is steadily replacing the inefficient, almost paralyzed Congress, which is paralyzed precisely because their constituents agree on almost nothing except the fact that we are drifting into unknown, fearful waters. It took two centuries for the Pax Romana to deteriorate to the point where everyone recognized the coming collapse, and a century and a half after that for the collapse—or rather transition—to come. It was a slow process. In our day we get speedy collapses. Progress!

What were the people of Rome really after? What did they expect from the vastly expanded powers of the Caesarian state? Cochrane tells us: "For the spirit which animated its economic, social, and political life was not so much that of expansion as of stability." Not growth, but *stability*; not progress, but the *status quo*; not the over-coming of problems that might lead to new problems, but the *accept-ance of existing problems.* The people wanted the fruits of the Roman Republic's more optimistic expansion apart from the roots of such progress, namely, traditional values that emphasized personal respon-sibility and family loyalty. Meanwhile, the bread and circuses drained the treasury, and the upper classes who were to finance the socialist programs started having far smaller families, using infanticide as one method of reducing family size.

What we should bear in mind is that *pessimism paralyzes action.* We should understand that a people who seek the status quo seldom find anything but decline, and even when they reach their goal (or seem to), such as China did after 1200 and the Eastern Roman Empire (Byzantium) did from 400 to 1200—using a gold coinage to achieve stability—the end is eventually defeat. The status quo cannot with-stand forever the pressures of optimistic expansion. When the faith of the culture is in tatters, and men grasp at the status quo in a frantic at-tempt to keep from sinking into oblivion, the culture cannot survive. Even status quo cultures need *some* faith—more than Rome had, and more than we seem to have.

Solzhenitsyn's July 9, 1975 speech to the AFL-CIO set forth the broad outlines of his analysis of the crises of our time. I recommend that every reader write for a free copy of the two speeches he delivered to the AFL-CIO; then, when you receive the pamphlet, *read it*! It is titled, *Solzhenitsyn: The Voice of Freedom.* It should be ordered from

> AFL-CIO
> 815 16th St., N. W.
> Washington, D. C. 20006

After tracing the history of Communist political tactics, Solzhenitsyn warned:

> In addition to the grave political situation in the whole world today, we are witnessing the emergence of a wholly new situation, a crisis of unknown nature, one completely different, one entirely non-political. We're approaching a major turning point in world history, in the history of civilization. It can be seen in various areas by various specialists. I could compare it only with the turn-ing point from the Middle Ages to the modern era, a whole shift of civilizations. It is a turning point at which settled concepts sud-denly become hazy, lose their precise contours, at which our familiar and commonly used words lose their meaning, become empty shells, at which methods which have been reliable for many centuries no longer work. It's the sort of turning point at which the hierarchy of values to which we are dedicated all our lives, which we use to judge what is valuable and what is not, and which

causes our lives and our hearts to beat, is starting to waver and may perhaps collapse (p. 42).

Political Bailing Wire and Political Nooses

People simply do not know what they want from government. That's not quite true; they want more goodies, but fewer "baddies." Polls indicate that the public believes the two least efficient and least trustworthy groups are *politicians* and *bureaucrats*. Does this mean that positive change is coming? Not in and of itself. These same people re-elect 95% of those incumbent Congressmen who choose to run. These same people go to bureaucrats for aid, and call for more aid, whenever some personal crisis strikes them or their families. So what we have is a contrast between belief in general results of government (negative) and belief in specific persons in, or actions of, government (positive). What we have here is *schizophrenia*. It is this schizophrenia which is paralyzing the political process. The result is momentum, except that the momentum is statist to the core. And if economic crises escalate—as I fully believe—then that *momentum toward the new Caesarism will be escalated*. Prof. Mishan is correct: the public will submit officially to an expansion of government power as never before.

Yet the public won't submit forever. The public will try to *evade* the very effects of the monster they have voted for. Milton Friedman once voiced the opinion to a group of us on the Board of Trustees of the Philadelphia Society that the Jews of the last hundred years have generally adopted the philosophy of democratic socialism. On the other hand, they have spent two thousand years evading big governments all over the world. The second tradition, he thought, would eventually win out. What he said of the Jews, I say of Americans. They have adopted the religion of democratic statism on a national level, if not in theory then at least in practice—every special-interest group wants to get on the dole and out of the pressures of the free market—yet they really resent this bureaucratic meddling in their daily affairs which is the inescapable consequence of the reduction of free market forces.

However, my optimism concerning the underlying preferences of the American people is a long-term optimism. In the *short run*, meaning throughout the remainder of this century, I expect a drift into statism. We are not talking about a dip or two in the Dow Jones Industrial Averages. We are not talking about 6% price inflation and a mere 3% real economic growth. We are talking about what Solzhenitsyn referred to: *the transformation of Western culture*. There are fewer than two dozen democracies left in the world, and most of them are socialist states. The trend of ideas is clear: *more State power*. The opposition to this idea is divided, incoherent, and unsure of its own foundations.

What we are witnessing is the final (I hope and pray) culmination of modern secular humanism. We are witnessing the final escalation of taxation and bureaucratic interference into the economy. We are witnessing the final act of modern socialism's theories of progressive economic development through bureaucratic guidance. As long as there is any production left anywhere in the world, the interventionists will tax it, sap it, and take credit for any growth that may remain after they have beat it into submission. Conclusion: *the total disruption of the international free market, including the domestic markets of the U. S., will probably have to take place before we reach the end of our productive rope.* To shake out the socialist heritage, we will have to shake out all taxable, confiscatable productivity. Only then will the public learn the basic truth: "You can't redistribute it if there ain't any."

This perspective sets my newsletter apart from most of the gloom and doom letters. I see lots of gloom and doom for a long time. I see it as not being anywhere near a resolution point. I think the slow, grinding erosion of freedom and productivity is almost inescapable. A world war could speed up the process, of course, and war is not out of the question. But if people are sitting around with a pile of Krugerrands, hoping to weather a storm of a couple of years, then I think they have underestimated the total nature of the crisis which is upon us. We are seeing *the expropriation of an entire generation*—my generation—which will pay the Social Security tax, the inflation tax, the rationing tax, and will retire with empty wallets, only to face the backlash of the next generation which realizes that there is no way to fund the Social Security system any longer. When that happens—and it will happen as certainly as the Federal budget will remain in deficit—a new era will be upon us, *the era of repudiation*.

The Era of Repudiation

Monetary inflation is repudiation. Price inflation is repudiation. Price and wage controls are repudiation. But when the repudiation is forthright, in nation after nation, because there are no sheep left to shear who are willing to stand still, then the final act of repudiation will have arrived. We are not to that stage yet, and until we are, there will be no fundamental changes in the direction we are headed. Only when there is a universal outcry against the disastrous results— unmistakable disaster—will the socialism of our era be reversed. Reagan's election is a hopeful symbol, but the American welfare State is not being dismantled. Eventually, it will bankrupt the economy.

That is where I become an optimist. I think the welfare State mentality will be reversed, possibly in my latter years. If not, then we will enter a period of true darkness, where hope in the future is really extinguished. That period will have to be classified as the new dark age. It will be the age of the local tyrant, the age of the war lords. The central government cannot hold the whole overcentralized bureaucracy together once the productivity runs out. It will fragment. It will be a new feudalism.

If it turns into that, then each family that can provide spiritual, intellectual, and financial leadership in a local community will have to sacrifice present income and take on heavy responsibilities. *Power flows toward those who are willing to bear responsibilities.* This is what our gold and silver should be all about. This is what our stored food should be all about. Most important, this is what our *education in freedom* should be all about. That's why I am so insistent that my readers read elsewhere. Take advantage of the information that is available in other forms and from other sources. This is what a *small family library* is all about. This is what church libraries should be all about (but seldom are—too practical, you know, to have books on economics and politics, and too controversial).

When the welfare State's debts are repudiated, the welfare State's ideas will be repudiated. When the treasuries are universally empty, the Keynesian and socialist experiments will be over. What then? *Freedom,* I hope, though it will probably take as many years to regain it as it has taken to lose it. And in some (most) cultures, it has never been tried. Men have little taste for it in most of the nations to which our tax dollars flow against our will and against common sense.

We have subsidized failure all over the world. The public is now afraid that universal failure looms ahead. The public is correct. *If you subsidize failure through universal doles, then the market will respond, producing even more failure*; it's the law of supply and demand. The government has registered a multi-billion dollar demand for additional failure, and we are sure to get it. Rome did. Why should we be any different? We are not facing some five-year economic setback. We are facing the painful transformation of a civilization—its ideas, its hopes, its presuppositions, its political institutions, and its monetary system.

Chapter 5

WHY NOT THE WORST?

The "doom and gloom syndrome" really is a syndrome. *Syndrome*: "A group of signs and symptoms that occur together and characterize a particular abnormality." We in the gloom and doom camp do indeed "characterize a particular abnormality." We see things in a unique way. We find signs of inevitable collapse in policies that are applauded by the reigning academic poobahs and their political mouthpieces. We see grim forebodings in news that sends the stock market up a hundred points in a week. The public regards us as a peculiar abnormality, though not quite so abnormal as we appeared to be in the mid-1970s.

Nevertheless, we have to face the reality of what it means to be a part of this syndrome. We constantly face a standard set of criticisms and rhetorical questions that bedevil us, since we are serious about our concern for the future, but at the same time, we ought to have some coherent answers. If we think the future will bring a combination of events that will be the worst of all possible economic scenarios—high inflation *and* high unemployment, no guns *and* no butter, etc.—then we have to face squarely the fact that some developments seem to be so positive. Consider, for example, the startling improvement in computer technology, or the falling price of calculators. How can this be evidence of a faltering economy?

I want to consider a series of questions that are offered by optimists and conventional interpreters of the world economy. I want to provide every reader with some answers to these questions, but more important, with a theoretical framework in terms of which each reader can interpret similar questions for himself and provide his own answers.

"The Economy Is Growing"

If everything is about to come apart, how is it possible that the economy is growing, and has been growing steadily, for several decades? Aren't we now experiencing far greater per capita wealth than ever before? Isn't poverty being eradicated?

Let me say from the start that the economy is growing. We are wealthier today than ever before. One of the failures of the defenders of traditional free market economics is that they underestimate the extraordinary power of the free market system. They simply don't grasp just how resilient and innovative the profit system really is. Prof. F. A. Harper once commented that he had discussed the problem of inflation with a European economist, and he was struck by the man's reply: "It takes a long, long time to destroy a sound currency." The economist made that statement to Harper in the 1950's.

The appeal to economic growth has its weak points, however. The major one is seldom recognized: the possibility of widespread *misforecasts* by entrepreneurs. Capitalists in mid-1929 were still building plants, hiring new employees, and expanding operations. Their activity unquestionably raised the *statistical indicators* of national prosperity. It looked at that time as though there was solid economic growth right through 1929. That's what the statistics said. But the depression proved that *the statistics were wrong*. Entrepreneurs had been misled by the fiat-money-induced boom of the late 1920's. They had made capital investments that the depression wiped out with a vengeance. In short, investment errors made the statistics look good in 1929, but terrible in retrospect.

This is one important feature of any economic catastrophe—or any catastrophe, for that matter. The earthquake in San Francisco in 1906 no doubt cancelled out a lot of "solid economic prospects" that some Chamber of Commerce tract probably outlined in 1905. Right up until the day of reckoning comes, conventional investors and planners do not reckon that it's ever going to show up. The statistics continue to look terrific until they are smashed on the shoals of reality.

What we doomsayers really are saying is this: *the statistics look good only on the assumption that no major unforeseen disruption hits the economy*. To say that it cannot possibly hit is stupid. To say that the statistics of progress are, in and of themselves, proof of long-term progress, is also stupid.

We like those cheap computers. We rely on them. They make our companies more efficient. They are magnificent devices. And if the money system is destroyed by *enforced* price and wage controls, we will find ourselves totally dependent upon highly sophisticated, totally stupid machines that perform garbage operations because the data are all wrong. As some skeptic once remarked, we have built computers that are so efficient that it would take a thousand scholars a million years to make a mistake as large as an IBM 360 can make.

The statistics of progress are no better than the entrepreneurial forecasts of risk-bearing entrepreneurs whose actions, within the framework of a decreasingly free market, create the productivity that these statistics chronicle. The statistics do not support the economy; the free economy, governed by hopefully honest governments of limited authority, make possible the positive statistics. *Destroy the free market, and you can kiss the statistics goodbye.*

"The Dollar Is Backed by Confidence"

All right, stop laughing. This one used to be very popular on campus and in *New York Times* editorials. As a matter of fact, it was acceptable to the *Wall Street Journal* staffers, too. This was the stock answer to those who said that money ought to be backed by gold. Public confidence in money was supposedly based on the rising productivity of the American economy—good statistics, in other words —and this meant that gold was superfluous. It was confidence in the minds of the users of a particular currency unit that determined its fate.

Then came currency devaluations, the collapse of the dollar on international markets, floating exchange rates, and the daily reports concerning the dollar's international performance. Now we're told that the dollar is somehow undervalued, and that the loss of confidence of the public, especially foreign sellers of excess dollars, is unjustified. The dollar ought to be as good as gold, or better, since you can earn 14% on your dollars by buying T-bills. But to keep what little confidence alive that there is, the rates keep climbing: 10%, 12%, 14% . . . . This is the government's way of buying confidence on the international currency markets.

The basic premise is correct. *The value of a currency unit is unquestionably dependent upon the confidence of users and potential users of the unit.* Men are willing to give up scarce economic resources for money because they are confident that other men will do the same thing for them in the future. Money can be used as a unit of account precisely because men expect the money to be acceptable in exchange at some future date.

Why should they be confident in any particular currency? For 6,000 years of recorded history, the answer has been the same: they trust the issuing agency. They trust the government. However, there are degrees of trust. A government which promises to redeem the paper currency on demand in gold or some other scarce commodity can break its promise, thereby converting the currency into a fiat currency, but no government ever abandons full convertibility and then inflates the currency unit massively in a single act. The abolition of full convertibility is a *sign*—recognized by very few at first—that the second process is about to begin. *But the skeptics still have time to hedge themselves against the erosion of the currency unit.* They can become long-term debtors, or buy real estate, or abandon all pension schemes, and cash in their cash-value life insurance policies. They can buy gold and silver (usually in the later stages of inflation, unless it's wartime). They can buy productive equipment. But they have time to act. Why? Because the public trusts the government still, despite the abrogation of the government's contract promising full redeemability. And those who display their distrust of government promises by clinging to the ideology of a fully redeemable currency—or even more preposterously, by clinging to an ideology which would prohibit governments from exercising a legal monopoly over money—naturally bear the brunt of the ridicule by the still confident lemmings who think it means nothing that the government is abandoning the full convertibility of the monetary unit into gold.

It is the later skepticism of the vast majority of initially trusting lemmings which creates the magnificent profit opportunities of the inflation-hedging entrepreneur. The public is skeptical concerning hard-money economics; the gold bugs are skeptical concerning the reliability of the bureaucrats. It all depends on where you place your confidence. There ought to be intelligent reasons for people to remain confident concerning the monetary unit. Since principled action is not highly regarded in our century, the pragmatists have opened themselves up to government confiscation. They have "confidence in confidence" in the same way that some vaguely religious people have "faith in faith." There should be good reasons for both confidence and faith. But are there?

"You Pessimists Will Destroy the Economy"

This is a fully logical conclusion, given the logic of the preceding faith system. If the dollar is based on public confidence as such—a confidence in no way related to government's promises or ability to restrain its spending—then skepticism concerning the integrity of the dollar (meaning the government) obviously threatens the continued operation of the confidence-based economy. The pessimist is like the person who warns the public against the latest Ponzi scheme, or chain letter, just when 40% of the lemmings have sent out their letters telling everyone to send a dollar to the name at the top of the list. Pessimism will bring the game to a halt.

This is quite true. Pessimism in 1930 no doubt contributed to the crises of 1933. The optimism of FDR, coupled with fiat money, provided some increased economic activity in 1933-36. But pessimism or optimism should relate to a basic set of operating presuppositions concerning the nature of man, the State, and the market. Pessimism and optimism are not things in themselves. They are not autonomous attitudes that can lift the economy by its bootstraps, or bring down the economy in flames. Pessimism and optimism need a framework of reality. Pessimism's framework of reality is substantial today, if only because optimism's framework is so unsubstantial—a house of cards in which everyone is supposed to have overwhelming confidence.

How could the pessimism of the doomsayers bring down the economy? There are not enough of them. Those who are pessimistic, and who know the steps that ought to be taken—a tiny minority of investors—seldom take even a majority of the necessary steps. They buy some gold coins, but never learn how to shoot. They buy a water purifier, but remain dependent upon the municipal water system to provide them with what they need. They buy some camping equipment and call it a survival investment. In other words, the constraints on the pessimists, both financial and motivational, are always sufficient to keep them from taking all the steps that they themselves believe are prudent. *They take risks* that the establishment optimists regard as nothing more than rational, normal, and unquestioned by sane people. Risks like staying on a job because of its pension benefits. Risks like buying cash-value life insurance. Risks like living in a large city, especially in the northeast. Risks like becoming dependent upon municipal monopolies for basic necessities. These are high-risk decisions.

So when someone accuses you of being the cause of the collapse that might hit the modern, highly specialized, highly interdependent world economy, you must understand that the critic is attacking you in terms of his theology, namely, his *confidence in confidence.* It is thin ice for an entire economy to rest upon, but it's all he has, and he resents the fact that certain people go around placing "thin ice" signs on top of the ice. He and his millions of fellow optimists are frantically skating on this thin ice, and if someone starts putting up "thin ice" signs, too many of the skaters might head simultaneously for the shore. The trouble is, the ice is connected by a narrow neck to the shore, and if everyone heads for shore at once, it's going to get crowded—just before the ice breaks. (That's why the Arabs don't ask for gold instead of dollars for their oil: the price of gold would become astronomical overnight, since there are so many buyers holding so many dollars, and so little gold in relation to the supply of dollars.) *Only a minority can get off the ice in time.*

If pessimism *alone* could destroy the economy, then the economy *deserves* to be mistrusted. It is not pessimism as such, but pessimism based on an understanding of human nature and government actions, which can bring down modern Keynesian economies. Of course, pessimism won't do it. What will do it is *a series of escalating crises that create pessimism in the minds of a growing minority of participants.* Like the hypochondriac who instructed the gravestone maker to put "See, I told you I was sick" on his headstone, the pessimist can point to reasons for his pessimism. After all, paranoids *can* have real enemies.

And if the grim forecasts come true, the critics will blame the pessimists for having killed the goose that laid the golden egg. This is why pessimists who successfully convert their pessimism to capital assets that survive the economic disruptions had better keep their successes to themselves. In an era of envy, it doesn't pay to profit visibly from "the misery of others." The fact that one profits in a free market only by relieving the misery (or desires) of others never enters the consciousness of the envious.

"The Promised Disaster Never Comes"

That depends. *Which* promised disaster? World War III has never come, either, but that doesn't mean that it never will. In fact, many of those who claim to be unconcerned with an economic crisis say that they're very worried about nuclear war. They want to cut back the military budget. They want more domestic spending by the Federal government on national necessities. (When was the last time you heard a disarmament proponent advocate reduced military spending in order to reduce government taxes and return the funds to the public? They love that "ratchet effect" of taxes once confiscated by the State staying with the State, even if the original justification of the confiscatory tax rates disappears.)

Just because a disaster hasn't come doesn't mean that it won't. In the words of the economist, E. J. Mishan: "Calling 'Wolf' frequently and mistakenly, does not mean that wolves do not exist." All it means is that some people may have their timing off, or they may have forecast the wrong disaster.

Those who prophesy a total, one-time shake-out of the economy, whether mass inflation or comprehensive deflationary depression, are probably being too optimistic. What we are witnessing is a *universal erosion process*, with some segments of the economy prospering, but with pensioners, marginal businesses, creditors, prospective urban home buyers, minority group members who have not yet entered the work force, and taxpayers in general falling behind, or at least facing a major squeeze every time the economy turns into recession. The erosion is steady in its escalation, but not equally painful to all people in every area of their lives. It is continual, so people get used to it, accepting it as normal. The *Wall Street Journal* ran an article on people in a small midwestern town where wives had engineered a boycott in the early 1970's in protest against rising prices. These same ladies universally admitted that they have given up, that they pay the asked prices in the stores, despite their grumbling. They think they have no choice. It doesn't pay to spend so much time shopping for bargains, one said; a person's time is too valuable. They have come to accept inflation—the erosion process—as a fact of life and absolutely inescapable.

This is the crisis of crises. When the voting public feels it cannot successfully deal with *the* economic crisis of our era, price inflation, then the crisis is here. When they want something done, but they don't understand what needs to be done, then they are being set up for "the man on the white horse," the man with the statist answers. People in the doom and gloom camp keep prophesying a crisis (though not the same crisis), but *the major crisis is already at the door and growing*: the acceptance of a philosophy which says that price inflation is now normal and that only "extraordinary measures" by the Federal government will be sufficient to reverse this trend.

This may not sound like much of a crisis. It is not a front-page headline. It may not sell a lot of newsletters. People want a one-shot crisis which will blast the present economy to smithereens and then allow them (newsletter subscribers) to pick up all the pieces because They Knew In Advance. Well, it is not that kind of crisis. It's far worse. It is such a *long-term crisis* that there really is little that a person can do to prepare for all its ramifications over the entire lifetime of the crisis. *It is a crisis of spirit, philosophy, and economic knowledge.* It does not progress in a straight line historically, as California's tax-cutting Proposition 13 demonstrates. But its roots —the philosophy of something for nothing through State coercion —have not been cut, and the next step has to be more monetary inflation, more price inflation, and then the call for "extraordinary measures."

I have stressed this aspect of what I regard as a present crisis because I am convinced that *most newsletter readers will not act in terms of what they know intellectually* until they see the newsletter writer press the panic button. Even then they really don't want to believe it. "You don't mean I should sell my 8.5% bonds in Consolidated Widgets, Inc. do you? Not *my* bonds! Somebody else's bonds, but not mine!" "You don't mean my pension fund is no good. After all, I've paid into it for years. Somebody else's pension fund, but not mine!" But the problem is the *money* in which the bonds and pension funds are denominated. A *"good program" cannot evade bad money.* And the money is universal. It's not limited in its effects to the other guy. So the crisis escalates right under the noses of the people who ought to recognize it, and they fail to take the *multiple strategies* that are required to mitigate *some* (never all) aspects of the crisis. They do not recognize the present looming disaster because *the disaster is a process, not a single event.* (Unless war comes. And war could come.)

Similarly, the critics of pessimism think that the disaster is a single, one-shot event, and when it doesn't come, they conclude that the pessimists were wrong and that no such disaster can come. They have taken the pessimists at their word. They too have defined disaster in terms of one earth-shaking or economy-shaking event, some *once-and-for-all conflagration* that nobody could overlook and which will miss those who have taken the *one-shot preparation* for disaster.

The disaster is not a one-shot event, and the proper preparation is not some last-minute, one-step action, like buying a few gold coins.

To speak of the crisis in this fashion may not be too exciting, and it is hard to motivate people to take evasive action, but it has advantages. It does allow the tiny remnant to take the proper steps, allocating at least some capital, steadily preparing themselves, building for the long-term future. It may be true that no one-step action will cure the problem, and no one-step program will save a family from a long-term, growing disaster, but the erosion process does give people time to build up reserves, financially and psychologically. The capital expenditure needed to protect a family is huge, but a steady program of investing in tools, hard assets, education, and precious metals, not to mention at least an acre of country property with living quarters on it, can mitigate the worst *predictable* features of the erosion process. (Unpredictable features, like terrorism aimed at a particular family, or pillage of a particular home, or a nuclear attack on a particular small town, cannot always be mitigated successfully.)

Let each man face the facts: *the crisis is now.* It will also be tomorrow, next year, and next decade. It will not go away. It will get worse. He who sits around waiting for the signal, "this is it!" is waiting for the wrong signal. When erosion becomes rapid, most people will hardly notice, since they will have been anesthetized to it. The signs of breakdown will be blamed on "outside agitators," like newsletter writers, gold bugs, speculators, or unpredictable acts of nature. Don't let a false understanding of the nature of the crisis anesthetize you.

(Maybe now is the time for you to turn to Appendix B and survey what you need to do. If not, just go on to the next chapter.)

Chapter 6

THE LAST TRAIN OUT

It would make a classic Alfred Hitchcock movie. The hero and his fiancee are standing at the station in some unnamed European city. The refugees are desperately trying to squeeze into the second and third class spaces. Our hero has money, or a ticket purchased beforehand, or some asset that will get him on the train. The Nazis (or perhaps the Soviets) are closing in on the city. He is a marked man, having worked for the underground against them. There is a spy following him, trying to delay him long enough to miss the train. Freedom lies ahead. Two more trains (possibly more) are scheduled for the afternoon, but no one knows whether they will ever be able to leave, or get to the final destination. Is this the last train out?

As investors on the fringes of conventional markets, we are trying to preserve our assets, or produce large capital gains. We are convinced that the key to investment success is to put our capital into off-beat investments that have traditionally done well in times of economic confusion. In other words, our investment strategy is based on the idea that the conventional markets are not where the long-term returns are likely to be. So we are inordinately sensitive to certain indicators of forthcoming disruptions. Historically, the *price of gold* has been one of these key indicators—all over the world.

There is a problem here. If the rise in the price of gold is "merely" inflation induced, meaning a response to the general rise in commodity prices, then we have little to worry about, other than that general rise in commodity prices. But gold almost always moves in huge leaps —$40 and $90 at a time—up or down. The rapidity of gold's moves startles investors and potential investors in gold. They think there is something frightening about such a rapid move upward in the price of the metal. They conclude that "this is it," the time of total disintegration is at hand.

Yet at the same time, they don't really believe it. They wonder whether they ought to buy now. If the day of final economic reckoning were really at hand, there would be no question. It would be suicidal not to cash in all conventional investments and buy gold, guns, and groceries. So people hesitate. Then they call some expert, preferably one who has told them long ago to buy gold.

50

This stage is the "lemming stage." Lemmings are those European creatures that run to the sea in the millions from time to time, for no known reason, to drown themselves. I used to be a gold coin salesman. I have been writing newsletters for several years. I have been following the market closely since 1963. And I can always tell when it's about time for gold to go down. I start getting calls from people asking me, "Should I buy gold now?" No; they should have bought in June.

I can remember a phone call I got from a conservative economist who had talked about buying silver from the time, in 1973, that it rose above $2.00 an ounce. He had talked about it endlessly. He had said he was convinced it would go up in response to government inflation. Finally, in March of 1974, I got a call from him. Did I think he should buy a futures contract in silver? The price was about $6.20 by then. No, I said, I thought he should buy a bag of coins and store it. But he was ready to make his move. "I've agonized over this for a year." he said. All right, I said, but make a quick, in-and-out move. Don't get greedy. Fine, he said. It was down the limit the next day. He bought. It went up. He could have made a good $1,000 profit. He stayed in. Then the bottom dropped out, as never before. It hit $6.70 or thereabouts, and dropped one full dollar the next day. He was wiped out on his investment. He didn't go bankrupt, but he lost all of his equity, and probably had to come up with a thousand or more in addition. He knew for a year. When *he* went into the market, it was time to sell. Silver didn't hit $6.70 again for five years.

Which leads me to *North's law of delayed investing*: He who knows what to do in advance and hesitates, will jump in at the top, or near the top, when what he knew would happen actually happens. I've done it myself on occasion. I touted Durban Deep mining shares in 1970, when Durban sold for under $2 per share. It went to $35 or so (maybe $40), fell to $18, and I got in on a sure winner—the one I had always known would win. It sank to its old $2.00.

Having seen this law of investing in action so many times, I now respect it. I believe in its predictability. Show me an investor who knows, on principle, what he should do, but who doesn't believe enough to put his money where his mouth or heart is...he buys in only in the middle (or near the end) of a panic run, when all the average investors catch on to this "sure winner."

It creates a real dilemma for me as an investment counsellor. When the calls started coming in after gold went above $195 in 1974, I knew what had to be happening at the coin stores. I called two of them. Sure enough, they were cleaning up. The salesmen were grinding out the commissions like wildfire. (I have a relative who sells coins for a living, and whenever he goes on vacation, the markets surge; it's a great contra-cyclical indicator.) Everyone was calling in to get on the last train out, or get on the bandwagon, or get on the gravy train. "All aboard!" cry the salesmen, and off they go.

Well, why not? The salesmen have worked themselves to a frazzle for months or even years trying to explain the logic of gold and silver. They face seemingly convinced listeners who refuse to take action. A world full of Scarlet O'Haras, all willing to think about it tomorrow. Then the wild ride comes. Only when the panic hits, only when all the conventional—or at least a solid chunk of *somewhat* more conventional—investors start getting on board, do they finally decide to think about it today, and even to act. They need psychological confirmation, a vote of confidence from their peers, a little lemming action. Then they call in their orders. Suicidal.

It makes cynics out of the coin salesmen. The salesmen know what the score is. Gold is probably peaking. Of course, it might go up $100 before it drops back $75. No one knows. Maybe this is the last train out. Maybe it's at least the next-to-the-last train out. But in any case, the commissions are beckoning, the months of rational discussion are about to pay off, and they take the order. "Is this the time to buy gold?" The honest answer: "If you have none, it's *always* the time to buy gold." And these are the people who probably haven't got any, since those who know the markets have already been buying in the nice calm period.

Psychological Paralysis

Those of us who have spent any time selling gold and silver are quite familiar with this universal malady. The person knows he should buy. He knows the dollar cannot be trusted. He has heard of the history of gold as a contra-government investment. But he simply cannot bring himself to take action. Why not? The salesman isn't a trained psychologist. All he knows is that this phenomenon is all too common.

My favorite story in this regard actually happened to me. I sold gold and silver coins in 1973. I was sitting at my desk when I received a phone call. A man with a British accent wanted to know what the price of British gold sovereigns was. He was interested in buying some. (This was prior to the legalization of gold, when we could not sell Krugerrands or Austrian 20 coronas.) I told him they were selling for $26 each. "That's impossible," he replied. "Why, I called not too long ago and they were only $13 each." He had called about a year earlier. "That's correct; they were selling for that when you last called in," I replied. "They sure were a good buy then. Did you buy any at that time?" Negative. Then came his classic, ultimate, incomparable reply: *"But nobody there made me buy them then!"* There was the sound of anguish in his voice. "Do you want to buy some now?" I asked. Negative. They were just too high. That was in early 1973. They were to hit $70 within a year and a half before backing off to about $50. He was right though; nobody made him buy them. Not at $13 each, $26 each, or $70 each. They hit $250 briefly in January, 1980. Two years later, they were back down to $90. They will go higher.

How can a salesman deal with such a prospective client? Tell him the market is sure to go up? That would probably be unethical, unless the seller has some technique of predicting gold price movements that he absolutely believes in. Can the salesman tell him that "now is the time to buy" if there is a chance that the person is buying in the midst of a panic? Should he tell him this? Is panic the only motivating force that will ever get this client to take the big step and get out of fiat money and into some precious metals? Is panic the only way to un-paralyze the person's psychological block? If so—and the person shows every sign that it is so—the salesman ought to tell him that "now is the time to buy." For the sake of the man's future, as well as the commission, now probably *is* this person's time to buy.

The problem stems from the fact that the best time to buy is never known by anyone, or at least not known by more than a handful of professional traders. We have three choices, each one geared to some-one's psychology. We can buy because:

1. *Gold is rising rapidly.* Everyone is getting on board. It is the final call for the last train out. The hordes are at the gate. "There's no tomorrow."

2. *Gold is collapsing in price.* It is at the bottom. The "weak holders of gold" are out of the market. All the bad news has been discounted. "There'll never be a better buying opportunity than this!"

3. *Gold's price is stable.* It is in one of its holding patterns. It has been stable for months. It's about to make one of its fast moves upward. "Get in now, before the lemmings come rushing into the market."

These are all excellent reasons to buy. They are all excellent reasons *not* to buy, because:

1. *Gold is rising rapidly.* The lemmings are into the market. The "weak holders" are dominant. These prices cannot possibly be maintained. Wait.

2. *Gold is collapsing in price.* The lemmings are getting out of the market. "Don't fight the tape!" It may hit new lows. Panic has just begun. There will be good bargains later. I'm worried. Wait.

3. *Gold's price is stable.* Why buy now? There's plenty of time. I can put my money into T-bills and get 14%. It may go into a panic downward spiral. No use getting in too soon. Wait.

Which attitude is correct? It all depends on the future. Sometimes the "wait and see" attitude is correct. It certainly was in 1975 when gold went from $198 to $160 and even to $148. Sometimes the "wait and see" attitude is incredibly costly, such as the one all too many took, from late 1976 to early 1980. When gold moved from $103 to $120 in 1976, the handwriting was on the wall. So many people knew it. So many people waited. Now they see. Too late.

The fact of the matter is this: most people *have not* bought gold, *will not* buy gold, and will not have the money to buy gold when they finally decide to make their move. The bulk of the nation's population knows very little about gold. The gold markets are a concern to a fraction of the investing public today. But that fraction is growing, and in mass inflation-price controls, it will continue to grow. The market will expand, and the price will rise, which is to say, the dollar will fall.

There will finally be a "last train out" for *some* urban dwellers, in *some* instances. When or where this will happen is problematical. If World War III breaks out, the price of gold (collapse of fiat currency) will be only too evident. But there will be numerous "last trains out" between now and then. As one of my subscribers once put it, "I've been on the last train out several times."

For the person who has heard of gold, but who regards gold speculation as crackpot, unpatriotic, premature, unwise, silly, doom-and-gloomy, or devoid of confidence, the second set of reasons will predominate. There are three good reasons for not buying gold. All of them have been used in the past. All of them will be used in the future. If everyone abandoned this negative attitude one morning, they would all rush out to buy gold, driving gold's price to astronomical levels in a few days, whereupon the first reason for not buying gold would reassert itself: "Gold is too high."

Gold Is Too High

This is the obverse of the statement: "The dollar, in relation to gold's present price is too low. The dollar, vis a vis gold, is undervalued. Buy dollars. Hold onto dollars. Seek dollars."

Well, maybe it's true. It certainly was true in 1975. The dollar was sinking, but gold was sinking faster. *There are no all-purpose ports for every conceivable storm.* If there were, everyone would try to crowd into them at every sign of a storm, and you, I dare say, would wind up at the end of the line once in a while. So would I.

So *which storm* are you predicting? *When* do you think it will hit? Once you have made up your mind, you can buy a space on the dock for your vessel. It will be there when you need it, but you may not need it for a few years. You still have to pay the docking fees, storm or not. In 1975, gold's docking fee looked rather steep. Right now, it doesn't look that costly, in retrospect.

What do you believe concerning the dollar? What do you think are its *long*-term prospects? What amount of your present net assets do you want to apply to a dollar-avoiding, highly liquid, easily concealed asset like gold?

What do you think are the short-term prospects for the dollar? Will it rally for a time? Is it better than other fiat currencies? Will foreigners decide to hold dollars at some price? Will the gold boom slow down or reverse itself for a while when the news about the dollar gets better? Will the lemmings finally swim ashore and go back to "business as usual"?

What do you think of gold's prospects in comparison to real estate in your area, or silver, or unregistered handguns? Is gold too high, right now, not in comparison to dollars, but in comparison to other effective *dollar-avoiding investments*?

What assets do you have now? Are you in need of extra gold coins, or would some other hard asset be better? Is there an auction coming up where you think there will be some one-time-only bargains? Where do you live? Have you a food storage program? Will food be higher, proportionately, a year from now, than gold?

Gold may well be too high today, if you are talking about gold in the short run (compared to dollars), gold compared to silver, or gold compared to food. But gold is not too high today compared to the dollar in five years, even discounting for interest available on dollar-denominated investments. So it depends upon the following considerations:

Your present geographical location
Your present mix of hard asset investments
The future of the dollar and gold over the next year
Your present evaluation of interest rates for real estate loans
Your need for liquidity
Your age
Your need for income
Your business opportunities for the next year

But, you say, these are the same old criteria for investing in *anything*. Right you are! My point exactly! Don't violate North's first law of speculation: *Never buy or sell in panic.* If gold is dropping, don't worry, it may go lower, but eventually it will go higher. If gold is climbing, don't worry (unless you have absolutely none), since it will eventually drop, before it goes through the roof, i.e., the dollar goes through the floor. Never forget, *gold is a political metal.* Governments, short of collapse, can take actions that will force down its price. Expect such actions. Fret not. (Unless, of course, you're in the futures market. Then you must fret, full-time, for as long as you're in.)

Is Now the Time to Buy?

If you have none, and you have agonized over the fact that you missed out on gold's big move, buy. You missed out on gold's big move. You cannot get even, ever. There is no way you can call back a poor investment. No matter what you do now, you cannot recoup, since a correct decision taken today could have been taken with a lot more capital had you not missed the big move. That capital is forever, irretrievably lost. As my father used to say, don't stand around looking up a dead horse's nose. Or something like that.

But why buy now? Because *you may not buy later*, that's why. You may put it off. Some people only act rationally under pressure. Some students only crank out the term paper the night before it's due. Sure, it would probably have been a much better paper had the student researched it diligently, three hours a day, and written two preliminary drafts. But the fact is, most students never write term papers this way. And the fact is, most buyers of gold never buy at the bottom, or even in the nice, calm periods. They buy in panic. So on the assumption that you ought to buy gold sometime, and you have put it off until now, *buy now*. The problem is not with gold; the problem to be overcome is *your own psychological paralysis*.

Here is my favorite (though difficult) strategy: buy the long-term durable goods that the lemmings have not yet rushed out to get. Buy the good which will be out of stock when the lemmings rush down to spend their depreciating fiat money. Buy the *next* object of lemming fancy, or the last one. Don't buy the present one unless you have none whatsoever.

I don't think today is the last train out. You may find the ticket, as denominated in gold, at its lowest price today. Gold may never again be this low. But do not forget, there are a lot of tickets that are good in exchange for a seat on the last train out. Gold is only one of them. Since they will all be going up as "exit day" approaches, buy a different ticket. The price of all the tickets is surely going up in general, but if you shop carefully, and avoid Lemming Street, you may pick up some bargains.

Stay out of panic runs in or out of gold. Do it on principle, as a means of self-discipline and training. Go in or out of gold in times of stability, when gold is off the front pages. In the long run, you will preserve more of your capital this way. You can get your tickets on the last train out at a much reduced rate.

Chapter 7

PROCRASTINATION AND PARALYSIS

Counselling people over the telephone made me aware of a phenomenon of human nature that I always knew existed, but at the same time, I never quite grasped its significance. It is the willingness of people to wait until the last minute, or later, to make a major decision. This flaw in human character can be incredibly expensive.

Let me give you an example. Several, in fact. A lady called the *Ruff Times* hot-line in 1979 to ask whether she and her husband ought to pay $12,000 cash for a new Peugeot diesel, or else put a small down payment on the car and buy gold with the difference. Her husband had made a $500 deposit that morning on the car, but he hadn't signed the papers. Which was the best way to go?

The best way to go was *away*, fast. She was asking the wrong question. The correct question was: Should we spend $12,000 for a Peugeot diesel? The answer was clear: no. Their income level could not sustain that much expense. The salesman, it seemed, had told them that a car like this would go 500,000 miles without major repairs, as preposterous a statement as "Invest in America by buying U. S. Savings Bonds!" Well, almost as preposterous. They were buying a foreign car, with the predictable problems of buying replacement parts in the future, a French car at that, which doesn't have an extensive repair network in the U. S. They were, in effect, tying themselves to the city, a suburb of Los Angeles. Diesel fuel was getting scarce, and unless a person intends to store it in 500 or 1,000-gallon containers (since diesel is safer to store than gasoline), it no longer pays to shell out a small fortune to buy a diesel automobile, even a comfortable one like the Peugeot. It would have been conceivable to buy one a year earlier for $8,000, but not in the summer of 1979.

What is my point? Simple: they had access to a toll-free telephone line for free consultation, yet they waited until the deposit was in the hand of the salesman. Why? Why do people wait until the last minute, never asking the proper questions, only to find that they have made an error of judgment? Even when the information is free of charge, they wait.

Time after time—several times each week, in fact—I spoke with people who told me of some investment they have just made. "I did the right thing, didn't I?" they asked. Sometimes yes, usually not.

Maybe they just bought a long-term annuity, or a cash-value life insurance policy. In any case, it was diametrically opposed to what I think is sensible, or what Howard Ruff had advised in print on several occasions. (These calls came through Ruff's hot-line.) They called in to confirm their faith in their own good judgment. They expected me to tell them they did the right thing. They were universally shocked to learn that they have been sold some turkey of an investment. Why hadn't they phoned in a week earlier, *before* they put their money on the line? Why did they wait for me to confirm them in their decision, rather than to counsel them before they signed the check? I cannot answer. Neither could they. When I asked them point-blank why they didn't call in earlier, they never could give me a straight answer, except the lame one, "I never thought of it." But once the ink was dry, they thought of it.

Part of this phenomenon is well known to salesmen. There is a period of "buyer's remorse"—second-guessing that takes place in the mind of the buyer after he walks away with his receipt. The buyer keeps asking himself whether he did the right thing. The salesmen naturally want to avoid all contact with the buyer for the first few days after the transaction, at least until the check clears. The buyer at this point is highly susceptible to suggestions from critics. *They* didn't buy the deal, so they feel certain he shouldn't have, either. Maybe they're correct, and maybe they're only envious, but their words carry weight, mainly after the deal has been transacted.

You have to know yourself before you buy. You have to know what your second-guessing will do after the deal is sealed. *You have to second-guess yourself way in advance.* After seeing this phenomenon first-hand, I'm convinced that this is one of the most difficult problems faced by rational investors.

It Got Away

Not buying is no answer, either. You can second-guess yourself both ways. Your friendly post-decision counsellor responds, "Boy, if you get an offer like that one again, let me know. Would I like a piece of *that* action!" Yes, on the assumption that the deal is presently unavailable to him, he would.

There is no better place to second-guess yourself for not buying than at an auction. You let it get away, didn't you? And now you're just certain that it was the deal of a lifetime. How could you have been so short-sighted? (Meanwhile, the wife of the guy who bought it is saying, "Henry, you told me that you wouldn't buy one of these things again. You remember the trouble we had the last time you came home with one. How much did you pay? . . . *You can't be serious* !!! For *this*?")

One rule of auctions should be understood in advance: *another item just like it, or close enough, will show up again*. Just wait around long enough. After all, this is Henry's second one. Maybe his third. (My favorite case like this was a former professor of mine who had bought a choice used book, only to discover that his own nameplate was in the cover. He had sold it to the store a few months before, because he knew he'd never read it.)

There is one problem with this universal rule: it isn't universal. There is one set of economic conditions that defies it, and sometimes abolishes it. That set of conditions is called price and wage controls.

Under a price control regime, *used goods* take on a premium. Used goods that are productive and immediately valuable under the conditions of a shortage economy are not that easy to locate. Sure, you may find lots of bargains. You may find all the items you can use of the items you can't use. But you can't always locate the items you can use, let alone those you really need.

The summer of 1979 may become known as the summer when the used diesel power generators disappeared. A 5,000 watt Lister or Petters-powered generator that was easily purchased in the spring could not be found by summer. New units, yes, if you had the $3,500 to $5,000, but not the less expensive used units. Waiting around on the assumption that there will always be another opportunity is not always that smart. If the psychology of the buying public shifts for some reason, then the rule doesn't hold up. There may not be another time around—at least not at a price like the one that was missed.

This is one of the truly devastating facts about panic buying under price or wage controls. Energy is operating under controls in the United States. It has been hampered for decades by price controls. So the public can dry up energy-related supplies, especially in the used goods markets, merely by acting in terms of panic. The rapid depletion of *lockable gasoline caps* is an obvious example. They disappeared off the shelves almost overnight in 1974, and it happened again in 1979. In between, you could buy all of them you could afford any time the desire hit you. Odd, isn't it, that the desire didn't hit you? Until the day it hit everyone.

The horror of price controls, when they are systematically enforced, is that *they don't give you a second opportunity*. You strike when the iron is hot, because there isn't much coal around to heat it back up later on. You have to know what you want in advance. You have to be ready to act when you see the opportunity.

The Discipline of Forecasting

The entrepreneur is the person who can predict the future state of the market, and who acts courageously in terms of his forecast. He has to put time and effort into studying the present state of the market, and he has to make plans about the future. Not only does he have to devote himself to understanding the likely scenarios of the future, but he also has to make plans about how he can get from now until then, meeting the demands of the future, with the minimum expenditure of resources. It is an incredibly difficult job even when you have reliable price data to estimate with. When these price data are distorted by price controls, it makes the task far more expensive and risky.

The entrepreneur can often make predictions about what you and I will be buying in the future far more efficiently than most of us can predict our future needs. There are several reasons for this. *First*, we assume that the market is a smoothly functioning system, and that when we want to buy some item, it will be offered for sale by several competing sellers. Thus, we don't have to give much thought to the details of making the purchase. The entrepreneur is being paid by all of us to make those decisions concerning production and distribution. *Second*, the entrepreneur can rely on "the law of large numbers." He can forecast the needs of many buyers precisely because we buyers are part of a statistically predictable class or classes. Our individual actions are not predictable, but as a collective whole, we are. I know, as an entrepreneur, that when I make a mailing to a list, to offer a *Remnant Review* subscription, that I am unlikely to get more than a 5% response, and I will probably get 2% or less, unless it is a very special list—a prescreened list, in effect. I don't know which buyers will act, but I know that a lot of them won't. Professional mailers who use lists regularly can be amazingly precise in advance—unless, of course, some unforeseen condition appears. The mail-order universe is guided by the law of large numbers. There are few deviations from certain statistical responses, and those deviations are eventually brought into line (e.g., through too many mailings to a "hot" list, or by the list-renter's decision to hike the rental fee for his list).

Competing entrepreneurs can therefore make very intelligent judgments concerning the future state of the market, even though you and I, as buyers in that market, may not even know what we will be buying in the future. It's a marvelous fact of the free, competitive market that such *predictability* exists within a framework of *non-coerced human action*. Of course, some entrepreneurs guess wrong, but if they continue to do so, they are removed from the business of forecasting.

What the *control economy* does is to destroy the key economic indicator used by successful forecasters: the freely fluctuating price system. When this goes, so does the ability of most entrepreneurs, at least those who are used to operating within the framework of legal markets. The Mafia may do well under controls, but that's another story. They can make offers to suppliers that the suppliers can't refuse. The rest of us can't make those kinds of offers.

Price controls force us to become frenzied entrepreneurs. They force us to become forecasters of what we will be needing in the future. We can no longer rely on the ability of competing entrepreneurs to deliver to us the goods we desire at prices that just manage to clear the market—the balanced equation of buyers and sellers. When supplies are curtailed by the profit restrictions imposed by price controls, we find that suppliers are no longer competing actively in the open, legal markets. They are increasingly pressured by the reality of illegal competitive bidding to sell to the highest bidders, and these bidders are offering their bids on illegal markets. Even in the face of threatened prosecution, market participants continue to make their offers. The suppliers of goods and services begin to shift production toward those who are making higher-than-legally-permitted bids.

It is this *transfer of production* in the direction of those buyers who offer higher-than-permitted bids which forces us all to become better forecasters. We know that supplies are going to dry up at the legally announced prices. We will have to pay more by standing in line, or by taking the chance that the supplier will run out before we make our transaction. Or we will have to pay more by buying items we really don't need in order to get delivery of the items we (and most of our competing consumers) think are crucial. Or we will have to pay more on some illegal market. But the inescapable fact remains: *a statistically significant portion of the buying public*, meaning you and I, *will have to pay more*. The price controls are supposed to protect us buyers. Instead, they guarantee that most of us will pay more, most of the time, compared to what we would have had to pay had the controls never been imposed. The question is not whether or not we will pay more. The only significant question is this one: *In what form will we have to pay more*? More time wasted in lines? *As entrepreneurs, we ought to decide today which form is least burdensome to us*. And having made that forecast, we ought to begin making plans to increase our supply of whatever it is that we intend to trade for the goods and services we need: time, disappointing visits to empty stores, or an acceptable unit of account in those future markets. (Unit of account: Gold? Silver?)

Do you begin to see what price controls mean for the average buyer? We all want to defer making key decisions until later. We always feel pressed by today's decisions. We want to delay as long as possible the consideration of the next series of major decisions. Our own nature impels us to put off until later the decisions that we could be making today. *The man who does not recognize this aspect of his own personality is going to have to pay extra under a price controls regime.* We tend to assume that the future will take care of itself. And in a godly, honest, free society the future usually does, precisely because profit-seeking professional forecasters enter the markets and assume the burdens of uncertainty. But it is the imposition of price controls which penalizes this class of professional forecasters, thereby reducing their effectiveness (raising their costs), or actually forcing them to enter the so-called black markets, both for buying their production goods and for selling them at the best possible price.

Price controls ruin us all by destroying the very class of businessmen who are willing to enter the gap of our own procrastination. The rewards to these people are reduced on the legal, visible markets, so they leave these markets—markets where most of us operate most of the time. The very place which law-abiding citizens prefer to operate is where it no longer pays entrepreneurs to participate.

We are all thrown back on our own resources, meaning personal, internal, psychological, entrepreneurial resources. And need I emphasize how inexperienced we are in making forecasts? I am not just referring to our woeful errors in forecasting what we will be likely to need in the future. I also mean our lack of experience in *supplying ourselves* what we need in the future.

Mini-Warehousing

I have long recommended that people begin to stockpile goods and tools for an indefinite future. I prefer to stay out of illegal black markets. I don't like the risks involved, and I don't like having to pay the higher prices that must be paid in order to lure prospective sellers out of the woodwork and into the "alternative markets." To avoid these costs, we have to plan ahead. We must act now.

What this means is that people must become their own future wholesalers. They have to start entering today's markets for durable goods in order to become "sellers" in the future—*sellers to themselves*. The government says that it is illegal to buy this or that good at prices above a certain stated level. So the goods dry up on the legal, visible markets. All those who intend to stay out of illegal markets, but who also intend not to see their future standard of living reduced more than is absolutely necessary by the shortages, must enter today's markets and start buying up those items that they think they will be needing in the future. Some people call this hoarding. I prefer to call it saving. Perhaps we can compromise and call it mini-warehousing.

We have to think about practically everything. We have to sit down and make a list of those items we use on a daily basis, weekly basis, monthly basis, and even yearly basis. A family without a *buying list*, with a *schedule of purchase* and a *budget* geared to these purchases, is not taking seriously the threats presented by price controls. This applies to consumer durables as well as to those durables used in our businesses. For example, I stockpile paper for my newsletter. I intend to begin stockpiling ink. But mine is a relatively simple product. What about the really complex production mixes? How can a person stockpile everything? Here is where entrepreneurship comes in. Here is what will make us or break us. Can we predict which items will be in short supply first, stockpile them, and use future income to stockpile the next items in line to disappear? To stay in business under price controls, this is exactly what businessmen have to do. Price controls make the life of a forecaster that much more complex.

Mini-warehousing requires a new discipline. It means that every consumer must begin to deal with an uncertain future—a future which is even more uncertain as a direct result of the price controls. If you think our energy forecasting difficulties have been nightmarish, just consider the implications of a general price freeze. Consider the implications of "gasoline lines" extended to the whole economy appearing unpredictably, producing panic buying, clearing the shelves of whatever item is on the minds of the masses of buyers. The gasoline lines of 1974 and 1979 were only a foretaste of things to come. You have to get psychologically prepared for these events under a general price freeze.

There is only one sure way of dealing with such crises psychologically: *have some reserves*. This means *moral* reserves, including a view of the universe which is personal, not hostile to our efforts, but controlled by a personal Creator who can intervene to help us. Second, it means having reserves of the *basic necessities*. To head off your own panic, you have to know in advance that the basics are taken care of as much as is humanly possible, given your own present financial limitations. *Don't discount panic.* Panic is basic to human nature, as basic as procrastination. You have to face yourself realistically. You have to have sufficient reserves on hand so that you know your flanks are covered. Then you can make more rational economic decisions under major stress. You have some leeway. You'll need this leeway.

Disciplined Impulse Buying

Impulse buying is usually inefficient. You buy what you don't need at prices you can't really afford. That's why major decisions should almost always be postponed until you can sit down and think about all your second-guessing, before you sign the dotted line. This is first-guessing, and it is the proper way to buy, *assuming times are normal.*

Times are rapidly becoming perverse—the real opposite of normal. We are facing the *normality of perversity.* Economics informs us of the kinds of disruptions we can expect. We have to take economics, and the disruptions, seriously.

Impulse buying now begins to make sense. Maybe there won't be "a second time around." Not at today's prices, anyway. So you have to train yourself to make impulse decisions that are rational, the same way a skilled athlete makes a move against an opponent, or the way he reacts to such a move. Most of us will never become O. J. Simpsons, but we want to do better than the average competitor.

What the systematic forecaster has to do is start thinking about his future. He has to assume that there will be a decrease of competing sellers to serve him. He has to start checking into prices, supplies, quality levels, and the most likely sources of supply of practically everything he buys. He has to know what a proper price for some item is, precisely because he has been monitoring prices in this area on a systematic basis. This means going to auctions, Good Will stores, flea markets, swap meets, and other wholesale centers. It means knowing what has to be bought, and then rapid, confident action when a buying opportunity appears. He who hesitates is lost. A stitch in time saves nine. And so forth.

It is discipline, training, and practice that make a good athlete. The same thing is true of any craftsman. This is what I'm recommending to every reader. *You have to become skilled in new markets*—markets that you have been able to rely on in the past. You have to get out and start shopping today. You have to gain familiarity with new markets, or else get the co-operation of those who can assist you in entering these markets. *Swapping skills in different markets is, in my opinion, one of the best possible swaps of all.* Search out others who can help you enter new markets. Regard familiar markets as sources of capital in future swaps; someone you know won't be all that familiar with your markets. You can trade expertise later on. This is why group planning makes sense. Each person can specialize, watching for sales, teaching others what to look for. *The more help you can give, the more help you can get later on.*

One of the reasons I am unenthusiastic about planning for in-dividualized retreats is that I know how much I need the assistance of others. The division of labor is reduced drastically by controls. Why reduce it further? Yes, I can see the idea of having a one-family retreat for a single major crisis, if you have a lot of money to spare, and if you need the protection. Joel Skousen recommends a three-stage retreat: a semi-autonomous survival home, a back-up retreat property, and an absolutely hidden retreat known only to you and as few builders as possible. But only a tiny handful of people have the money to buy all three, not to mention the motivation. So we will have to content ourselves with stages one and two, and perhaps only stage one.

What we need is co-operation. Impulse buying is mandatory the longer controls stay on and are really enforced. Buyers who know how to buy should accompany one or two close friends on a visit to an auction, or to some off-the-beaten-path source of supply. Trade off markets from time to time. Help each other out.

This is not hypothetical speculation. I am absolutely serious. Maybe you don't have a lot of money. Maybe you're short on time. It doesn't matter. Even if you only make two or three visits a year to the "alternative markets," it pays to do it. If nothing else, you will establish rapport with sellers. They will know your face. In times of critical shortages, not everyone will be welcomed with open arms at these auctions. You are paying your dues early. You are establishing your right to be there. You do what you can to get yourself on good terms with the available sellers. *Personal contacts* count for plenty when times are tight.

And you have to have the guts to buy. Make the offer. If you know you'll need it in the future, buy it now. All right, if another one shows up later on, you can buy it, too. Keep the first one for trading in the future. Or sell one of them. Or use one of them for spare parts. But you must condition yourself to *buy in advance, even when you're not absolutely certain it's a good deal.* You have to pay the freight of bad decisions early, while you have time to recoup your losses. There will come a day when you'll have one opportunity, maybe, and no opportunity to recoup. That's when you had better know when to buy.

Impulsive buying, like all other instincts, can be disciplined. Those who refuse to learn the skill of rational, selective impulse buying will pay far higher prices when panic hits. Panic is, of course, the ultimate form of impulse buying. No one is immune to it. But it is possible to get a handle on it. The more panic buying can be avoided, the better off you are. *Panic buying is undisciplined impulse buying.* Disciplined impulse buying is steady, determined buying that is based on the full realization that panic is quite possible in the future, and *it is necessary to stockpile goods now in order not to get caught up in a panic buying mania later on.* Disciplined buying is pre-panic buying in a stage of the economy in which panic buying is looming, even breaking out sporadically. Like the panic in the gasoline lines which led to shortages of used diesel home generators, so panic in other areas can touch off new waves of impulse buying. *Buy before panic hits*: this is the rule of disciplined impulse buying.

You must say to yourself, "I can't safely put this off forever. The only questions are these: When, where, what price, and how much panic when I finally enter the market?" Price controls make these questions mandatory. It isn't a question of *if*, once the controls go on; it's only a question of *when*.

Get the word "maybe" out of your vocabulary when it comes to shortages. Act!

The Mistake Paralysis

Whatever your income level, wherever you are in terms of planning, you must reduce your mistake paralysis. Clearly, the rich man can make a lot more mistakes with his capital than a middle-class investor. But the ultimate mistake is to ignore the signs of the economy. The real mistake is saying that do-nothing litany to yourself, "But [   ] is so expensive now." Of course it's expensive. It's expensive because it's increasingly important as a hedge against disaster. You missed it before; that's no reason to miss it again. Whether it's gold, silver, ammunition, used generators, land, equipment, raw materials, or whatever: it's more expensive precisely because people are convinced that it will become more and more important in the future. Unless conditions change, the price will probably go higher. And for conditions to change to your advantage, everyone else has to change his mind, selling off whatever it is that you want to buy inexpensively, while you maintain your confidence and buy it up at a bargain price. Question: *What is your guarantee that you won't play the lemming again?* What will prevent you from following the pack? You had better know yourself very well if you play speculation games with survival needs. Trying to save 20% could kill you.

Will people throw away their economic futures because they're trying to save a miserable 20%? Absolutely. Why? Because they are kidding themselves. They really don't intend to buy at all. If gold is at $500, they will tell you that they're willing to put half of what they own into gold, but they're waiting for $400—a 20% drop. And if it comes, will they buy? Many won't. They hold out for that elusive 20% more. They never buy because they always hold out for that *additional* 20%. They're not after a 20% saving, but an additional 20%, forever.

So make some mistakes. Take some chances. Buy something you know you'll need when controls squeeze supply channels. You may pay too much. But you'll lock in your price and the product now. You won't second-guess yourself in advance to the point of paralysis. Think through what you need, step by step, budgeted dollar by budgeted dollar. Discipline yourself. Set up a schedule. But be prepared to deviate from it when a seeming bargain appears. So the price drops afterward, or a better quality item comes on the market. Better to have a mini-warehouse that is 75% of what you need, even if you paid 50% too much, than to be caught in a crisis with 50% of what you need, but bought with just the right amount of money.

Don't shoot for perfection. Don't wait for the very best deal possible. Why not? Because the very best deal possible takes *time*. That's what your enemy is, time. If you wait around for the very best deal possible, in terms of money, you may be frozen out of the market when money dies. On luxuries, you can afford to shop around, waiting for that incomparable deal. On necessities, you can't afford to be choosy. For those things in between, you can do some shopping, but don't shoot for the very best deal. Don't waste your resources, but remember, the key resource available to you in a control economy is time. Above all, *don't waste time.*

So we're back to the original point: the question of *procrastination.* This is what fritters away your time, and you cannot possibly afford to waste time. You have got to break free of *the last-minute syndrome.* In a crisis imposed by price controls and rationing, the last-minute syndrome can turn out to be just that: the last one. When it comes to the basics, you cannot afford to be a part of this syndrome.

Chapter 8

THE BLOW-OFF

By training, I'm an economic historian. My doctoral dissertation dealt with the economic thought of the New England Puritans during the first 90 years of Massachusetts and Connecticut. One of the interesting aspects of the New England Puritans after about 1660 is that they increasingly became convinced that they were living at the end of the age, that a terrible moral and economic collapse was imminent, and that the judgment of God was about to be visited upon their little communities. What happened, in contrast to their prophecies, was that New England got rich. New England, under the leadership of the distasteful merchants and the distrusted lawyers, became an important trading center of the British Empire. The biggest problem the economy faced was not the judgment of God; it was the horde of British customs agents that flooded into Boston. Customs agents, unlike God, could be bribed, so the problem was capable of being solved...at some price.

The reason why I bring up the experience of the New England Puritans is that in some ways, we in the "hard-money" camp have gone through similar trials and tribulations. We have seen ourselves, as the Puritans did, as voices crying out in the wilderness. We have not convinced the leaders of sophisticated culture that they have adopted immoral and unworkable social and economic policies. We have cried out for years, even decades, that present-day economic policies would eventually lead to an economic disaster. We have tried to put dates on the forthcoming disaster, as some (though not all) of the New England Puritan pastors did after 1660. We have tried to console each other at "revival meetings" (monetary conferences) that we are right and the conventional experts are wrong. (Actually, the New England Puritans didn't have revival meetings; it was the advent of revival meetings in the 1730's that killed off what was left of New England Puritanism.) And like the New England Puritans we have been ridiculed as "old-fashioned moralists" who do not understand our problems and modern solutions of the contemporary wizards.

Some of my readers have been "in the trenches" for years. They have watched this economic mess develop along the lines they long predicted. Other readers have come into the "hard-money camp" relatively recently. Remember, in the late 1950's, there were almost no pro-gold newsletters around. The newsletter industry was far smaller, and the publishers were generally conventional men—skilled technicians, stock market experts, and so forth, but not self-consciously anti-inflation, pro-gold economists. The dean of the "unconventional" letter writers, Col. E. C. Harwood, was around, but he was pretty much alone. (He died in 1980.) In short, ours is a relatively new movement, and our track record as an industry (or sub-industry) has been proven only in recent years. The professional and conventional investing specialists have only grudgingly acknowledged the accuracy of our predictions about gold and silver, and it took $300 + gold and $10 + silver to wheedle even grudging praise out of them. As far as the general public is concerned, they still aren't even aware of the newsletter industry.

This means basically, that *you're alone*. In your industry, your community, your church, or your service club, you don't have many people to discuss these issues with. The danger with being alone is that you're liable to go off the deep end, predicting some looming cataclysm, making a lot of noise in order to attract the attention of your sleepwalking colleagues. *What if the cataclysm is postponed?*

This is why I recommend to all of you that you *keep your principles visible and your assets hidden*. You tell people what economic reasoning says will result from certain policies, *if* those policies are pursued. Then you may choose to offer your reasons for believing that today's political order guarantees the continued pursuit of disastrous policies, but you refrain from using phrases like "absolutely inevitable." *Don't make an idiot of yourself prematurely*. They may remember your skill as a prognosticator twenty years from now, ten years after some economic disaster, but between now and 1990, it is possible that you will look like a real wacko. (Possible, but not probable.)

Economic Boom

I want to warn you against a very common mistake inside the "hard-money" circles. People assume that an economic collapse is a rapidly appearing event, and one that will go away in a few years. I have harped on this theme for many years, but it needs repeating: *economic disintegration can be marked by an economic boom*. If we define a boom in terms of high employment, increasing per capita income, techonological innovation, more leisure time, reduced mortality, and so forth, then why should the presence of some or all of these pleasant criteria be a cause of alarm? Because the price of sustaining some or all of these symptoms of prosperity may be—and in fact *is*—the erosion of the currency unit, the expansion of Federal power, the overspecialization of production, the increasing reliance on imported materials (when war is looming), the misallocation of scarce resources which will eventually lead to depression, the increase of political pressures leading to price controls and rationing, and so forth. Like the Puritans of old, we may misinterpret the nature of the crisis which faces us. We may make fools of ourselves by predicting continually the imminent collapse, when in fact *the really dangerous developments are presently basic to our economic prosperity.*

For example, we newsletter writers have a tendency to use the words "depression," "collapse," "panic," and "liquidation," yet the very phenomena we worry about are the free market's means of *restoring the economy to health.* The depression is the market's way of reestablishing consumer sovereignty in the market, to cure the previous misallocation of scarce resources that was caused by monetary inflation. *The disaster is, in fact, today's enforced maintenance of the boom conditions by government bureaucrats and the money creators.*

When we tell people of the trouble that is coming, we become *prophets of doom* in their eyes. They may sense the frantic nature of today's economy, but they still want to believe that we have tapped the cornucopia. They want to believe that today's Keynesian system of government intervention really works. So they reply, "We've never had it so good." That, after all, was the reply of non-Puritans to the Puritan pessimists of the late-seventeenth century. "Why raise such a fuss? The system has worked, is still working, and will continue to work, *as long as pessimists like you don't weaken men's faith in the system.*" They believe in perpetual motion, and they resent the critics.

If you're going to preserve your assets in times to come, you have to fix your eyes on the star of *economic and moral principle*, and not get sidetracked by the arguments of pragmatism. The preservation of capital is not simply the discovery of some secret formula. The preservation and expansion of capital is based on a willingness of men to learn the fundamental rules of investing in various areas of the economy, and then to invest their time and capital in terms of these rules. There are formulas that are used in every profession, which is why financial calculators are so handy. But fortunes will be lost and missed by those investors who think that a financial calculator is a substitute for the strict adherence to economic principle.

Therefore, don't allow yourself to be misled by short-term movements in the economy. In January of 1980, subscribers to pro-gold newsletters watched gold and silver peak. They may be asking themselves whether they were wise not to sell out. They are asking themselves this question: *Did I miss the final blow-off?*

This is the wrong question, or if it's the proper question, then we

had better try to get it answered by asking ourselves the following subsidiary questions. (In my opinion, these are the fundamental questions; the question concerning the blow-off is the subsidiary question.)

1. Has there been a fundamental change in U. S. political
   economy?
2. Have voters decided to return to a philosophy of limited
   government?
3. Has anyone taken his hand out of your wallet lately?
4. Is a tight-money policy in effect today? If so, will it last?
5. Is anyone running for President by calling for *specific* budget
   cuts?
6. Has the average investor figured out what is happening to him?
7. Have money managers abandoned the "prudent investor rule"
   for gold?
8. Is the Soviet navy afloat? Are our sea lanes secure? For how
   long?
9. Are investors still making long-term credit commitments
   (bonds, etc.)?
10. Do people still take Eliot Janeway seriously?

We look at the economic boom, and we are tempted to say to ourselves. "The crisis isn't coming. The boom will never die." Then when
we see a seemingly frantic move into gold and silver, we are tempted to
conclude that *this* is the final blow-off. I think several thousand investors previously made this mistake, sadly, and I suspect a lot more
of them are about to make the same mistake now.

There are at least two variations of the mistake. *First*, the mistake
called *deflationism*. There are several newsletter writers who say next
year will be the year of the deflation. They said the same thing last
year, and in 1979, and right on back to 1974. There are some of them
who are convinced that they are going to be correct, once, and that
successful prediction will make them famous. True enough; it will also
bankrupt their clients, unless they are smart enough to recommend *inflation* hedges in the name of the coming deflation. That, of course, is
precisely what they do. They tell people to buy gold and silver—traditional inflation hedges. The *second* mistake is to argue that the traditional inflation hedges are finished, or in another variation, to argue
that the traditional inflation hedges never were inflation hedges, and
besides, the threat of mass inflation is over anyway. I call this variation *conventionalism*. A man makes his reputation as a prophet of
doom, and when everyone flocks to him after *some* of his dire predictions have come true, and the fellow starts getting a hearing in the
establishment press, then he panics. *He starts worrying that the prophesied collapse really isn't coming, or if it does, that it won't last very
long*. I call this the *Jonah syndrome*. The prophet Jonah came to the

people of Nineveh and prophesied their imminent destruction, whereupon they converted, and God's hand was withdrawn. Jonah, like too many prophets of doom, was outraged (Jonah 4:1). God had made him look like an idiot in retrospect. Better that Nineveh should perish than convert, better the wrath of God than the embarrassment of the prophet. After all, hadn't he spent all that time in a whale's belly? And now *this*?

The problem with any prophet of doom is that the prophecy comes true only in part, and then it seems to get dispersed on the shoals of conventionality. The prophet gets an audience when the skies darken and the earthquake shakes, but then the collapse is delayed. Instead of reminding himself that these convulsions are mere down payments on things to come, he concludes that the crisis has shot its wad, and the good times have overcome the tremors. The prophet assumes that the *judgment* is a *straight-line phenomenon*, which finally peaks in a wave of panic and disintegration. Except in times of war, this is not the way that crises occur. They occur in waves, and they are interspersed with periods of relative calm.

The classic example of this phenomenon was *Germany, 1919-23*. Here we had the worst inflation ever suffered by an industrial nation, yet it was not a straight-line phenomenon. Constantino Bresciani-Turroni, whose book, *The Economics of Inflation* (1931), is still the standard account of the great German inflation, comments: "The psychological crisis which had occurred in the second half of 1919 was gradually calmed, and it seemed that a certain faith in the mark was again established among the German population. In the first months of 1920 a reaction to the sharp depreciation of the preceding months appeared. As the Reichsbank observed in its Report for 1920, there was a tendency on the part of the German population to sell foreign exchange possessed by it; exchange which the Reichsbank willingly bought against marks" (p. 57). *From February of 1920 until July, the value of the dollar actually fell in relation to the German mark by about 60%* (p. 30). Anyone who had shorted the mark in early 1920 was hurt. The depreciation resumed in mid-1920, but not in a straight line, for the mark rallied in late 1920 against the dollar, a rally which continued through May of 1921. Then came the incomparable disaster, which only ended with the destruction of the mark in late 1923.

Considering the response of the German public, we can only conclude that the great mass of the population did not really understand what was happening until that final year of inflationary collapse. Bresciani-Turroni comments on the fact that internal prices lagged behind the fall of value of the German mark on the international currency markets. There was a rent control system, and German railway fares were kept artificially low. However, there was a far more significant reason for the lag:

> To these must be added a cause of a monetary nature; in numerous classes of society, especially in the country in 1919 and also in the following years, in spite of the continual depreciation of the currency, great quantities of notes were continually hoarded. Even in September 1922 a bank director asserted that "the German population preserves considerable quantities of notes." By such means the rise of internal prices was retarded (p. 133).

Only in 1923 did the German population quit buying the nation's treasury debt certificates. At the beginning of 1922 the treasury bills issued were *still* being bought by citizens, and half the debt was held outside of the central bank (p. 63). In April of 1923 it was 75%, and by July of 1923 it was 93% in the possession of the Reichsbank. "To every addition of Treasury bills there now corresponded an equivalent increase in the issues of notes." The fate of the mark was sealed—sealed by the disastrously late perception of the public of the effects, if not the cause, of monetary inflation. The public began its "flight into real values," meaning the flight out of the German mark. *It had taken three years of monetary inflation for the public to catch on.* So the central bank printed the money and bought the T-bills. No one else would in 1923.

The point I'm trying to make is this: *Don't allow the continuation of the economic boom to hypnotize you!* Don't allow the inevitable (oops—there's that word) ups and downs of the economy to divert your attention from the general drift of prices, namely, upward. If the great German inflation was not a straight-line phenomenon in every segment of the economy, then you should not expect our drift into inflation and controls to be an easily predictable, easily discounted, easily hedged straight-line phenomenon. The boom goes on.

Bailing Wire

One reason why we should not expect straight-line erosion is because the government bureaucrats and politicians are not about to see their long-touted system go under without a fight. They will do what they can to keep the system running until the next election. This means that we can expect far more ludicrous economic directives to emanate from Washington, with far heavier sanctions being applied.

As the government lashes out against "speculators, profiteers, and disturbers of the Keynesian peace," people are going to be hurt. The response of the profiteers is predictable: to raise their prices in order to compensate themselves for the added risks of doing business. *When the Federal dinosaur starts to swing its tail, get out of the way.* There are no automatic, easily discovered, conventional ways to avoid a hypothetical straight-line erosion of the economy. When Washington starts to react to the economic fragmentation that is the result of Washington's policies, the bureaucrats will replace the red tape with bailing wire, and when that fails, they will bring out the handcuffs and straitjackets.

You must be prepared to deal with your own local problems in terms of your own resources. While I believe in trends and general movements in the economy, I am convinced that *localism* still is fundamental, and that we have to devote time and resources to dealing with local problems. I am convinced that the key to political success is localism. We should be willing to do what we can to make an impact locally. We have to find local bread-and-butter issues and use them to construct a political barrier between the Federal bureaucrats and ourselves. I am therefore a great believer in county government, especially in counties that are not burdened with large urban concentrations of votes.

One possible project that could become crucially important in the future is the capture of *local Civil Defense units*. These units have been neglected for decades. Now they are becoming important again, if not in the eyes of the public, then at least in the eyes of the Federal regulators. If your community has a Civil Defense unit, you might get your church or other conservatively minded organization—if that organization is not easily identifiable as a "right wing extremist" group—to offer to help out the local administrator. Hold a seminar presented by the local official. Volunteer to do the stamp-licking or other chores. Get to know the guy and be on a first-name basis with him. You want to help out. People who help out have a tendency to attract responsibility. *You want to be in a position of responsibility in your local Civil Defense unit if what I think may happen in the next 48 months really does happen.* It is likely that Civil Defense agencies will be in a position to have advanced information in important areas in the future. Also, you want to be sure that you or other trustworthy people can serve as foot-draggers if Washington attempts to use the Civil Defense agencies as tools of economic centralization in the future. You can't be successful if you wait to organize *after* a military attack or threat of attack on the U. S.

Conclusions

Investors who expect a single, definitive blow-off are probably going to be very disappointed in the future. Occasionally such blow-offs occur. Germany in 1923 is an obvious example. But we seem to be years away from that. In fact, we should be more concerned with Germany in 1946-48, the era of the controls. There was no final blow-off in that second German inflation. It was a grinding down of productivity, an erosion process.

What can speed up this process is a war, or preparations in expectation of a war. I would therefore warn you to forget about "the great inflationary blow-off," as well as "the great deflationary contraction." What you should be extremely concerned about is *the great wartime straitjacket.*

When you hear about gold at $700 or $900 or even $2,000, the blow-off hasn't arrived. When you hear about $100 silver, the final blow-off hasn't arrived. When you hear about a $250,000 reward for information leading to the conviction of anyone who requires payment in gold or silver, rather than payment in legal tender paper money at the legally frozen price of some item, *then* you should start worrying about the blow-off. It may not be a strictly economic blow-off. It will probably be a political blow-off, in which personal freedoms are smashed, the free market is disrupted by controls, shortages begin to paralyze certain neighborhoods or classes in urban areas, and wholesale confiscation of visible property takes place in the name of American patriotism.

The issue is personal freedom, not the price of gold. The price of gold is a very good indicator of the market for freedom—the higher the price, the less the domain of freedom—but the really important issues are moral and political, not economic. If you allow yourself to become hypnotized by rapidly rising or falling dollar-denominated prices for pieces of metal, then you will probably make some disastrous decisions, such as selling off your gold in order to buy back in later at a really good price. Gold should not be regarded as a means of increasing your holdings of paper money. *Gold should be regarded as an admission ticket to the free markets during a future period of bureaucratic tyranny.*

The blow-off that should concern us is not the dollar-denominated price of some marketable commodity. The crucial blow-off is the *blow-off of personal liberty in a wave of political centralization.* Subsequently, we can expect to see a *blow-off of the unworkable straitjacket economy.* But this blow-off could take a generation. I assure you that you will find good and profitable uses of your gold and silver coins in between these two fundamental blow-offs, and afterward as well.

Chapter 9

FEAR AND THE DIVISION OF LABOR

Like most free market defenders, I have long been bothered by the depression of the 1930's. The ideology of Keynesian economics is based on a belief that the free market failed in the 1930's, and that some form of government intervention into the economy is mandatory if the capitalistic system is to be preserved. Of course, on an ad hoc basis, this same message is offered by every trade association, manufacturing group, and special-interest lobby on Capitol Hill. They all parade in front of our legislators, telling them that the free market idea is wonderful, especially in the case of their suppliers, but in their own special and unique situations, government intervention is mandatory for the preservation of capital—*their* capital. "Parity, not charity," yell the farmers, not understanding that parity is legislated, mandatory "charity." Everyone wants to get on the dole, all in the name of capitalism. Thus, when all voices cry out against the idea of a free market mechanism, it is difficult to get an audience for the message of freedom. And when you do, somebody in the audience asks, "If freedom is so hot, why did we have a depression?"

Well, why did we? And why do we call the phenomenon a depression? According to William Manchester's book, *The Glory and the Dream*, President Hoover had coined the word in preference to the more traditional "panic." He thought it sounded less frightening. In retrospect, the term "panic" has been used to describe the bankers' recession of 1907, meaning a stock market crash that affected primarily high finance institutions, not the whole economy. "Panic" is the mild word today; "depression" sends fear through the hearts of those who remember, and knee-jerk spasms of Keynesian intervention among those who don't.

The followers of Ludwig von Mises use Mises' theories of money and the trade cycle to explain the depression, or any depression. It was the expansion of fiat money through the fractionally reserved banking system which created the boom of the mid-1920's, and it was the stabilization of money, and the concomitant rise in short-term interest rates, that produced the crash of 1929-30. This is argued most forcefully in Murray Rothbard's book, *America's Great Depression* (1963). To explain the extension of the contraction, the Misesians

76

point to other government interventions into the economy, most notably the Smoot-Hawley tariff in 1930 and Hoover's Reconstruction Finance Corporation. Then Roosevelt's massive intervention made the paralysis permanent until the mass inflation of the war years hit.

The more I think about this explanation, the more questions I have. I agree that the crash of 1929 was caused by new stable money policies of the Federal Reserve System. But why was this contraction so terrible, when the monetary boom of the Civil War years did not produce anything comparable in 1866 after the inflation stopped? Why was 1930 followed by the horrors of 1931 and 1932?

Unquestionably, the Smoot-Hawley tariff was an economic disaster. This has been recognized by almost all historians of the period. It restricted the ability of European governments to repay war debts, normal commercial debts, and just run-of-the-mill debts. It closed off portions of the American market to foreign producers, thereby closing off their markets to American producers. The international division of labor was sacrificed for the short-run political gains of the tariff. It was wealth redistribution from the consumer and more efficient producers on both sides of the various borders to the less efficient producers on both sides of the borders. Still, can this explain the extent of the depression? The United States is a big country. The proportion of its trade component out of the total production system is now and has long been quite small—under 10%. (Under 5% in 1930.) If we are to argue that the Smoot-Hawley tariff was the major sign of intervention in the 1930-32 period, then we have to ask this question: Was this intervention sufficient to produce the disaster which followed? If it was, how did it achieve so crucial a position?

The chief argument of Keynesians against the free market is this one: the flexible pricing mechanism was not sufficient in the 1930's to clear the market of the goods and services offered for exchange. In short, demand did not equal production, which a freely flexible price system is supposed to make possible. Why did a glut of labor appear? Why were there two million youths on the road, riding the rails? Why was 25% of the labor force unemployed in 1932? And more interesting, why was 1933 the single greatest year, proportionately, in the history of the Dow Jones Industrial Averages?

The End of an Era

When we think of the 1920's, we always think of the Roaring Twenties. We feel compelled to capitalize the words. Indeed, the twenties roared. They roared on the highways, for the Model T had launched a new era of mass production and price competition, making kings out of common men. They roared in the speakeasies, where violating the law brought a sense of release. They roared in fashions, in sports stadiums, and in the movies. They roared most of all on the stock exchanges, where the little man was promised a piece of the action, on margin. (They did not roar on the farms, however.) A dream was offered to Americans, and they fell for it.

The dream became a nightmare. The dream was an ancient one: easy riches, good times, and unlimited progress. People were told that the old laws of economics were abolished. There would be no more depressions (that is, "panics"). The new engine of industrial technology, mass advertising, easy money, and cheap transportation had overcome the ancient fears that men have faced since the first man made the first tool. There was enormous optimism about the future. The new age of Freud was upon us, when sexual repressions and guilt could be overcome through free expression. (Freud, by the way, was not at all optimistic in this regard, but his popular interpreters were.) War was abolished. The world had been made safe for democracy. Now Americans could stay at home, enjoy life, and let the laws of compound interest multiply their capital without end. In short, the promise of the 1920's was this one: no limits to growth, and few costs either.

The Viking Press published a delightful little book in 1931, *Oh Yeah?* It catalogued the statements of optimism from 1928-31. Some of these have become classics in retrospect. Consider the following:

> Stock prices have reached what looks like a permanently high plateau. I do not feel that there will soon, if ever, be a fifty or sixty point break below present levels, such as Mr. Babson has predicted. I expect to see the stock market a good deal higher than it is today within a few months.
>
> Prof. Irving Fisher (Yale)
> Oct. 16, 1929

> Looking to the future I see in the further acceleration of science continuous jobs for our workers. Science will cure unemployment.
>
> Charles M. Schwab
> Chairman of the Board
> Bethlehem Steel (Oct. 16, 1930)

> There is no cause for worry. The high tide of prosperity will continue.
>
> Andrew W. Mellon
> Secretary of the Treasury
> (Sept. 1928)

> Comparatively few people are reached by this crash.
>
> Julius Rosenwald
> Sears Roebuck & Co.
> (Nov. 9, 1929)

Fisher lost a fortune in the years following his optimistic pronouncements. Schwab did better; he drew $250,000 a year from Bethlehem Steel in the honorific position as Chairman of the Board, as payment for past services. When he died in 1939, his estate was nonetheless bankrupt by over $300,000, with assets of $1.4 million and liabilities of over $1.7 million. The depression had taken its toll. On Feb. 7, 1931, he had stated simply: "I am not predicting anything." Roger Babson, who had made himself famous by predicting the crash, started saying that the crash was all over in the summer of 1930, and he kept saying so through 1931. As he said on May 9, 1930: "I go further and say that 1931 should offer the greatest opportunities of any year for generations." *Oh Yeah?* closes with a quote from Calvin Coolidge (Jan. 20, 1931):

"The country is not in good condition."

What took place between 1930 and 1933 was a revolution. It was a revolution in attitude, in ideology, and most important, in public confidence. The professors of renown had lost their self-confidence, and the Keynesian prescriptions of more government spending found no real resistance in American academic circles—at least none that has survived. Mises' former student, F. A. Hayek (who won the Nobel Prize in 1974), was an eloquent opponent of Keynes in England, but he was not read here. In any case, he was not listened to after the late 1930's. The public had its first experience with the credibility gap of the Federal government. Governments had lied before, of course, but not for so long and in such a crisis of collapsing expectations. The old arguments were lost on the former believers. The Roaring Twenties disappeared into the decade-long despair of the thirties.

Depression

When Hoover renamed panic, he made a tactical error, but his choice of a new word was superb. Depression is just what the 1930's created. In the psychological sense, depression was the essence of the economic crisis.

Manchester's book has a lot of faults, but he has a great ability to help reconstruct the psychology of the average worker. The fear that gripped men who were out of work for months at a time must have been terrifying. Private charity funds began to dry up, and about 30 million people were on local public welfare by 1932. Those who had believed the promises of the 1920's had a rude awakening in the early years of the thirties. Men who wanted to work hard enough, and were willing to take low enough wages, could find work eventually, but evictions, bankruptcy, and failure were common. When we are talking about the entire Western world, the magnitude of the collapse becomes apparent. This was literally *the end of an era*. From that time onward, the logic of socialism has made tremendous strides, and the market, despite its remarkable recovery everywhere, has continued to have a bad press. Those who write seldom understand what a market is or how it works. In an age of pragmatism, it is easy for those in political power or in the universities to take credit for something they did not accomplish through welfare, bureaucracy, and taxation.

No one (after 1932 anyway) ever accused Franklin Roosevelt of not being able to sense the concerns of the voting public. When he stood before the microphones to deliver his inaugural address, he uttered these famous words:

> This great Nation will endure as it has endured, will revive and will prosper. So, first of all, let me assert my firm belief that the only thing we have to fear is fear itself—nameless, unreasoning, unjustified terror which paralyzes needed efforts to convert retreat into advance.

The paralysis of fear: here was the political problem. Roosevelt challenged the "money changers" who had lost confidence in the system they had built. Then he ended with these words (which he followed up the next week by closing the banks):

> I am prepared under my constitutional duty to recommend the measures that a stricken Nation in the midst of a stricken world may require. These measures, or other such measures as the Congress may build out of its experience and wisdom, I shall seek, within my constitutional authority, to bring to speedy adoption.
>
> But in the event that the Congress shall fail to take one of these two courses, and in the event that the national emergency is still critical, I shall not evade the clear course of duty that will then confront me. I shall ask the Congress for the one remaining instrument to meet the crisis—broad Executive power to wage a war against the emergency, as great as the power that would be given me if we were in fact invaded by a foreign foe.

The next hundred days saw the greatest peacetime expansion of executive power in the nation's history. The stock market started upward in its greatest percentage performance ever recorded. As Will Rogers wrote on the day of the inaugural, for publication the next day: "If he burned down the Capitol, we would cheer and say, 'Well, we at least got a fire started somehow.' "

Fear had done its work. The paralysis of unemployment made it possible for Roosevelt to reverse some of the basic principles of American constitutional law. He simply arrogated power to himself and to the Executive, and that power has not reverted to the states or the people since that grim year of 1933.

Why had the depression lasted so long? Why had the traditional answers failed? To some extent, the traditional answers had not been tried. The old answer had been to cut Federal spending and cut taxes. Hoover raised spending, ran a huge deficit, and raised spending again. This was a kind of half-hearted Keynesianism, and it reflected a half-hearted Liberal's way to handle the problems which the market had handled successfully in previous "panics." It helped shake the faith of the business community. It kept the market on its back. It led to the escalation of fear.

Nevertheless, the market was free by today's standards. It was not a plaything of the Federal government. It was made up of the decisions of acting men. Yet the masses of Americans, like men around the world, stayed scared. They saw prices falling, banks closing, and suffered a shrinking money supply. So they hoarded money. Sure enough, prices continued to fall. The downward spiral continued, as monetary deflation came out of the collapsing pyramid of the banking system. Over 6,000 banks went under. People who had savings accounts and mortgages in the same bank discovered that the bankruptcy wiped out their savings, but the new owners of the defaulted bank owned the mortgage. They were in debt at pre-1929 prices, and their assets were gone. (The FDIC and FSLIC today insure against this two-way switch, but they guarantee protection only by means of the printing press.) Terror, perhaps, is too strong a word, but a constant sense of crisis was maintained for almost four years. In the face of this universal despair, the U. S. Constitution did not survive intact.

Fear paralyzes. Men are afraid to make long-term investments. They prefer to hold cash and take advantage of lower prices later. The interest rate actually approached zero in 1932. Below zero, the only reason for depositing money is for the safety of keeping it in a vault; the interest rate becomes, in effect, a storage fee. You pay them to store your money. But they can't loan it. So until confidence is restored in the political, legal, and economic structure, there will be very little investment. This is what people want. The market responds. Falling interest rates will not lure most people back into the loan markets with their money, and rising interest rates scare off potential borrowers.

Machines lie idle; businesses fail; projects begun under one set of asumptions become uneconomical under the new conditions. The future is too risky for people to invest in it. Entrepreneurs who normally are willing to bear the burdens of uncertainty are repelled by the wholly new conditions. They pull back. They reduce risks by putting money in government bonds. (Short-term U. S. securities paid .14%

in 1932.) Men want a partial guarantee before they commit new capital, or accept loans from investors. They want *security*. Franklin Roosevelt convinced them that the Federal government can, at least in the short run, provide security. He gave them hope in *a new world view*.

Conclusions

The old faith is wearing thin. The old confidence is beginning to crack. But this time the precedents are on the side of the Executive. Do Something, men cry. Give us tariffs; give us parity; give us a guaranteed minimum wage. What we are given is the highest increase in taxes ever legislated by one bill (the 1977 Social Security bill), yet not a single lobbying group, not a single foundation, not a single special-interest representative came to Capitol Hill to challenge this bill. No one has even bothered to produce estimates on unemployment and reduced capital investment which will be caused by this bill. The old religion still lives, and the priests of Social Security are still secure in their temple. But the pragmatic public is willing to turn on former heroes at the drop of a hat (or the drop of the Dow Jones).

What's next? What politician will pull what rabbit out of what hat? What is the next answer?

Unlike many commentators, I am not afraid of panic. Short of nuclear war, I really don't expect a massive, rapid panic. I expect a grinding, long-term erosion of purchasing power, efficiency, and freedom. I expect depression in the psychological sense—universal fear, universal confusion, universal despair. When it comes, it will create the scene of a new transition. The fear I have is that it will lead to the age of the Caesars and the destruction of the division of labor. When men fear the future. . . .

Fear *does* paralyze. In a way, this is one advantage of monetary inflation. It gives most people—younger people—hope that next year will be better, that prices will stabilize eventually. In any case, it allows people to go into debt and pay off in cheap dollars. Inflation does not seem to paralyze men the way they were in the 1930's. *But its destruction is long-term*. The erosion of all fixed-income investments is insidious. It steadily transfers the wealth of one class—conventional savers—into the foreign bank accounts of the few successful members of another class, the speculators. It creates envy on a massive scale. It takes longer before inflation is revealed as just as terrible a destroyer of capital as depression is. Indeed, it is usually followed by depression, unless price controls have devastated the economy so thoroughly that there is nothing left of the capital structure to destroy through deflation.

Controls will give temporary hope. Rationing will give temporary hope. The occasional beating of the shortages will give temporary hope. But we are seeing the end of an era, the Keynesian era. The question, still unanswered, is whether or not the command economy will replace "moderate" Keynesian intervention, or whether the free market will, through the revival of black markets. The war will be on, with the open confiscators battling against the underground free markets.

Fear, I am sad to report, favors the State. The big fear lies ahead—fear so total that good men will lose faith in everything but power. Be prepared.

Chapter 10

BANANA PEEL INVESTING

One of the great tragedies of inflationary times is that inflation destroys the seemingly solid, familiar, prudent investment strategies. *Habit* can be a killer when the environment in which habit developed is rearranged by the forces of price inflation. You cannot imagine how deeply ingrained habitual patterns of thought really are. After you have done a few years of professional financial counselling, you understand. It is extremely difficult for people to rethink fundamental presuppositions, slogans learned in youth. Yet they *must* be relearned if a person is to survive.

People in the United States are hard-pressed to remember bad econmic times, except the 1930's. *There* was one economic disaster in this century that people remember, as far as Americans are concerned. Yet the overwhelming majority of Europeans born in 1900 have witnessed three great cataclysms in their nations' economies (five if you count the war years). We Americans forget that such events are possible.

First, Europeans learned about *inflation and price controls* during World War I. They learned about shortages, rationing, and lines in front of stores. But patriotically they invested in war bonds, forfeiting present income for promises of future returns. Those living in defeated nations after 1918 saw their bonds collapse. But those in the victorious nations also saw the erosion of their assets through inflation. The French franc declined, 1918-1958, by well over 99% of its original purchasing power, with the bulk of this loss coming before the late 1920's. In 1918, the French franc was worth 18¢. In 1920, it was down to 9¢. By 1922, it was at 6¢. By 1926, it was at 2.5¢. It recovered somewhat in the late 1920's, and by 1936 it was at 6.7¢. From then on, it was all downhill. In 1957, it was worth less than one-third of an American penny—and the American penny was only a shadow of its 1918 self. Only DeGaulle's austerity budget and currency revaluation saved the French franc from total destruction, and it cost him a recession in 1958. But in retrospect, it was worth it. Comments Sidney Homer, the bond expert: "France survived the disasters of the first seventy-five years of the twentieth century largely at the expense of her *rentiers* and other holders of franc assets." (*A History of Interest Rates* [New Brunswick, New Jersey: Rutgers University Press,

84

1977] p. 432.) A rentier, just for the record, is a person who receives a fixed return on some paper money investment.

Second, Europeans learned about *deflation and depression* in the mid-1920's (Germany, Austria, Hungary) or finally in the 1930's (France, Britain, and everyone else). The crisis was as severe in Europe as it was in the United States. But consider the average German or Austrian. He has gone through wartime shortages, a military defeat, the post-war mass inflation, the depression of 1924, a brief recovery, then the great depression. On top of that came Hitler, with all the controls on currency exchange, and in 1936, price controls. Another war broke out. More shortages, more controls, more rationing struck all Europe. Then came the post-war recovery, which meant more inflation and controls in the defeated nations, more rationing, and starvation for some.

Consider the effects these events have had on the generation which went through them. It is almost inconceivable for geographically insulated Americans to imagine. We missed the mass inflations of the 1920's, and we evaded the controls of the 1940's and 1950's. Besides, the shortages were for "a good cause." Nixon imposed controls, which were clearly disrupting, but they were not seriously enforced. The inflation of 1965-81 has made an impression on Americans, but in no way can it be compared to Germany in 1923 or France in the early 1920's. The feelings produced in most Americans seem to be vaguely hostile, but few people know the cause, and fewer still are ready to bear the deflationary and depressionary effects involved in eliminating the cause. Inflation is tolerated.

So the Europeans have some advantages for forecasting purposes. Frenchmen are prone to buy gold coins for long-term capital preservation. Germans resist inflation. Austrians still mint bullion gold coins and the magnificent silver coin, the Maria Theresa. Their experiences have prepared them better to make accurate predictions about the future, assuming that the future is inflationary.

Americans, on the other hand, still have very little idea about what is going on. They cling to clichés and attitudes that are outmoded and suicidal. If they happen to be Certified Public Accountants, they get paid by well-intentioned professionals to put these outmoded clichés into force. In short, we all believe the government, and the government's private tax experts, the CPA's. (There are a few exceptions to the CPA rule, such as Vernon K. Jacobs, the editor of the very fine newsletter, *Tax Angles*: P. O. Box 976, Farmingdale, NY 11737; 12 issues, $50.)

Let's consider two of the typical banana peel slogans that lead directly to suicidal decisions.

"What Will I Do For Income?"

This is one of the most popular. I spoke with a man in mid-1977 who had a million dollars invested in 6% tax-free (ha ha) municipal bonds. There are of course, no such things as tax-free municipal bonds. There are *income*-tax-free municipal bonds, which is another description of *inflation*-tax-paying bonds, or capital-erosion bonds. (Here is a basic rule of all tax-avoidance investing: ask the seller or advisor which tax the investment *does* pay; if he can't spell it out in the grim details, find a new salesman or advisor.) The man wanted to know how to protect himself from inflation. Sell the bonds, I told him. "But I need the income. I'm retired, and I just can't live on less than $60,000 a year, after taxes." Well, I can understand how a retired fellow like that has budget problems. I'm sure we all can. But at least he understood the capital-erosion aspect of price inflation and municipal bonds. Could he sell some of them? No, he could afford no income loss. Could he invest in short-term T-bills, to escape the fate of long-term fixed-return investments. No, that would mean paying income taxes. Well, could he put it into income-producing real estate, get the depreciation, and enjoy a rising value for his assets? No, he didn't want any management problems. But he insisted that I had to give him an answer: How could he preserve both his capital and his income in a time of inflation? There is no way, I assured him. "Yes," he said, "I know." Meanwhile, the chat had taken 20 minutes of my time.

But at least he knew. He was simply trying to get his income while it lasted. Psychologically, he had already adopted the late Prof. Mises' philosophy of inflation-hedging. When asked what the best hedge against inflation is, he replied: "Age."

Widows are the real losers in inflation. They have a bit of capital, a meager pension, a pathetic annuity. All of it disappears, inevitably, relentlessly, in times of inflation. They are paralyzed with fear. What can they do? They can go back to work, if they are physically able. But often they are not. They could set up trusts for their children or relatives, with the income coming to them until they die, and the assets going to the relative on their death. This would give a real incentive to relatives to treat them well, since the assets were coming to them eventually. But how many people ever use trusts? Interested people can check out the following books, and then go to an attorney for assistance, *after* knowing what to ask for, and *after* checking management fees:

How to Avoid Probate
by Norman F. Dacey
(Crown Publishers)

*How You Can Use Inflation
to Beat the IRS*
by B. Ray Anderson
(Warner Books)

The point is, a person does not need to become a total dependent on some relative; the trust assets can serve as a compensating device to reward others for taking on some of the burdens for caring for an older person. But it is unwise to delegate the responsibility of selecting the trust's investments. Trust your own judgment.

Still, the quest for income is illusionary, if we mean passive income (coupon-clipping income). People with *long-term bonds* do not have income, as normally thought of. They are *eating up their capital*, month by month, because the longer they keep their capital tied up in promises to pay paper money in the future (the return of principal), the more surely their principal is disappearing. It is the consumption of capital just as surely as if they had their money in a checking account and continued to spend money. Their money in a bond contract will be returned, but at a drastically reduced purchasing power. Yet people are absolutely hypnotized by "income" off of fixed-return investments. I really mean it: *hypnotized*. They cannot perceive reality. You tell them—I tell them—over and over, you ought to sell the bonds (now selling at a ghastly discount, precisely because they are depreciating assets), buy gold coins, and sell the coins when you need the money to live on. The coins can appreciate with inflation, so you may stay ahead of it; bonds are unable to stay ahead of inflation. What is the answer? "But I need the income!" My carefully thought-out logic makes absolutely zero impression. It is too confusing. It is not familiar to Americans. (I never have to explain this process more than once to anyone with a European accent, no matter how faltering the voice at the other end of the telephone.) Income means that familiar, comforting check in the mail. That's the American Way. That's what a person needs in old age. After all, we all remember 1933. Yes, we do. It, too, hypnotizes us.

Let me return to Economics 101A (before grade inflation, it was Econ 1A). Why does an asset command a price? Because it's scarce. But scarcity means greater demand than supply at zero price. So once again, *why* does some asset command a price? Because it promises to produce a *future stream of income*. Why does a gold coin command a price? Because it is believed to be capable of providing a future stream of income. What about dehydrated food? The same answer. What about diamonds? The same. How about newsletter subscriptions? Yes, yes, oh my *yes*! Keep that future income coming!

But there is a hitch. In fact, there are two. *First*, and most important for this topic, that future expected income stream is discounted by the rate of interest (or better yet, the *expected rates* of interest over the life of the asset). Thus, if the asset provides fixed monetary returns (bonds, annuities, preferred stocks), then the present price of the asset should be computed as follows:

$$\frac{\text{net annual return}}{\text{interest rate}}$$

Yes, I know the formulas are more complicated. So buy a financial calculator, and it figures it out for you. But for the average person, this is warning enough. *The larger the denominator, the less the fraction is worth.* One-fourth is less than one-half. The 4 on the bottom is larger than the 2. So when the figure on the bottom increases from, say, .06 to .12, the value of the present price drops. Why? The income stream hasn't dropped. The same number of dollars is going to come in. Those checks won't stop coming. True enough, but *the discount is higher,* simply because people value present dollars compared to future dollars a lot more than they did when the interest rate was 6% (.06). They see that the future dollars won't buy so much, and they hike interest demands. Who wants depreciated money dumped in his lap? A person wants a compensating income, so lenders demand higher rates of return. "Far away dollars" are worth less, so the discount increases.

Meanwhile, the nice little lady with her 6% bonds (let alone the 3.5% ones her husband bought back in 1963) has no idea what's happening, since she never learned how to read bond quotations in *The Wall Street Journal*, and her banker keeps his mouth shut unless he's trying to lure her into a 4-year time deposit paying 12%

Why do people insist on clinging to depreciating assets? The lure of passive income is too great. It all seems so easy. Just cash those checks. "It's like money in the bank, my boy." Yes, sir, it certainly is. A bank that is steadily going belly-up. Only in this case, the *money* is going belly-up.

The *second* hitch involves the solvency of the outfit promising to pay that future income stream. Will it stay solvent? But this is less important than the really crucial question, *the solvency of the monetary unit.* As far as I'm concerned, long-term interest rates are way too low, given what I expect price inflation will become in the 1980's. When interest rates finally rise to keep pace with price inflation, thereby wiping out the principal of fixed-return investments, they will still be too low, since the speculators will still underestimate future price inflation. Let me simply point to a most fascinating bit of history. In Germany in November, 1923, the stock market one day charged a short-term rate of interest of—you won't believe this— 10,950% per annum. Quit hunting for the decimal point, Charlie; it ain't there. (Homer, *History of Interest Rates*, p. 467.)

"I Can't Sell Now; the Taxes Will Kill Me!"

This is another classic banana peel investment decision. It fails to grasp the nature of taxation. First, given the present value of an asset, the capital gains tax is *subsidized* compared to regular income tax rates, at least for smaller transactions. It always has some element of subsidy, even for big dollar sales. Second, the slogan rests on an assumption: if I hold now, things will get better, later, tax-wise. Do you really believe this? Third, it assumes that the asset will appreciate between now and sales time. Fourth, it assumes that someone will be psychologically able to stop using this slogan in his economic decision-making sometime later. It's like the alcoholic who says he can stop drinking anytime.

Inevitably, somewhere in the back of a person's mind is this killer assumption: "When I really have to sell this asset, I won't have to pay the tax. It will be mine, all mine. I will have beaten the system."

Dumb, isn't it?

All right, it might possibly happen. Let me outline *the ultimate scenario for beating the system*. One, a person buys safe, small-town income-producing real estate, using the Lowry-Nickerson methods. He mortgages them to the hilt. He trades for more property. Rent controls are not imposed on his type of rental units (lots of luck), which are single-family units (quads or under). He continues to pyramid, paying bankers rather than tax collectors. Meanwhile, the rental units keep rising in value due to the inflation. Finally, in a wave of inflationary panic, he sells one or two units at a huge paper profit, pays the capital gains taxes, pays off the mortgages, gets completely out of debt, and waits for deflation, which happens the following Tuesday. Down comes the paper-money value of his real estate pyramid, down comes his paper-money income, down comes the government, in comes a tax revolt, down comes the welfare State, and he is sitting pretty holding real assets, still rentable, but in a nice, low tax bracket. The estate tax does not gobble up his empire, since deflation has lowered its value. He owes nobody anything. He has beaten the system.

It could happen. I know one economist in Pennsylvania who has bet his future on some such scenario. Only he knows it's a real long shot. But in the meantime, he pays practically no income taxes. And the bankers love him. He pays them lots of interest.

The fact is, an asset should be sold at that point when it ceases to be regarded by the holder as the very best producer of future *real* income that he can own. If something else will probably perform better, sell now, pay the tax, and buy the better asset. Remember, *you will have to pay the tax sometime*. If you don't, then your estate will. Or your widow's estate. So sell it now.

I am now going to offer a piece of investment advice that is *absolutely sound economically* and *absolutely abhorrent philosophically*. You must continue to invest in terms of it and vote against it. That principle is this:

The Government Really Does Own the Tax Portion of Your Assets.

If you keep this principle in your mind, and in your gut, you will not be tempted to hold onto some clinker of an asset longer than economically necessary. You are holding the government's taxable portion of your assets as a kind of zero-interest loan. If you lose the asset, you pay nothing. If you make a killing, the government will want its share. Economically speaking, though not philosophically speaking, *you are a trustee of the government's assets.* The government permits you to manage its wealth for as long as you are willing to maintain ownership. But as soon as you decide to forfeit ownership, the government wants its money, assuming you have made a paper-money-denominated profit.

There comes a time to say, "Buzz, off, bureaucrats. Here's your blood money. I'm not managing it for you any more." But what good is this slogan? After all, haven't I already argued that you can't beat the tax system, and if a person reinvests what's left, and does well, he will have to pay again later on? That's true, assuming one's next purchase leaves a *record* of some sort.

What if, just for the sake of argument, a man converts his present assets—for which numerous records exist—into cash? All taxes are paid. Then *cash* is taken out and used to purchase *used goods* that will be income-producing assets in the future. Assets like unregistered hand guns purchased at a gun show, auction, or swap meet. Assets like farm equipment. Assets like tools. Assets like dehydrated food, perhaps the ultimate barter device. Assets like experience in the "alternative markets." Assets like gold and silver coins, purchased for cash, or from an outfit that doesn't keep records that have names on them. This is one reason for taking out cash at regular intervals and increasing the amounts removed steadily, so as not to arouse suspicion. Keep the cash on hand ready for "cash discount" bargains.

So pay the capital gains tax this time, and hide your assets. Your *real income* will be preserved in a crisis by *real assets* that leave phantom records, or none at all. Use some of that extra cash the statisticians tell us you have lying around your dresser drawers. And if you don't have that much, get some. Don't hoard it. It's working capital for the record-less markets.

Your greatest tax worry should be with the *inflation tax* and the price controls-induced *shortage tax*. Your accountant, I dare say, has not discussed these with you. The CPA gets paid by offering his clients

nice, safe, "quick fix" tax solutions, like setting up a Keogh or professional corporation retirement program—with the assets invested in
nice, safe bonds paying 10%. Or managed by a reliable insurance
company. In other words, he can show you how much *income tax*
you've saved. But if he's like most accountants, he thinks in terms of
the myth, "a dollar is a dollar, now and later." That kind of thinking
will destroy you within a decade.

Tell your CPA you appreciate his services; pay him his due, but you
don't have to use him for your "off-record" investments. Remember,
the tax laws are not very clear about barter items, and in any case, enforcement is necessarily restricted. Sell your turkeys, buy some
barterable assets for cash, and pay your taxes. *This* time.

Remember my strategy: *mini-warehousing.* If you buy consumption
goods now, at today's lower prices, and consume them later, when
prices are higher, you will owe no taxes. But if you buy an investment
now and sell it for paper money later at a *monetary* profit (though
possibly at a purchasing power loss), you *will* owe taxes. So buy the
goods now. Avoid future taxes.

Chapter 11

HOW MUCH TIME DO WE HAVE?

It is indicative of the present moral, political, and economic disruptions that the West faces that people are seriously asking this question of themselves and of others who are supposed to know the answer. Not that many people are seriously asking it, of course. That kind of question is limited to those who have something to lose and who are convinced that the present drift of world events can lead only to a situation which threatens everything they have built up over the years. Thoughtful people who have both *capital* and a *sense of history* are clearly in a minority in any period. They are no less a minority today.

Nevertheless, the question seems to demand an answer. The question is almost, though not always, rhetorical. It is prefaced with some observations. They run along these lines: "The country is going to the dogs. The government is getting bigger, stupider, and fatter every day. We are getting taxed to death. People don't have a sense of workmanship any more. The Protestant ethic is dead. Everyone wants to get on the dole. It just can't go on like this forever. How much time do you think we have?" Being a full-time predicter, I answer a question with a question, a time-honored prophetic response. "How much time do we have? *To do what?*"

Ultimately, the individual who asked the question has something in mind, or more likely, a whole package of ideas. The problem is, he has not sat down to think about what he is really asking. *Time is a resource.* As I have said in other contexts, it is *the* resource. It's the one irreplaceable resource. You only go around once in life, as some scholar has observed. (Or, in the immortal words of Hud, the cynical anti-hero of the movie: "Nobody gets out of life alive.") If time is a resource, then we have responsibilities for the effective use of that resource. *Just what is it that a person is trying to accomplish?* Until he asks that question and begins to answer it, the question, "How much time do we have?" is meaningless.

What the person is implying is that he thinks that his capital, including his life style, will run out on him before time does. The person really isn't asking about time. He is asking about his *hopes and dreams* concerning the time that he thinks he has remaining. When a starving man asks another starving man how much time they have left,

92

they are really concerned about time. When an affluent man of the industrial West asks the question, he is talking about his familiar life style, unless his most pressing concern is nuclear war. Few men have that as their most pressing concern.

If you want to know what is wrong with America today, here is a good place to start your research.

Redeeming the Time

Time, like any other capital resource, can be used productively or squandered. If you consider the growth of television over the last three decades, you will get a picture of what wasted time is all about. Men all over the world seem baffled about what to do with leisure time. Never before in the history of man has so much "free" time been available to various cultures, and like sailors on shore leave, men have squandered their capital with a suicidal vengeance. In contrast to this vision of zero-cost time consider the words of the apostle Paul:

> See then that ye walk circumspectly, not as fools, but as wise, redeeming the time, because the days are evil. Wherefore be ye not unwise, but understanding what the will of the Lord is (Ephesians 5:15-17).

The history of Western culture cannot be understood apart from an understanding of the implications of this message. The Industrial Revolution was a systematic attempt of capitalist entrepreneurs to redeem the time—not necessarily in a spiritual sense, but economically. The Protestant ethic, above all, was an attempt to deal with the limits of time, to see to it that it was not wasted. Protestant businessmen in the sixteenth and seventeenth centuries became convinced that thrift, hard work, foresight, rational calculation, and a close attentiveness to ledgers will lead to a better, more productive world. This outlook permeated the West, even after the theology of the Puritans had faded. So when we look around us and lament the loss of that older vision, let us not be naive: the heart of its vision was *the effective use of time.*

Unquestionably, the West is in the process of erosion. We have lost our bearings even as we have lost time. The Marxists, with their distorted concept of linear time, borrowed from the Hebrew-Christian concept of linear (start-to-finish) time, are conquering the world in front of our eyes. Theirs is a sense of destiny, a sense of purpose, despite the fact that Marx's evolutionary universe was rigorously Darwinistic, that is, devoid of purpose. The purpose is now man's or more accurately, proletarian man's. Victory is inevitable. The Marxists seem to beat us in the world market place of ideas because of their optimism concerning the future. They are redeeming the time.

What is our conception of time? There are few questions more crucial to survival over the next twenty years. Just what is it that we expect to achieve over time? The West, which was once geared to the future, invested where its dreams were. It still does, which is why we are facing a looming capital shortage. Its dreams are in the present. "The future is now," coach George Allen said. As more and more Americans agree with him, we can expect rising interest rates, lower production, more demands for leisure time, more pressure for the four-day "work" week. *Output per man hour is headed for the rocks*, which means that our future income per capita is in jeopardy. This is one reason why I strongly recommend the purchase of high quality durable goods, especially tools.

The 1978 coal strike was a grim promise of things to come. They weren't debating over wages. They were debating about fringes, especially pensions. They were debating about future productivity, too, since someone has to pay for those pension benefits. Workers want raises now and a guaranteed income later on, when they retire completely. Other unions are likely to follow suit over the next few years. People simply expect income apart from present thrift (savings) and future productivity. *The "English disease" is spreading fast.* So is the English sense of time. It is the concept of time shared by the drunks described by Isaiah: "Come ye, say they, I will fetch wine, and we will fill ourselves with strong drink; and tomorrow shall be as this day, and much more abundant" (56:12).

The Reality of Crisis

The question, "How much time do we have?" seems to imply another: "What kind of crisis is coming?" It makes a lot of difference whether we have mass inflation, or mass deflation, or price controls and rationing, or a direct expropriation of private property by the State. It makes a difference whether we have taxation through inflation, or property taxation, or income taxation, and in what proportions. It makes a difference whether the banks collapse or not. The time schedules involved are very different. Our strategy of planning will be very much affected by our choice of crisis, especially if we guess incorrectly.

By now, most of my readers know how I feel. I think the crisis, *short of World War III*, will be erosion, controls, rationing, black markets, steady reductions of per capita income, the destruction of pensions, bonds, mortgages, annuities, and all other forms of long-term credit. I think the crisis will last until the end of this century, at the very least. I see it as a transformation of Western culture. In short, my time frame is longer than that of most of those who are pessimistic about the economy in general. Nevertheless, just because my time perspective is longer, I in no way want to underestimate the magnitude of the crisis. When a nation's concept of morality shifts, its concept of property rights shifts with it. Our system of property rights has created the enormous wealth which we all enjoy. That enjoyment cannot possibly remain widespread if we see the alteration of the concept of the rights of private ownership.

What am I getting at? Simple: *tinkering won't do it*. No change in Presidents will do it. No technical solution will reverse the drift. No one-shot solution can possibly work. Please, for your own sanity and the preservation of your perspective, *don't get on some cure-all bandwagon*. That's what millions of Americans did in the 1930's, and we are witnessing the results today. It led away from the concept of personal responsibility for one's own conditions within a framework of political and economic freedom. Simple one-shot solutions are invariably tried by even simpler hot-shot politicians.

This is not to say that technical solutions cannot help. In fact, I offer two. They are quite simple. They would not cost the public much. They would cost the politicians plenty. To get either or both into law, we would have to have a political revolution. *First*, abolish withholding taxes on all income (Dr. Milton Friedman's gift to us in the 1940's—streamlining government, ho, ho). Let's unstreamline government. Make everyone pay it all at one time. Taxes should hurt. Let people go into debt to pay. Let them know what government costs. No more "refunds" from the government. No more over-withholding, the government's way to force us to file annually (to get our money back, without interest). *Second*, establish tax day on the second Monday of November. We go to the polls on the second Tuesday of November. Have you ever wondered why April is the month to pay? Wonder no longer. Minor technical revisions, right? Bounce it off your congressman sometime. Buy 1/4-ounce or 1/10-ounce Krugerrands while you're waiting for an answer.

I view our crisis as one similar to *a man who is sliding down a very steep cliff*, tearing his pants, digging in his heels, and praying for a handhold before he goes over the edge. Perhaps I should describe it this way: most people prefer not to acknowledge that the cliff lies before them. Some are already sliding down. Not many have gone over the precipice. But when controls go on, the bulk of the population will be pushed over the edge—not to fall straight to the bottom, but to begin that long, bloody slide down the steep incline. More and more will go over the ledge, and these are the ones who will call for further Federal intervention. Further intervention will push still more people over the edge.

What I am looking for is almost universal *fiscal bloodletting*, but not a universal crash. (Again, I am discounting war, although I am very fearful that the Soviet Union will be willing to take far greater risks in the early to mid-1980's—their version of John Foster Dulles' "brinksmanship" of the 1950's. War cannot be ruled out, but few of us will take the steps necessary to protect ourselves from nuclear war, so I don't spend much space discussing it.) A crash is conceivable, but we should go with the better odds. The ability of governments to create fiat money and impose "popular" solutions to price inflation must not be underestimated. In the international division of labor, the United States has begun to exercise its particular specialized skill in creating green paper with ink on it. Government may not do many things well, but it can print fiat money.

So when you wonder "how much time we have," think in these terms: *How much time do I have to accomplish those ends that I have set for myself in each period of escalating crises?* If I am correct in my analysis of the *multiple levels of crisis,* and the variations in each level, then each man should have *separate plans* for each period. He should have separate goals. He should have *separate budgets,* including a budget for his *time.*

Any man who is not setting up budgets for a future series of crises really does not take seriously the threat of those crises. The existence of a budget indicates a person's willingness to plan for a particular expected future. "No budget" is still a budget; it reflects a person's unwillingness to plan for the future, either through despair or unconcern. Again, we are called to redeem the time in terms of a vision of the future. The man without a budget has abdicated.

Budgets: What Is Available Today?

I recommend buying systematically those items that will be in short supply later on, but which are taken for granted by most buyers today. You should buy all those items that, in a panic wave of buying, you think you would be tempted to buy. I try to schedule my own buying in terms of *future panic.* I never want to be a buyer of anything—gold coins, guns, ammunition, tools, toilet paper, gasoline, food—during a panic. *Panic buying is an indicator of inefficient prior planning.* I realize that anyone can forget some item, or not quite get around to buying it, but no one should be caught short in too many areas. This is why systematic budgeting is mandatory. A balanced program of buying and storing goods is sensible. Once you have one basic group of items, go on to the next; don't try to buy everything in each group all at once. Don't buy all your coins now, or all your tools, or whatever. Buy only those that are vital in the *preliminary stages* of a *series* of crises. There will be items available for an advanced stage after the preliminary crisis is noticeable. Never forget this fact: *not everyone sees the future in the same way.* The idea is *to keep one or two stages ahead of the panic.* It will always come in waves. Different communities will have different problems at different times. The coal shortage isn't hurting Louisiana much these days. Some future hurricane may eliminate 70% of New Orleans (the most vulnerable city to hurricane waves in the country), but New Jersey residents will not notice. You must prepare for the problems most likely in the community where you reside, or intend to reside, in the next stage of any crisis.

Today, we should be planning in terms of basic goods that are easily available. My "Shopping Guide for Survival" in the price controls book is a handy introduction. [*How You Can Profit from the Coming Price Controls* ($14.95): American Bureau of Economic Research, 3536 N. Wellington, Indianapolis, IN 46226.] Bullion coins, a few weapons, ammunition (which will probably be controlled first, especially handgun ammo), dehydrated food, tools of your future expected trade, books on survival and crafts, and similar basic supplies should be purchased now. Once controls appear imminent, a person should step up his purchase of durable goods, such as a 3,500 or 4,500 watt generator (such as the Onan), spare parts, and more coins. Once controls are announced, it's time to buy a car, or at least get spare tires, plugs, etc. It would also pay to buy at least a small bit of ground at least 40 miles outside a major city, put a used (10 year old) mobile home on it, sink a well, put in a septic tank, and keep the generator ready at home. This will be a major purchase. It is wise to have a credit line open, to get your land and a liveable shelter. The controls, once imposed, will inevitably create disruptions. You can hold off for a time, but when controls go on, fast action will be imperative.

Fact: *you can't afford to do everything right now.* The idea is to do a *little each week,* if possible. Get a proposed timetable, with warning signs, that you think will apply in your community. Get a budget outlined to fit each stage of the expected escalations of disruption. Be systematic. *Know what you're willing to give up* at each stage in order to finance the purchases you will have to make. If you do this, even in a very simple outline, you are really serious about the possibility of government-created disruptions. A very simple beginning is your own self-testimony that you are doing your best to redeem the time, period by period.

Conclusion

How much time do we have? *To do what?* How much time do we have? *To meet what kind of crisis?* How much time do we have? *To meet a crisis period of what duration?* How much time do we have? *To spend how much capital once we think we know the answers?*

If someone told you, to the day, how much time "we" have, what would you do about it? Really and truly, what would you do differently? If the answer is "not much," then it really doesn't matter how much time we have as far as your budgeting is concerned. So the question is more of a curiosity than a piece of information in a program of crisis-evasion. Do you really want to know?

If you really do want to know, then decide for yourself, once and for all, do you think it will be deflation (prices falling, so hold cash), inflation (prices rising, so hold precious metals), price controls (black market supplies, so hoard goods)? Do you think it will be a period of terrorism, or revolution, or intermittent breakdowns of the public utilities (water, power, garbage collection)? Will it be martial law? Will it be rationing? Will it be world war? What do you think the most likely scenario will be? Until you *budget your time and capital* in terms of one or more of these possible scenarios, you ultimately think it will be good times as usual.

Have you spent a weekend looking for a piece of ground? When you do, you will have taken a preliminary step toward serious breakdown. You don't have to buy in panic now, but have you at least looked? Have you bought a copy of Les Scher's *Finding and Buying Your Place in the Country* (Collier, $7)? These are simple steps. Use this spring for enjoyment but seriously. Spend a weekend just snooping around. Pick up a rural local paper. So it costs you a weekend. So what? Don't assume that you will always have time to shop. It is time spent in advance planning that will keep you from gross mistakes. It's the assumption that you have unlimited time, meaning an unlimited guarantee on your present comfortable life style, that can cost you too much gold or too much debt later on. If you're short on capital, you will have to spend time. If you're *short on time,* then don't begrudge the capital and the expensive mistakes.

Prepare for one stage at a time. And most important, have something productive in mind for you to do at each stage: productive when you're doing it as well as productive for the next stage. A man without a *sense of meaning in his work* is not a good candidate for long-term survival. Spend capital now in order to assure yourself that you will be productive and useful to others, in the market and in other spheres of life, in each stage of the long-term series of crises that confronts us. Man does not live by protein powder alone.

Read Appendix A, Joel Skousen's list of items you need to buy (pp. 252-73). Don't be paralyzed by its size. Just pick out a few items to buy each week, and buy them. Get started today.

Chapter 12

THE SOURCE OF YOUR SECURITY

Lay not up for yourselves treasures upon earth, where moth
and rust doth corrupt, and where thieves break through and steal:
But lay up for yourselves treasures in heaven, where neither moth
nor rust doth corrupt, and where thieves do not break through
nor steal: For where your treasure is, there will your heart be also.

(Matthew 6:19-21)

Like so many conservative Americans, I bought a copy of Alek-
sandr Solzhenitsyn's *Gulag Archipelago*. Also like many conservative
Americans, I put off reading it. But in 1978 I devoted Sunday after-
noons to knocking off a couple of hundred pages, which means about
a hundred pages, plus a nap, plus other interruptions, plus a weekend
skipped, etc. But line by line, chapter by chapter, I plowed through it.
It was a most rewarding exercise in self-discipline on my part. I
learned things that my courses in Russian history and Soviet government never quite communicated.

The Gulag Archipelago will remain a classic. If any book is read in a
hundred years that appeared in our generation, it will be this one. Or,
if things go badly, if any book is prohibited in a hundred years, it will
be this one. What sticks in the mind—my mind, anyway—is the extent
of *the insanity and destructiveness of the Soviet regime.* Those who
survived did so on a seemingly random basis. A few people ran away
when they learned of their impending arrest, but very few. No one
resisted. No one yelled, screamed, or beat up the arresting KGB officials. They went meekly to the slaughter. Jews in Germany, kulaks in
Russia, citizens in every totalitarian state seem to have this one thing
in common: *they do not make a scene,* even when their worlds are collapsing around them. And the monsters who run the State, meaning
other faceless citizens under the command of truly demonic elites,
take every advantage of this meekness.

Thomas Molnar, the conservative scholar, suffered under the
regimes of both the Nazis and the Communists. He once made a very
significant observation. He said that the way you could sometimes
escape from a Nazi-dominated village was to dress up as if you were
going out for a stroll. You and your wife and children would create no

unusual appearance. You might even tip your hat at the military policeman or other official. With nothing more than the clothes on your back, you would march down to the train station and buy a ticket for the next town down the line. Station by station, you could get your way closer to the border. Then you could risk a silent crossing in the dark of night, or by bribing a guard. Significantly, he noted, those with lots of possessions seldom took this approach in the early days of military law. They would sit in their homes and hope for the best. This is exactly what Solzhenitsyn notes. The result was too often the loss of everything, including personal liberty.

When I was studying economic history in graduate school, our professor, Herbert Heaton, told us this fascinating story. One friend of his in England, before Heaton came to this country, was a Jewish scholar named Pribram. (I think it must have been Karl Pribram, but I'm operating from a 1966 memory.) Pribram had been working on a long-term study in German economic history. When the Nazis came to power, he had forebodings about his future. From then on, he made carbon copies of every document he typed up for his files. He sent the carbon copies, piece by piece, to Sir John Clapham, the British economic historian. He trusted Clapham not to steal his material. Finally, since the Nazis allowed people to leave Germany, including Jews, Pribram left. He was not allowed to take anything with him. Few Jews took this route to freedom, although of course several thousand did, but this was hardly a majority of those who had the opportunity; it was a mere fraction. When Pribram arrived in England, he had his notes. He could continue his studies. Most of his fellow refugee scholars had to leave everything behind. This included Ludwig von Mises, who had to abandon his library, a very difficult thing for any scholar to do. Both Pribram and Mises enjoyed fruitful careers later on, however, which those who perished under Nazi rule could not do.

What am I getting at? Simple: *a crisis can overtake any of us in our tracks at any time.* The flooding in the hills of southern California in 1978, the freezing cold in the Midwest and Northeast, and similar disasters can sweep unsuspecting people away. Their hopes, dreams, and careful plans do not avail them if the crisis is great enough. An all-encompassing disaster waits for no one to get his house in order. That wood stove and year's supply of food at home could not help those caught in the blizzard on the Ohio turnpikes in 1978.

Solzhenitsyn describes in detail a long-forgotten event in the late 1920's. He calls it "gold fever." This was a period in which Stalin was consolidating his position by exterminating his former colleagues in the Presidium—the standard practice of violent revolutions to consume their founders—and to centralize the nation's production system. The New Economic Policy (NEP), inaugurated by Lenin to reverse the starvation of the "war communism" period, which started in 1922 and lasted until this period of Stalin's rule, had decentralized small businesses, thereby encouraging increased output. Solzhenitsyn writes:

The famous *gold fever* began at the end of 1929, only the fever gripped not those looking for gold but those from whom it was being shaken loose. The particular feature of this new, "gold" wave was that the GPU was not actually accusing these rabbits of anything, and was perfectly willing not to send them off to Gulag country, but wished only to take away their gold by main force. So the prisons were packed, the interrogators were worn to a frazzle, but the transit prisons, prisoner transports, and camps received only relatively minor reinforcements.

Who was arrested in this "gold" wave? All those who, at one time or another, fifteen years before, had had a private "business," had been involved in retail trade, had earned wages at a craft, and *could have,* according to the GPU's deductions, hoarded gold. But it so happened that they often had no gold. They had put their money into real estate or securities, which had melted away or been taken away in the Revolution, and nothing remained. They had high hopes, of course, in arresting dental technicians, jewelers, and watch repairmen.... Nothing—neither proletarian origin nor revolutionary services—served as a defense against a gold denunciation. All were arrested, all were crammed into GPU cells in numbers no one had considered possible up to then—but that was all to the good: they would *cough it up* all the sooner!... Only one thing was important: Give us your gold, viper! The state needs gold and you don't. The interrogators had neither voice nor strength left to threaten and torture; they had one universal method: feed the prisoners nothing but salty food and give them no water. Whoever coughed up gold got water! One gold piece for a cup of fresh water.... If you in fact had no gold, then your situation was hopeless. You would be beaten, burned, tortured, and steamed to the point of death or until they finally came to believe you (Vol. 1, pp. 52-53).

The Chinese Communists used a different technique in the early years of their revolution. The situation there was different. When a Communist force would enter a village, they would try to get access to weapons. This was during the Japanese war period. The details are provided by Raymond de Jaegher, a Belgian Roman Catholic priest, who was a Jesuit missionary in China at the time, and his co-author, Irene Corbally Kuhn, in their neglected and important book, *The Enemy Within* (1952). I hope that their account eventually gets a wide hearing in the anti-gun control camp. They wrote:

Every Chinese family that had any property at all, even just their cooking utensils, their bedrolls, a few primitive farm tools, yearned for a gun. A gun meant protection. Farmers banded together to share common ownership of one rifle; wealthier farmers and landowners had a few rifles. Indeed, rifles were a rich medium of exchange, and in those times people preferred them to cash.

The Communists needed all the rifles they could lay their hands on beyond what they were allowed to have legally, if they were to increase in power and numbers. Persons were arrested on the slightest pretext and forced to pay a certain number of rifles. In fact, everyone arrested was faced with the alternative of handing over rifles or being shot. Always the people were punished for misdemeanors, big crimes, or no crimes at all by being fined in arms instead of money, a typical Communist trick which was used as part of an ascending spiral of ever-increasing demands to achieve maximum control over the population.

When the Communists first arrived and took such pains to make a good impression on the populace, they stressed their determination to save China from the Japanese. They appealed to people for funds over and above regular taxes, for a "war fund" and "to help the government." Many rich men, seeking to win favor with the authorities, contributed to the fund and then and there unwittingly sealed their doom, even as did good decent citizens who gave willingly and generously, often at great sacrifice. The Communists merely waited for the right moment and then applied the screws.

It was a simple procedure. They would call in a rich man who had given fifty dollars in the drive to "help the government."

"You are rich," a Communist officer would tell him, fixing him with an accusing eye. "Your contribution of fifty dollars to your government is not enough. You must now give arms. Bring ten rifles here tomorrow." He would name the hour, dismiss the man, and put his chop on the order.

No one could buy rifles easily in China in those days, and since the man's life depended on his getting them, a black market quickly developed. The Communists encouraged this, as they encourage any illegal or irregular enterprise which will serve their purpose. A rifle worth fifty dollars on Monday then acquired a greatly inflated value on Tuesday; when the desperate man finally tracked down his quota he had spent a small fortune.

As the weeks went by and more and more such fines were levied by the Communists, it was seen that the process was continuous. The man who was fined ten rifles at first was neither shot nor imprisoned that time, but just when he began to breathe easily once more, he would be arrested again and fined ten rifles. It was much harder for him to get the guns the second time and the deal cost him much more. By this time, too, he knew he was only buying a little time and that he would have to resign himself to a third arrest and a third demand, and so on, until one fine day. . . .

In this way the Communists got a fine haul of arms (pp. 42-43).

The story of how the Communists expropriated a class of people, simultaneously expanding their control over the population by disarming it, is not something to be ignored. We have to ask ourselves, what would we have done? Would we have left town as soon as we saw what the goals of the invaders really were? Would we have left after that first arrest? Or would we have sat around quietly, waiting for things to get better, hoping that the demands on our dwindling resources would finally be reduced? Think about it.

Here is the almost universal fact: people do exactly what the Chinese landed gentry did. They allow themselves to be skinned without a whimper. Why do we believe that we would act differently?

The Soft Underbelly

Totalitarians rely heavily, confidently, and continually upon their understanding of human nature. They realize that *men are incurably habit-oriented,* willing to suffer almost any disruptions in their wealth or freedom if they are permitted to believe that the basic outline of their lives will be left unimpeded. If the authorities are very careful to give the next victim the impression that today's victim may be the last, or that there are other victims in line, then most people most of the time will sit quietly and wait to be sheared. This reduces the costs of control to a minimum. In that graphic phrase of Solzhenitsyn's, "A submissive sheep is a find for a wolf."

Part of any serious program of economic and political survival is that of mental and psychological conditioning. It is not sufficient to stock up on your supplies of dehydrated fruits and Krugerands. The rifle you bought is no better than your determination to use it and your ability to use it. This means you have to have some sort of guideline about when and under what circumstances to use it. In a time of true terror, which I hope never comes, but which cannot be dismissed lightly, each man must have a *mental line* drawn, over which his opponent cannot step at zero risk. *The drawing of that line is probably more important than other physical preparations.* Where a man's treasure is, there is his heart. What am I getting at? Simple: *all of your preparations should be aimed at preserving your freedom first, and only secondarily aimed at protecting your wealth.* Your wealth is simply a tool for expanding your productivity under freedom. Your wealth must not be allowed to capture you, to chain you to the ground while the wolves plan your demise. Get this into your mind early: *your wealth is your tool to utilize freedom, not your enemy's tool of dominion over you.* The soft underbelly of America is here: our inability to understand the proper use of wealth. We cling to our wealth as if it could save us in a major crisis. As toolmakers, we have learned to worship the products of our hands—silent gods that neither speak nor give counsel.

We have confused means with ends, and we have worshipped means. So did those Chinese landowners.

Yet no bureaucracy is perfect. There were and and always will be ways out, although few people find them. Solzhenitsyn's account of Andrei Pavel is instructive:

> On the other hand, the NKVD did come to get the Latvian Andrei Pavel near Orsha. But he didn't open the door; he jumped out the window, escaped, and shot straight to Siberia. And even though he lived under his own name, and it was clear from his documents that he had come from Orsha, he was *never* arrested, nor summoned to the Organs [security system], nor subjected to any suspicion whatsoever. After all, search for wanted persons falls into three categories: All-Union, republican, and provincial. And the pursuit of nearly half of those arrested in those epidemics would have been confined to the provinces. A person marked for arrest by virtue of chance circumstances, such as a neighbor's denunciation, could be easily replaced by another neighbor. Others, like Andrei Pavel, who found themselves in a trap or in an ambushed apartment by accident, and who were bold enough to escape immediately, before they could be questioned, were never caught and never charged; while those who stayed behind to await justice got a term in prison. And the overwhelming majority— almost all—behaved just like that: without any spirit, helplessly, with a sense of doom (Vol. 1, pp. 11-12).

He adds this footnote one page later:

> And how we burned in the camps later, thinking: What would things have been like if every Security operative, when he went out at night to make an arrest, had been uncertain whether he would return alive and had to say good-bye to his family? Or if, during periods of mass arrests, as for example in Leningrad, when they arrested a quarter of the entire city, people had not simply sat in their lairs, paling with terror at every bend of the downstairs door and at every step on the staircase, but had understood they had nothing left to lose and had boldly set up in the downstairs hall an ambush of half a dozen people with axes, hammers, pokers, or whatever else was at hand? After all, you knew ahead of time that those bluecaps were out at night for no good purpose. And you could be sure ahead of time that you'd be cracking the skull of a

cutthroat. Or what about the Black Maria sitting out there on the street with one lonely chauffeur—what if it had been driven off or its tires spiked? The Organs would quickly have suffered a shortage of officers and transport, and notwithstanding all of Stalin's thirst, the cursed machine would have ground to a halt!

If...If...We didn't love freedom enough. And even more—we had no awareness of the real situation. We spent ourselves in one unrestrained outburst in 1917, and then we *hurried* to submit. We submitted *with pleasure!*...We purely and simply *deserved* everything that happened afterward.

The Three Worlds

If a person is to be successful in the possible scenarios before us, he has to live in three worlds. I am not speaking of the much-touted "multinational person." The world will not be rebuilt by multinational nomads, however useful their tax-haven-protected newsletters may be. I am speaking of something much more fundamental. The three worlds are, in order of importance (greatest to least important):

1. The residence of the heart (where your treasure is...)
2. The residence of the body
3. The future residence of the body

Why couldn't the Europeans known by Molnar have just walked out of their homes and headed for the border? Why couldn't the Russians have acted like Andrei Pavel? Why didn't those Chinese landlords just walk away from the Chinese Communists to join Chiang's forces? After all, that's what the Red Chinese did in the 1934 Long March, when they escaped Chiang by walking thousands of miles to isolation and safety. I think the difference between the landlords and Mao was the location of their treasure. Mao's treasure was in an ideal of a Communist revolution. His heart was in the utopian future. So he walked away. He escaped, survived, and lived to return in force. He knew where the treasures of his enemies were buried: in their traditional way of life. So he dug up their treasures, family by family, until there was nothing left of that traditional way of life. Hoping to save their lives, his enemies forfeited their lives and treasures. They would live or die in Mao's kingdom, at the discretion of the Communists.

We must live in the present, where we make our daily income. We have to build in terms of what we have now and where our responsibilities are. We have to hope that our present circumstances will not be disrupted. We have a lot of treasure buried here. But to insure our own safety, *we have got to rethink the meaning of treasure.* It had better not be in bricks and mortar. How many alumni have financed the destruction of capitalism by blindly (and not so blindly) contributing to their old alma mater to buy a little phony immortality, the Crittendon J. Armbruster economics building? It is not bricks and mortar, but the *use* of bricks and mortar, that should capture our imaginations. Andrei Pavel knew this when he jumped out of the window and headed for Siberia. The present is worth only part of our sacrifice. We hold our possession of the present only on a lease, not as a permanent title.

We have to live in terms of the likely future, not our hoped-for future. We have to sacrifice present enjoyments in order to build up the survival capital we expect to use in the future. That capital had better be mobile, and if not mobile, then at least isolated. One tank full of gasoline away we should have at least a spot of ground, a septic tank, a well, and a building, if only a used mobile home bought at a steep discount for cash from someone living in a trailer court nearby. (The equity in a mobile home drops to about $4,000 after seven years, so it's not that great an investment. Any county which has restrictions on mobile homes is run by Liberals, cartels of mobile home park owners, or ecologists; you don't want to live in that kind of county.)

Conclusion

You dare not put your trust in *things*. Things are means to certain personal ends. Let them capture your heart, and you have offered crucial leverage to the tyrants of the world. Things can be confiscated anyway; sacrificing your future for the sake of them, only to be removed from them, is the very act which *The Gulag Archipelago* warns against. Mobility is a more important asset for short-run maneuvering, since isolation and invisibility may be initially dependent upon mobility. But in the long run, nothing can protect a person from the external crises of life. Robbers break in, and rust erodes. You can't take it with you. But if you have it buried in the wrong place, it sure can take you with it.

Chapter 13

THE FOUR G'S

Predicting the future is a necessary and preposterous task. The whole idea of "the" future implies that there is a single future for all earthly participants, which we know is false, short of a supernova which destroys *everyone* simultaneously, or some other cosmic event. There are a myriad of individual futures, which is why the newsletter industry is flourishing. The general audience magazines have been dying off for two decades, as the reading public has begun to recognize their distinctions. The financial newsletters try to target a certain segment of the reading and buying public and then provide information that helps these narrowly defined readers try to deal with their futures.

The difficulty with publishing a newsletter like *Remnant Review* is that my promotions and my editorial content favor the idea of personal privacy. I am a fanatic about this, and I am unwilling to send readers imitation census forms which are supposed to be "completely confidential." A few years ago, the *National Observer* (now defunct) sent out a form like this, and the editor later found out the supposedly confidential forms had been coded. He was outraged at his staff, and he was informed that this was standard policy within the publishing industry, which was true. The publishers rent their mailing lists, and the large-circulation magazines like to be able to segregate their subscribers for more profitable list renting. I know that my readers would resent getting such a form from me, so I really am not quite certain just which kinds of people presently subscribe, except that I know they read newsletters generally, and that they buy books that are concerned with financial survival.

When I sit down at the typewriter and begin to compose a particular issue, I have to make some strategic guesses concerning the personal concerns of my readers. I go by instinct to some extent. I don't try to predict a single future for every reader, but instead I try to present several possible futures that would seem to be probable for many readers, and which will probably influence everyone to some degree or other. I do not expect every reader to take every piece of advice I offer, since any single idea is influenced by questions of age distribution, financial resources, geographical location, experience in the markets,

107

employment possibilities, and so forth. The best inflation hedge, for example, is short-lived parents coupled with your 87th birthday and a nagging cough.

Let me give you a recurring example. Most of my readers, I suspect, have money to invest. This means, usually, that they are *short on time*. Newsletter readers are time-conscious, which is why they want their information distilled and direct. However, I find that some readers have more time than money, and they tend to be more price-sensitive than time-sensitive. When I include a suggestion to buy an item like the *Cache-It,* I assume that people are going to put high-value, low-volume items (coins, gems) in the plastic tubes, which indicates that they have more capital than spare time. The *Cache-It* sealed tubes are fairly expensive, even on special. So one reader wrote me a letter telling me that the item was a rip-off, and that he can find equally good materials locally that can be used to construct an inexpensive equivalent. Well, that depends. Technically, I think he may be correct, though the screw-on caps make the *Cache-It* unique. The list prices of the various tubes and caps may well be cheaper than ordering a *Cache-It* from SI. But I contend that for most readers, it would be more expensive to go this route. You must always estimate the value of your "spare" time. (Time is never "spare"; it is allocated rationally in terms of one's personal value-preference scale. It always has a price tag on it.) *What is a man's time worth* to find out what kinds and sizes of tubes there are, what size caps are needed, where the best prices are available, and then drive down to buy the materials ("I'm terribly sorry, sir, but the clerk you spoke to seems to be mistaken. We stopped carrying those last fall."), drive home, and put them together? Isn't it cheaper for most subscribers to write a check, drop it in an envelope, add a stamp, and put it in the mailbox? It is for me. (Order from SI, Inc., 16809 S. Central Ave., Carson, CA 90746. They come in 6 sizes. For more details, call toll-free: (800) 421-2179.)

However, I am always open to suggestions, since some readers may be long on time and short on cash. But when I make a suggestion, I am always alert to the key problem: *it takes a lot of effort to follow through on a complex decision.* The easier it is to act, the better it is for the reader, even if the reader has to pay more. I believe in price competition, but given the innate resistance we all have to change, I have come to the conclusion that *ease of action* is more important than price. I am interested in low prices, but only after I have located the simplest, quickest means of taking action.

With this in mind, let me get to this chapter's topic(s), what I have called *the four G's.* There is nothing unique about the topic, since other newsletter writers and survival book writers have always emphasized at least two of them. But I want to reaffirm my belief that these are absolutely fundamental for any hedging strategy, and that if you have not begun to take steps on all four, you have made a mistake. There are some readers who will not want to deal with all four, since they think that one of them is superfluous or questionable, but I want everyone to consider the whole package. The four G's are: gold, guns, groceries, and God. (Some readers might add or substitute "girls," but this is an investment book.)

Gold

Most of you know at least the basic reasons for advocating gold. Gold has been the most familiar currency in man's history. A gold coin can find a relatively liquid market in any city in the free world. Gold's price is being quoted on some market throughout the day: London, New York, Hong Kong, and even Chicago. There are numerous buyers, so sellers can "play the auction" knowing that price spreads, dealer to dealer, will be small. Furthermore, the familiar gold coins don't have to be assayed, and counterfeits are irrelevant for common-date coins, since there is slightly more gold in most counterfeits than the restrikes issued by the various national mints. (The reason for this is internationally honored laws regarding counterfeiting: it's not a criminal offense if the counterfeit has an equal or greater quantity of gold than the official restrike—a restrike being the common-date coin which is kept in production. Rare coins, including U. S. gold coins, are counterfeited by criminals, given the profit potential, so you need a reliable dealer to buy from.)

I am partial to the ¼-ounce Krugerrand, the Austrian 20-corona, the Mexican 10-peso, and the U. S. $20 gold piece. I want liquidity, and I want to give up as little gold per transaction as possible. In mass inflation, who wants paper money change?

Several years ago, Deak & Co., which has offices in most major cities (Deak-Perera), sold Vietnamese taels of gold, thin ½-ounce strips of 24-carat gold, which could be cut with scissors to make weight transactions. These taels circulated throughout Southeast Asia, and they were the accepted means of payment for buying your way out of the country in 1975. Deak & Co. is the world's leading dealer in foreign exchange (cash basis), so the firm had a lot of these in 1975.

The secret of owning gold coins is knowing when *not* to sell. The best time not to sell is now. Eventually, you will want to sell some of them, but that will be later. *Buy now, sell later:* this is how you profit from gold in a time of international turmoil. (Bartering gold for *things* is something else again; some seller may want gold rather than money, and instead of trying to educate him, you give him what he wants.)

Also, *buy gold in between panics*—1970, 1975, 1981—and not when the lemming phenomenon is in operation. Psychologically, I don't like to "fight the tape." I don't sell when it's rising or buy when it's falling; I buy and sell when the dust has settled. Except when I panic, of course.

The real secret of buying gold is to buy when you can afford to and when you are psychologically prepared to. I recommend *steady buying,* which tends to reduce your reliance on panic for motivation. You get better prices this way. The idea is not to beat the market. The idea is to not get beaten *by* the market, and panic buying is a tried and true way to get beaten.

Guns

There are several reasons for buying guns. First, they seldom depreciate. You can sell all you have, for cash, on demand, any time you need to. You don't need to advertise. Word of mouth is sufficient. As a barter item, a handgun and 200 rounds of ammunition cannot possibly be beaten, and the worse the economy gets (deflation or inflation, black markets or no markets), your market will be expanding. If the government bans the sale of either ammunition or handguns, and you already have a supply, you become the immediate beneficiary of a law. You get the monopoly of supply, precisely at the time when others will be scrambling for the product.

Second, you need protection. When it comes to a crisis, you need more than gold. Kurt Saxon, a specialist in the survival field, was quoted in *New West* magazine (Feb. 25, 1980). Let's say, Saxon speculates, that one person has an ounce of gold, and another person has a high-powered weapon, such as a .44 magnum. "Who in his right mind would trade that revolver for ten ounces of gold? At the end of the transaction, one of [them] is going to have both the gold and the gun." When you're dealing with a person in a life-and-death situation, you had better be the fellow with the gun, not because you intend to steal from him, but because you don't want him to command the situation.

What guns do you need? For hunting, I recommend a Remington 700 BDL, 30-06, with a Weaver or other scope. I wear glasses, so I chose the 4X wide angle, and it's fine. You need a shotgun, preferably a pump action, 12-gauge, with interchangeable barrels (you want a 20-inch one, plus a longer one for hunting). I think a Remington 870 is a good one. A pump action is good for left-handed shooters. In fact, a leftie might want to buy a Remington 760 30-06, since it's a pump action rifle. For a lighter weapon that doesn't kick much, I would suggest the Ruger "Mini-14," which shoots a .223 round. It's a good rifle for wives and daughters. The Ruger 10/22 is a good .22 rifle.

For strictly defense shooting, the experts differ. Some like the old M1 Garand (but not the ones cut by torch by the government, and welded back together by private entrepreneurs). Others like the Springfield Armory M1A, which shoots the .308 round. These are semi-automatic rifles; each time you pull the trigger, it shoots. You don't mess with a bolt or a pump action. I think you should consult a self-defense expert before buying any strictly defensive weapon, since you're talking about a $1,000+ expense. Macho men love the Heckler & Koch 91, which shoots the .308. (The accessories are expensive.)

What about handguns? Here I have modified my thinking in the last few years. I no longer have as much use for the .357 magnum. I have no use at all for the .38 "special," except as a barter device, especially when you're bartering with someone who might try to shoot you. What you want is the good old .45 automatic, either the Colt Combat Commander (slightly smaller) or the Colt Mark IV. You want a reliable weapon, one you can drop in the mud. You want a weapon which is easy to load. This means a magazine full of rounds, not a round wheel full of empty shells. You may also want a weapon that kids cannot shoot by accident. No child is going to "rack" a .45 to load the chamber. It is just too stiff.

The handgun, however, is only part of it. You need training. You need to handle it safely. You need to know how to draw, aim, control, and pull the trigger. You need to know how to draw, unlatch the safety, aim, and put two bullets in a man-sized target at 20 feet in a second and a half, total. About 90% of you can be taught to do this in five days of supervision and practice. I had never fired a .45 in my life, and I had virtually no training in handling a pistol. I found myself a great teacher, and I learned how to do it. Though the training was gruelling for me, and the pressure was intense, I can recommend it without reservation. And speaking of reservations, you'll need one. The course is booked up six months in advance. Contact:

> John Brook
> American Pistol Institute
> Box 401
> Paulden, AZ 86334
> (602) 636-4565

The senior instructor is Jeff Cooper. Cooper reminds me of Col. Tim McCoy, the old cowboy actor, who was also a real cowboy. Cooper is a scientist of shooting. He took 15 years to study the best defense shooting techniques of the fastest, most accurate shooters in the world of practical shooting. He analyzed these techniques, and devised a simple program of instruction. It works. It works so well that it is not open to everyone. But if you're interested, you can find out. A week costs $400 (you pay for ammo, housing in town, and a rent-a-car to get you to the camp, daily, or a motor home for a week).

I also recommend the services of a good gunsmith. You *must* get your weapon working before you go to the school or anywhere else.

Sports West, Inc.
2200 W. Alameda Ave.
Denver, CO 80223

This firm offers the various modifications to the .45 that Jeff Cooper recommends. There are a lot of them. The two most important: 1) high visibility sights; and 2) a good trigger job (3.5 to 4.5 pound pull, crisp). A *partial* listing of useful modifications: adjustable high visibility sights; dehorned edges (rounding); enlarged ejection port; bevelled magazine well; extended thumb safety; throated barrel and polished feed ramp. There are at least 50 possible modifications, and the price adds up fast. (Anyone buying all this owes it to himself to subscribe to *Combat Handguns*, which is geared to practical shooting: $13.50/6 issues. Write: Subscription Dept., Harris Publications, 79 Madison Ave., New York, NY 10016.) A good holster (such as Gordon Davis' "Liberty") will cost around $40. I also recommend the stainless steel magazines (never call them clips, the experts tell me) for the Colt .45. If all else fails, just buy a fully modified Colt .45 Commander or Mark IV from Sports West. It can be arranged through your local gun dealer for about $10 or $15 extra as a broker's fee to him. Contact Sports West for details on how to order. As of mid-1981, expect to pay $500+ for the weapon and modifications.

Buy a copy of the *Shooter's Bible* in any gun shop. It's comprehensive.

People are always concerned about registration of guns. All guns must be registered by law. It is possible, however, that not every gun in the country is registered. One reason for this is gun shows. Gun shows are meetings were buyers and sellers congregate and exchange used guns (unregistered) for cash (unregistered). In Texas, for example, the gun shows can involve up to 1,500 tables, where weapons and paraphernalia of all kinds can be purchased. Only Texas residents are supposed to be able to buy. That's what the law says. However....

It is my opinion that it is worth a trip to Texas to participate in either the Dallas or the Houston gun show. Drive in, bring cash, and drive out. News concerning the dates of the better gun shows nationally, including Texas, is available by subscribing to *Shotgun News*. For subscription information, write

Shotgun News
P. O. Box 669
Hastings, NB 68901

Groceries

This year should be the last year for reasonably priced dehydrated food. The 1980 recession forced farmers to reduce the acreage under cultivation. The anti-recession monetary inflation will drive up prices next year. The weather patterns are being disrupted by volcanoes, but also as part of a larger, ominous trend, according to Cliff Harris, who provides professional consultation in meterology: (406) 862-5154, $20/call. War, inflation, price controls, rationing, riots, breakdowns in transportation, drought, crop failures, government regulation, foreign aid, and petrochemical shortages can (and probably will) combine to raise food prices. Only a full-blown deflationary recession will lower prices further, and I do not predict a deflationary recession.

When you buy a food storage program—and if you take this book's advice seriously, it's "when," not "if"—you should buy a wide enough variety of foods to supplement the standard wheat, soybeans, and milk diet. Food aversion is a real problem, especially with small children. Buy canned goods for *rotation,* a 6-months' supply: fruits, canned tomatoes, etc. Fully packaged food storage programs are available from several companies, which are listed in Appendix C. But if you simply can't or won't spend the money on a fully packaged program, then at least buy your wheat, get storage cans, find out about storage from a local Mormon Church or survival center, like SI (call for their book list and catalogue: 800-421-2179). Book: I recommend *Making the Best of Basics* ($6.95). The company which sells the least expensive wheat in bulk that I have located is Walton's: see Appendix C: "Food Storage." For organically grown wheat, Arrowhead Mills is excellent. For latest prices, write:

Martens Products   Arrowhead Mills
P. O. Box 359   P. O. Box 671
Lafayette, CA 94549   Hereford, TX 79045

For those of you who are short on funds but long on time, these firms can sell you what you need. If you know you don't have the time, then pay the price for a pre-packaged food storage program. But do something.

God

One good way to survive any major crisis is to find out why it's worth surviving. An even better way is to find out why it's important for someone else to have you survive. Finally, find out why the most important Person to please happens also to be the one who possesses the power to get you through the trials.

There is no doubt in my mind that those who will survive in good shape will be those who are dedicated to something more than personal survival as such. They will cooperate in order to maintain a basic division of labor. They will not cooperate with Caesar and his bureaucratic associates. They will help each other. They will also know why they are cooperating. Some of these groups will be underworld organizations, and most of them will be underground organizations, if tyranny comes. As organizations, they will fare better than lonely individualists, except in those rare (and unpredictable) instances where fully trained loners happen to escape the traps. If you won't pay the enormous personal price of becoming a mobile, ruthless, rootless loner, then you need trustworthy friends. If your friends are motivated to serve something more important than themselves and the local group, then they will probably be more reliable.

On the practical, anti-statist implications of Christianity, two books by R. J. Rushdoony are good, *Bread Upon the Waters* (1969) and *Law and Liberty* (1971), available from Fairfax Christian Books, 11121 Pope's Head Rd., Fairfax, VA 22030 ($4 for both). For a spirited defense of Christianity against theological liberalism, see J. Gresham Machen's *Christianity and Liberalism* (1923), published by Eerdmans Pub. Co., 255 Jefferson Ave. S.E., Grand Rapids, MI 49502 ($3.95). Both authors are Presbyterians.

For a relatively simple, one-volume introduction to *practical* Christianity, you can buy my book, *Unconditional Surrender: God's Program for Victory*. It sells (postage included) for $11. Order from

> Geneva Press
> 708 Hamvassy
> Tyler, TX 75701

Chapter 14

RETIREMENT

There is only one solid answer to the problems of retirement: *don't retire.* The only better one is to retire as a multi-millionaire, but it's a possibility limited to very few. Even Nelson Rockefeller said he didn't want to retire. He chose instead to return to the free enterprise system. (This amazed me; I hadn't been aware of the fact that he was ever in the free enterprise system.) All those who seem to be able to afford to retire want to stay on the job. This should tell us something. What it tells us is that it's nice to be on top.

It shouldn't surprise us that some aging coal miner wants to retire. Or that others who have physically difficult, or boring, dead-end jobs want to retire. But the fact of the matter is this; they really can't afford to retire. The price inflation of the 1980's is not going to permit many people to retire in comfort, and virtually no one can do it without watching huge chunks of his capital blow away. The *inflation tax* is the *retirement tax.*

Nevertheless, the public still hasn't caught on. They continue to retire at age 65 or earlier, despite the new Federal law which prohibits mandatory retirement at age 65. This ill-conceived law is one more example of bad results from good intentions. That the Federal government should intervene in the decisions of private businesses in this way is bad enough. The irony is that the age 65 retirement practice grew out of the old Social Security law. Paul Woodring of Western Washington State College investigated the origins of the practice and discovered that New Deal Brain Trusters assumed that Social Security would apply primarily to industrial workers. They didn't even bother to consult with those whom the law would immediately affect. They just arbitrarily picked 65 as the year to begin Social Security payments. Private industry picked up this figure from the government, and an American tradition was born. Now the bankrupting deficit in Social Security is looming, and the Federal government is trying to kill off the tradition the bureaucrats created. They want to raise retirement to age 68.

I am a great believer in continued labor, but I am strongly opposed to the new Federal law. On principle, it's a bad law. It is no business of the

Federal government to monitor the policies of hiring and firing by private companies, state governments, or agencies other than those created by or part of the Federal government. What we will very likely discover is that the least productive, or least risk-oriented workers will cling to their jobs, lowering overall corporate productivity. One of the great restraints on Japanese productivity, especially in the domestic (as distinguished from export-oriented) firms is the burden of less efficient workers who cannot be fired. A company should be permitted to hire or fire as it sees fit. For large corporations that are already bureaucratic and increasingly inefficient, mandatory retirement is what enables them to recruit hard-driving, energetic younger men. Those men now will be tempted to join small firms, or start their own companies, since the attrition rate will slow down in the larger firms. The benefits of free contract once offered to the corporate world are steadily being eroded.

The problem should be seen as one of philosophy, not legislation. What we have created is *a national system of supposedly guaranteed living.* Children get their benefits—education at State expense—while older people get theirs—retirement at State expense. People in the middle years are expected to pay. They, in turn, are supposedly benefited by a semi-monopoly, since both kids and older people are kept out of the labor force, which increases wages for those inside. It's a crazy-quilt system of redistribution. We simply refuse to allow the free market to operate. We refuse to let such factors as price competition and innovation prove to buyers the benefits involved. Instead we want *certification:* How old are you, how many degrees did you earn, how many exams have you passed, what color are you, what sex are you, and so forth? Bureaucracy begins to replace the market in a semi-medieval world of government protection. Everyone wants to know what his *privileges* are, not the market value of his productivity. "I'm 65, so you can't fire me." "I'm a minority group member, so you have to hire me." "I'm a token, and the government says you need me." One thing seems to escape the legislators: people can always say: "I'm productive and priced competitively; you'd be crazy not to hire me, but if you are, your profit-seeking competitor may not be."

The Golden Lure

The trap has been set; inflation is now about to spring it. What trap? The trap of *third-party retirement planning.* People have had faith in the competence of third-party experts. They have assumed that the Social Security system is solvent. They have assumed that their state or local pension fund has been fully funded. They have assumed that the trust department of the local bank—or even more foolishly, of some

New York City bank—is staffed by competent, profit-seeking entrepreneurs who understand inflation, markets, and risk. (They do understand risk, so they have invented the "prudent investor rule" which enables them to waste most of their investors' capital in ways that will enable them, the trustees, to evade future legal action on the part of the sheared. They understand *legal* risk, and they put their clients' dollars into investments that are sure-fire losers during times of price inflation. Safety first, meaning *their* safety, is their motto.)

The logic of the pension is faulty. It assumes that individuals can transfer the responsibility of their futures to a faceless, nameless board of supposed experts, and that those faceless experts will put the interests of the investors first. It assumes that long-term credit positions can be taken in an almost irrevocable form—such as a corporate retirement program—without a loss of capital. It assumes that the best managers of one's retirement plans are third-party experts. This aura of expertise is deadly, for it lures the unsuspecting into a trap. It encourages them to believe what the market daily demonstrates to be false, namely, that retirement fund managers (or mutual fund managers, or bank trust department managers) can systematically and consistently outperform the market. They can't. Or if some of them can, it's random as to whether your firm has hired them rather than some outfit that consistently performs in a mediocre fashion. The odds are against your firm's picking an outfit which will be able to outperform the market for 40 years.

What are the realities of retirement programs? As of 1974, about 30 million workers were "covered"—a most misleading term. This amounted to about 45% of the privately employed wage and salary labor force. The average pay-out per beneficiary (retired person) in 1974 was a paltry $2,000 per year, or about $170 per month. In recent years, these benefits have not kept pace with price inflation, and there is little reason to expect that they will keep up in the future. After all, the managers of the retirement funds put the bulk of the assets into stocks and bonds, neither of which have performed well since price inflation really got rolling over a decade ago.

This is a grim prospect for anyone who has made himself dependent on a private retirement program. What if the employer's program goes bankrupt? What about the loss of capital due to mass inflation, or a war, or a series of social disruptions? The average reserve for each "covered" worker in 1974 was $6,500. In short, each worker had "saved" $6,500 for his entire retirement years. Naturally, older workers had larger reserves, but that average figure isn't enough to give one a lot of confidence. If the average is $6,500, the top end for a worker at the end of his retirement years couldn't be much above

$14,000. That won't go very far in an age of mass inflation. (The figures appear in the *Social Security Bulletin* [June, 1976], p. 6.)

This *massive shift of personal responsibility* has come in an era of increasing government intervention. Men have been encouraged to believe that some other institution will always enter the scene and correct any errors made by the inefficient or thoughtless. Government, or the corporation, or the Federal Reserve System will always solve the problems at hand. So people allow their employers to extract present dollars from them in exchange for depreciated future dollars. The government even gives people an income tax break to do this. (Not a tax break as such. The government doesn't offer tax breaks to the middle class. It offers only *certain kinds of tax breaks,* and virtually all of them are cancelled out by some future tax: income tax, estate tax, gift tax, or whatever. If the government offers a temporary tax break, it is only to allow the taxpayer time to accumulate more capital for later tax collection purposes. Forget this basic law of taxation, and you will fall for almost any sleight-of-hand tax dodge that the government can come up with this year. "Step right up, folks, and take advantage of this fantastic offer." "Put your pre-tax dollar under this little shell—uh, shelter—while we revise the tax code once again." And on and on.)

What must be understood from the very beginning of a person's working career is this: *a pension fund is a retirement program designed by a committee.* Let this sink in. A corporate pension fund is something like a camel: a horse built by a committee. The committee selects its members in terms of proven, measurable criteria, such as an M. A. in finance from Stanford, or a B. A. in portfolio management from Harvard. People who shudder at the thought of the Trilateral Commission's running the country don't give second thought to the fact that their pension fund is being managed by people who graduated from the same schools, who bank at the same banks, and who read the same textbooks (Keynesian) as the members of the Trilateral Commission. (It occurs to me that Jimmy Carter was a President designed by a committee, and it showed.)

The thought of your future income's being determined by a committee that, by definition, believes in the "prudent investor rule," believes in the present-day "mixed economy," believes in the integrity of the banks, believes (or did right up to the end) in New York City bonds, and believes in the laws of Keynesian fiscal policy, should give you many sleepless nights. Yet the unsuspecting masses have slept soundly, knowing that their futures are in good hands with all-Statists.

Long-Term Credit

A pension is a form of long-term credit. It permits a person to give up dollars of today's purchasing power in order to receive future dollars. Do you really believe that those future dollars will be greater in purchasing power? If not, manage your own retirement portfolio. Most important, keep it out of long-term credit instruments that are denominated in dollars.

What is true of the pension plan is doubly true of the *irrevocable annuity*. You give up dollars with present purchasing power in order to receive dollars with the purchasing power of 1990 or 2000. This seems to me to be the world's worst investment decision. Even if you buy a Swiss annuity, you are betting on the survival of the world economy, the investment acumen of the Swiss firm who sold you the annuity, the continued existence of a free Europe, and the continued existence of free flows of currency (out of Swiss francs and into dollars) on *legal* markets. Frankly, I would hesitate to bet my future in terms of these presuppositions. Deny any of them, and you ruin a Swiss annuity, and we may see all of them denied sometime during the next 20 years. (Still, I'd prefer a Swiss annuity to a domestic one denominated in U. S. currency.)

In any case, a person's decision to invest in a retirement program should be based on the assumption that *he will never stop working*. He wants the program as a *supplement* to regular income, which he does not intend to forego. He may decide to use the real estate management approach as his way of creating a new job for his supposed years of retirement, but he should never, ever become dependent upon passive income, especially passive income managed by a third party. That is suicidal, whether or not the government offers special income tax breaks to indulge in such suicidal tendencies. Inflation destroys passive income.

Does this mean a person shouldn't rely on the income derived from those second trust deeds? That's what it means. But what about those AAA-rated utility bonds (2001)? AAA-rated by whom? In terms of what assumptions about the dollar, American society, and Keynesian economics? What about those other absolutely guaranteed credit certificates? That's the problem: they're absolutely guaranteed...*in dollars*. And who guarantees the dollar?

Two Steps to Take

The *first* and most important step a person can take is this: don't retire. Inflation will not let a person retire. He may not be able to work at his present job on a full-time basis, and he may not be able to do the work he likes most, but he must continue to work for as long as his faculties permit. His retirement income will inevitably be small and declining. Thus, it must be regarded as Social Security must be regarded: a minimal supplement to normal income, at best. A person who has to pay into a retirement program should accept the fact psychologically the way he accepts Social Security deductions: it's a tax that has to be paid. It's not a benefit; it's a tax. It's not a guarantee for the future; it's a drain on present resources. It probably has to be paid, but it's no blessing.

How to get out of your pension fund? Can you become an *independent contractor?* If so, perhaps you can quit, get your pension money, pay the taxes necessary, and start investing in something else. Then allow your ex-employer to hire you back.

Another approach: quit, take your money, and then get rehired by the same outfit even apart from independent contractor status. Sometimes it can be done, especially if you play straight with your employer and tell him the real reason why you're quitting.

Can you start a *moonlighting business?* There are numerous books on this, like Don Dible's *Up Your Own Organization* and Peter Weaver's *You, Inc.* There are real tax breaks involved, namely, short-term tax deferrals, which are the best ones the government offers. Can you create a new company, or offer a service locally, that will supplement your income? Could it become a full-time job after retirement from your present job? If so, give it careful consideration. This could be the most important single economic decision you ever make.

I have never understood why teachers retire altogether from teaching. Why not start a private school? Why not continue in the profession? Why not demonstrate a little entrepreneurship?

The *second* consideration is *geography.* How high is the cost of living where you are? Most people are located in expensive urban centers because that's where the jobs are. But this means that they compete in a giant auction for the items in short supply, most notably living space. Why stay in a $100,000 home when you could sell it, move to a smaller town, and buy a decent $40,000 place, pocketing the difference (after taxes)? Or why not move to that small town now, establish the $100,000 place as a rental, and then get a *tax-deferred exchange?* You might wind up with a couple of nice duplexes that generate income in a safe place, and the government doesn't get a penny until you sell for money.

It is not easy to move. You will miss old friends. You will not be able to see them as often, see them grow poor, see inflation erode their savings, and take comfort from the fact that they're doing as poorly in the expensive city as you are. You may not see the grandkids as often, assuming your children are still in the same city where you are, and will be able to stay there in a time of turmoil. Of course, the grandkids might like to visit you on the farm. And your children might get their survival property in the only way they ever will, namely, because you have the vision, capital, and inclination to move out of the city now. But rationally, you have to move soon.

Should you move into a retirement community? Just what you need: the elephant burial ground for the white middle class. Congested streets, lots of old people complaining about their illnesses, lots of time for golf, puttering around, and being generally unproductive. Take yourself out of the land of the living, focus your interests on the present, remove yourself from those who have a stake in the future. Hook up your future to those public utilities (water, power, sewage disposal) and pray for stable money. No thanks.

The Need for Income

Admittedly, if you're out of the work force and your skills are rusty, you may be trapped. If you have no energy, or your body is really handicapped, then what I've written won't do you much good. This is the horror of inflation: it strikes at those who are most defenseless. Yet it's standard operating procedure for every enlightened, Keynesian government in the West. This is the politics of envy come home to the generation that voted in its existence. This is the New Deal after 45 years, namely, the Raw Deal. This, frankly, is the revenge of the Invisible Hand.

I recommend that people buy 90-day Treasury bills for liquidity. The trouble with T-bills is that they have to be purchased in units of $10,000 (with $5,000 units above the initial $10,000 in any given order). They can be purchased directly through the regional Federal Reserve Branch (no commission) or through a bank or brokerage company (small commission). By buying through the regional Federal Reserve Bank, you save money but increase the paperwork. For full information, write to the Federal Reserve Bank, Washington, D.C. and ask about the purchase of T-bills. The interest on these bills is not subject to state income taxes.

Another way to buy T-bills indirectly is to invest in the Capital Preservation Fund of Palo Alto, California. They pay less interest, however, and the interest is subject to state income taxation. But you only need $1,000 to open an account. You can write a check for $500 or more at any time.

Capital Preservation Fund
755 Page Mill Road
Palo Alto, CA 94304
(800) 227-8380 (USA)
(800) 982-5873 (California)

There is another strategy which is generally overlooked. A person can buy a resource which he expects to rise in value and then sell off portions of it in future years, generating the income necessary for survival, while taking advantage of the more favorable capital gains tax rates. For example, if you expect the value of gold to increase more than 10% or 12% per annum, you can buy gold coins like the South African ¼-ounce Krugerrand, store them, and sell them to the dealer from whom you purchased them. Or sell them to a local coin dealer. Or swap coins for goods.

This approach sounds strange. People hate to "touch their capital" when they spend money. Let me tell you right here and now, inflation is touching everyone's paper money investments. *Touching* is not the right word; *grabbing* is closer to it. If you have a long-term, fixed-income investment, price inflation is wiping out your principal. So why not be smart? Substitute a hard asset like gold or silver coins, including numismatic (collectors) coins, for your long-term, fixed-income investment. You may see your capital increase even faster than the rate of price inflation, plus you benefit from capital gains tax treatment of your profits if you hold for 12 months or more.

But whether you choose the T-bill approach or the hard asset approach, your need for income will inevitably erode your capital if you cannot gain regular earned income. This is always the preferable approach. You should work as long as you can, while you can, and save your capital for emergencies, or for the day when you can't work, or for your heirs.

Longer Life

The Bible says, "six days shalt thou labor" each week. You will notice that it never mentions retirement. Caleb, who along with Joshua, was the only person of his generation who entered the Promised Land of Canaan, prided himself on his good health, and at age 85 he took as his heritage land which was more difficult to work (Joshua 14:6-12). He was not afraid of work. He regarded it as a blessing to be able to work as efficiently as younger men. This is the proper attitude to take. Good health is not an asset to be squandered away in meaningless leisure. Leisure's function is to refresh us, to re-create our energy (hence, "recreation"), to enable us to work harder, better, and longer after our time of refreshing.

One man who has led the fight against mandatory retirement is Millard Foist. Foist began a study of retired railroad workers, and he found some most interesting conclusions. Using statistics supplied by the American Association of Railroads, he found that the average life of retired railroad workers was about 2.5 years beyond the date of their retirement. However, retirees who began new careers added almost 20 years to their lives. Foist is convinced that the best thing a person can do after retirement is to start a new career. "New learning means new life and new health. It makes you more productive. A new career is something to look forward to. People hate to face retirement. They almost brace themselves as if they're going to fall off the face of the earth, and that's almost what they do. If you want them to be happy about changing, prepare them to develop a new career." So he went out and started a tool and die company, and he found that the older workers were more efficient than the younger ones. They were absent less, worked harder, had better reading and writing skills, and had more knowledge of their craft. (*Los Angeles Times* [Dec. 23, 1976])

When people decide to start living, they will start working. When they are ready to die, they can retire. It is significant that the Social Security System penalizes those who continue working. Full benefits are not given to workers who earn over $5,500 a year until they reach age 72.

What most men need is a job to "retire into." It is important that they begin preparing for such a job several years before age 65. If it takes extra education, then pay for it. If it takes extra capital, use some of that Keogh or IRA money to get it. Cash in that retirement program. Invest it in yourself. Who better to invest it in?

If you really have some basic skills, would your present employer bankroll you after retirement? Have you ever asked? What if you had a project in mind, or a willingness to be a sales representative in an area not considered desirable or lucrative by the younger man with a family (or expensive tastes) to support? Would your boss see the advantage of putting some of the company's money into financing you after retirement on a strictly business deal? If not, why not? If he won't, how about the boss of the company's closest rival? The closer you are to age 65, the more carefully you had better consider this. If retirement is about to hit, or perhaps has already hit, I'd get on the phone and start calling up those ex-employers who might see how much you're still worth. Ask. The worst thing that can happen is that they will say "no." And there are often several people in a corporation who can be asked. All you have to show them is that you can earn more money for them than it will cost to put you or a rival in the field or on the job. Tell him you don't need the medical insurance coverage if he absolutely can't arrange it. You don't need the pension plan. All you need is the assignment, or some capital to work with, and a contract.

Can your hobby be converted into a source of income? Why not?

Can't you at least teach people the skills of that hobby?

Can you paint, clean up messes, repair broken things, babysit, teach kids how to read, or any of a thousand other projects? If not, why not? How much will it cost you to learn how? What about the adult education programs available locally? Can they help? While I'm typing this, there's an older gentleman rototilling my yard. He'll earn some cash for his efforts. I'll save time, so I can write. Everyone wins. Except, perhaps, the tax collector.

Conclusion

The secret of retirement income is retirement output. The secret of getting ahead is to compete. Col. Sanders started Kentucky Fried Chicken when he was a relatively poor old man. He died at age 90, a rich elder statesman of the fast food industry. Almost everyone can contribute something of value to others in the community, and usually whatever it is can be sold at a profit. There is too much to be done to waste skilled people's talents. If you can work, you should work. In any case, price inflation is going to make you work. If you don't, you'll eat up your capital and wind up a charity case. It's better to work than be a charity case.

If you're retired and looking for somewhere warmer and cheaper to live, buy Peter Dickenson's book, *Sunbelt Retirement* (E. P. Dutton, $9). It surveys the best retirement cities in the dozen Sunbelt states.

If you're really interested in starting a small business, read Richard M. Whyte's *The Entrepreneur's Manual* (Radnor, PA: Chilton Books, 1977).

*   *   *   *   *

(Late addition: The tax-cut legislation of August, 1981, inserted a restriction against the use of "collectibles"—gold, silver, antiques, precious stones, art, stamps, etc.—in Individual Retirement Accounts (IRA's) and Keogh retirement plans. If this provision is not repealed, the advice in this book concerning retirement plans must be modified. This special-interest legislation favoring the banks and the savings and loan industry testifies once again to the danger of trusting government-approved retirement program tax deductions. The rules can be changed at any time. Individual retirement programs should be used sparingly. Corporate stocks that are resource-oriented, including the about-to-be-introduced mutual funds in strategic metals, might be one investment approach for these accounts. Keep at least half the funds in a high-yielding money-market fund. Ultimately, you cannot trust governments to give you any long-term tax breaks. What they give with the large print, they take away with the fine print.)

Chapter 15

GOLD FEVER

It's governments that you have to rely on. Basically, you can't rely on a metal for solvency.

William McChesney Martin
Los Angeles Times
March 19, 1968, Pt. I, p. 12

Martin, the conservative (everyone said) former chairman of the Federal Reserve Board, uttered these classic words almost on the day that the London gold pool collapsed, and the short-lived two-tier gold pricing system was adopted. The whole world was running to buy gold, it seemed at the time, and Martin wanted to reassure the public that the policies of Lyndon Johnson were far more reliable than hoarding gold. The policies of Lyndon Johnson lasted about a week and a half after this quotation appeared in print. Johnson announced on March 31 that he would not seek another term. The next day— April Fool's Day—the stock market went up 20 points. ("If that S.O.B. had died," one of my more radical friends commented, "it would have gone up a hundred.")

Meanwhile, in France the Marxist revolutionaries in the universities were tearing up the country's political order. General Westmoreland asked for 200,000 more troops. The Democratic Party's summer in Chicago turned into a nightmare of radical disruptions, vilifications of Mayor Daley, and the squashing of the hopes of Hubert Humphrey. It was, in short, a poor year for comparing the benefits of government to gold. The Great Society was running a $29 billion deficit, and fiat money was pouring into the economy.

Then we elected Richard Nixon.

All right, I voted for Richard Nixon, too. But I had a valid reason. I was evening the score with Howard K. Smith for his 1962 T. V. documentary, "The Political Obituary of Richard Nixon," in which Alger Hiss appeared as a critic of Nixon. That scene had stuck in my mind for six years. I wrote to Smith in 1971 and told him that I had settled accounts with him and would not vote for Nixon in the future. I let Nixon and McGovern fight it out, hoping that each would destroy the other. ("Turkeys in bottle," to paraphrase the old WWII phrase concerning Hilter and Stalin: "scorpions in a bottle.") They did, too, eventually.

125

Gold has gone through the wringer three times since 1968, in 1970-71, 1975-76, and 1980-81. Gold is a political metal. Its fluctuations are usually in inverse relation to the fortunes of politics. When the government is pursuing monetary expansion, gold rises. When the government is losing a war, gold rises. It is conceivable that gold could rise in good times, as a result of its industrial applications, but it would not be rising in $80 clips. Therefore, when gold is rising, the political order is sinking.

Which Form of Gold?

There are various strategies for buying and selling gold. Gold is available in many forms. Some are more appropriate to one period than another. You can trade gold for "almost gold" in certain cases. You should be aware of all the variations.

First, and most important, there is gold as a *survival hedge*. Most of you know these avenues. There is the South African Krugerrand, the widely-recognized gold coin. It has advertising from South Africa to increase its market. It also has pressure from numerous sources to decrease its market by convincing sellers to remove it from their operations. Some companies have been pressured to stop selling it. So have several medium-sized banks. I think that the Krugerrand is still a good investment, since a ban on imports would raise its premium somewhat. But a ban on sales—an unlikely possibility, I think—would reduce its *legal* liquidity. Therefore, I tell people to have some Krugerrands, but to put money in other gold bullion coins, such as the Austrian 20 corona. (It is indicative of the economic knowledge of the anti-Krugerrand forces that they know nothing about the other bullion coins and do nothing to criticize their sale. Where do you think the Austrians buy the gold that goes into their coins? Where do we buy most of our gold, for coins or jewelry or whatever?) I especially like the ¼-ounce Krugerrand. Why? Gold is a survival money, but it should be used sparingly per transaction. Therefore, for greater liquidity, you should have some smaller bullion coins, even when they have a higher premium over gold content. Other small coins are the *ducat* and the Austrian 20 corona. The smaller Mexican coins are getting more difficult to buy. I would suggest that at least two-thirds of a person's gold *bullion* coin investment be in these smaller coins.

Of course, pre-1965 *silver coins* are the ultimate American survival money. Again, buy dimes, the smallest unit of account. Gain greater liquidity by getting the largest number of transaction units per fiat dollar of present investment. You get 10,000 possible transactions in a "bag" of dimes, instead of 4,000 transactions in a "bag" of quarters, or 2,000 in a "bag" of half dollars.

What do I mean by "liquidity"? I mean the ability of an owner of an asset to sell that asset: 1) rapidly, 2) with minimal transaction (brokerage, advertising) costs, and 3) without having to offer a large discount. This usually requires a wide, integrated, familiar market filled with specialists in exchange. It also requires an asset which is homogeneous, that is, with easily recognized features that are interchangeable with other easily available assets like it.

What are the pitfalls of bullion coins? They will fall in price when gold bullion does. So for a person who already has 25% of his liquid assets in gold bullion coins, or $25,000+, there are reasons for holding one's capital in other forms, *if* a person is prepared to sell off these other assets and move strongly into the bullion coin market a few days after a major gold drop occurs, or possibly even the day after.

The other pitfall is the possibility that gold bullion coins will be made illegal at some point in the future. I do not expect this short of world war or open tyranny. One sign that it might happen is the issuing of internal U. S. passports to all adult citizens. Some bureaucrats have run this one up the flagpole (such as the now retired bureaucrat, Frances Knight). If it comes, then the President may decide to reverse the freedom of gold ownership. This is one reason to buy cash-and-carry, or to buy from a firm in a "street name," or to buy from a firm that takes the names off of the transaction receipts after a few months. Hold a receipt in a separate location from the coins. Don't leave a "trail of paper" for third parties to investigate at their discretion. They're your coins. You want to prove your purchase price when it's time to pay capital gains taxes. But keep the receipts separate from the coins. You must reassert your right of privacy all the time. Get used to acting in a private way as soon as possible.

Illegal gold coins are like illegal, unregistered hand guns: more valuable to own *after* they are illegal than before, more important for your welfare after than before. The possibility of bullion coins being made illegal is a very good reason for buying them *now*. It is a good reason for *start drawing out an increasing percentage of cash* each time you deposit a check, so as not to raise suspicions. You need "silent money" to make coin purchases. If you use the mails, write a money order or send a cashier's check. When you buy either the money order or the cashier's check, do it where they don't know who you are. If the bank requires you to sign for the cashier's check, make your signature illegible. Also, shop around buying small cashier's checks; some banks may not require you to sign.

Numismatic coins: If you want increased safety from the gold dumps, faster appreciation than bullion coins (short of total collapse), and a way to hold capital profitably until the day the Treasury sells gold, then numismatic coins are for you. These coins have increased in value by 16% or more every year for a decade. They are very good investments. They are not quite so liquid as a bullion coin, but I think they are better than diamonds, and they can appreciate as rapidly as diamonds. (I am not saying never to buy diamonds; I am saying to buy rare coins first.) One good way to start is to buy *type sets* of U. S. gold coins, starting with the smaller, rarer coins (while they are cheaper) and buying the more common U. S. gold coins. Any good coin specialist can give you advice, but one easy way to get it is to buy from Numisco and subscribe to their excellent newsletter, *The Numisco Letter* ($48). You can call them toll-free at

> 1423 W. Fullerton Ave.
> Chicago, IL 60614
> (800) 621-1339

Numisco also offers another fine service: *a managed account in rare coins.* It takes $50,000 to get in, but if you want a so-called passive investment, meaning one actively managed by someone who knows what he is doing, I would recommend it. I think you should buy and take delivery of some rare coins, but if you are worried about storage, or if you want the benefits of entrepreneurial trading without having to do the trading yourself, I think the Numisco fund will outperform the more conventional investment funds that have been sold to you in the past. The firm is competently managed, and I trust its director, Walter Perschke.

The reason why I like these coins as an investment is that they appreciate because of scarcity of the coins, not because of the scarcity of the metal. They are also less likely to be outlawed by the government in case of an anti-gold-bullion campaign. I would recommend that a person buy these for any retirement program, such as a Keogh plan. For anything short of disaster (for which you have your bullion coins), the rare coin is as good as diamonds or stamps, and probably a good deal more liquid. If I had $100,000 to invest and had no coins at all, I would buy two bags of silver coins, $20,000 of mixed size bullion gold coins, and at least $15,000 in rare coins. (This is on the assumption that I wanted to avoid the time-consuming nature of real estate investing and the inevitable visibility and taxability of real estate. Rule: *any private property that is protected by law is difficult to protect from legislation.*) You need liquidity *and* capital gains. Coins give both. See Appendix B: Portfolios.

Another reason why I like rare coins is that so few people are into the market yet. When word gets out, there will be a lot of new bidders driving up prices. Also, it takes times to get knowledge about coins, and *The Numisco Letter* is not well known yet. This means that sophisticated investors who get knowledge now will be able to reap entrepreneurial rewards over the next five years or more. Those who bought bullion coins will become interested in rare coins. As more people buy bullion coins, the potential market for future numismatic buyers increases.

I would also suggest buying five or ten U. S. *$20 gold pieces* (double eagles). Some Americans in the future may only want to trade for a "real American coin." I recommend the St. Gaudens design over the Liberty.

Gold mining shares: I am not an expert in the stock market. I am willing to mention the stocks only because they are an aspect of the metal market. In this area, I come as a man who lost a good chunk of money in 1975, so don't run out and invest your life's savings on what I say here. Buy you may want some of the data.

First, *there is no mining stock that pays dividends.* Get this straight: mining shares do *not* pay dividends. They dig gold out of the ground (thereby depleting the firm's assets), sell the gold, make some money, and pay the owners a share of these profits. Long-life (low-cost) mines pay a higher return, but are less likely to boom in a panic gold market. But if you were to buy gold coins, put them in the ground, dig them up every quarter, sell a few off, and spend your paper money, you would not be fundamentally different from the manager of a long-life gold mine. You would be depleting your assets: so is the mine. Understand this before you buy.

There are differences from the "coins in the back yard" example. You are investing in engineering talents and gold-exploration talents. Unlike your hoard of coins, the mining company may know (or think they know) where more deposits are. So in this sense, as an owner, you are an entrepreneur. If they find gold, you can reap *speculative* rewards. But these are not based on the present holdings of the mines. They come as capital gains.

Second, *the investor in mining invests in management.* He also invests in the political regime. It is simpler to hide a sack of gold coins than it is to hide two miles of mine shafts. South Africa has to raise money for arms. The mines have to pay taxes. The Soviet threat, for the moment, is not that great, and the Afrikaners are a mean bunch of S.O.B.'s, unlike the British in Rhodesia. They are of Dutch extraction, not English, and they will not be shoved around easily. I honestly believe that the South African regime could survive longer than the U. S. regime. But the investing public doesn't see it this way. The mines are in a reverse leverage situation: costs of mining, including taxes, are going up.

Another fact is ignored. Where investors had to "bury gold" in their South African back yards in 1974, because it was illegal to buy gold bullion, and few investors knew about gold coins (double eagle, sovereign), today they know about coins. The survival market is vastly larger today than in 1974. The coin market is vastly larger. Thus, the *mining shares are left for conventional investors who are becoming slightly less conventional.* The real gloom and doomers are putting their fiat dollars into gold coins, not shares. The mining shares have stiff competition from a newly developed industry, gold bullion coins.

So my philosophy of gold mining shares is simple: *shoot craps.* If you want a paper-money-denominated investment, which mining shares are, then bet on a panic price in gold which will make the mines profitable. Will this panic price occur? I think it will. A major war could do it, but if it's world war, then no one can be sure the mines will be kept open, not to mention the sea lanes from South Africa. So...it's a good reason to put money into North American mines. If panic occurs next time, it is likely to be international panic. All the major nations will be affected. A Soviet challenge in Western Europe would be one such cause. A betting man should bet on eventual currency panics.

I believe gold fever will hit the black markets in the 1980's, perhaps the early 1980's. To take advantage of this market, you will need "unregistered gold" for barter, or for sales for fiat dollars to pay off debt. Then you will need rare coins, which are more likely to remain legal. Buf if the panic is allowed to hit the legal markets, you will want to be a seller of high-risk exploratory ("penny") gold and silver mining companies. These may go ten to one or more. When the guy who is afraid of South Africa's chances and who can't afford Homestake or Dome mines starts looking for a gold mining investment package, his broker at Merrill Lynch will finally find out about the Spokane Exchange. That's the day your ship comes in, loaded with paper money (suitable for paying off mortgages 20 years early). For more data on this market, call America's lowest pressure stock market broker, Jerry Pogue, and beg him to tell you something about the mines:

National Securities Corp.
500 Union St.
Seattle, WA 98101
(800) 426-1608 (toll-free)

An investment of $5,000 in five mines might be the way to get started. (No widows and orphans, please.) Then sit back and wait for gold fever. If it doesn't hit, you will probably lose half your money (discounted for inflation), but if it hits, you'll get the leverage of the commodities markets with a fraction of the risk and worry. I think these might be *a good investment for a child's trust.* Parents can give away up to $10,000 each this year without paying a gift tax, and if the shares ever take off, the trust can sell off the shares, pay capital gains taxes, and get the advantage of lower tax rates, meaning a larger transfer of wealth to the trust. If the trust has some income-producing real estate in it (strongly advised), the shares might help to reduce the mortgage debt of the trust. I would not have too much of this in the trust, but $5,000 out of a total of, say, $15,000, might be smart.

Let me give you an example. I bought shares in Gold Standard Corp. in 1975. I paid 10¢ a share. The last time I checked (March, 1982) the price per share was over $1.75. Not a bad investment! These crap shoots can pay off *big*.

Conclusions

If you have no bullion coins, *now* is the time to buy. "But gold is too high," you say. This is the same as saying, "the dollar has finally stabilized, and good times are coming." Never say the first, if you have no bullion coins, unless you are absolutely convinced of the second. "Gold is too high" means "the dollar is too low." The dollar, my friends, is never too low. When it comes to inflation, "there's always room for more with Dollars."

Chapter 16

CLICHÉS AGAINST GOLD

Today, people are talking about gold. Back in 1967, nobody talked about it except people like Harry Schultz, Bill Baxter, and a handful of skeptics. Then came Harry Browne's book, *How You Can Profit from the Coming Devaluation* (1969), followed two years later by the devaluation. Sure enough, those following Browne's advice—advice criticized widely by the professional economists, investment counsellors, and government experts—made a pile of money. Nevertheless, the same old clichés are still heard today. The same tired explanations of why gold is such a poor investment are put into print by the same tired critics, who are still telling their readers and other victims about the "loser's game" of gold and silver. Here are my favorite anti-gold explanations.

Gold is too speculative. Let us quote the former dean of the anti-gold bugs, Eliot Janeway. Janeway is a genius, and there is no doubt that anyone who has read his columns for ten years, and did precisely the opposite of what he has recommended, is a rich man today. Janeway's track record is fantastic: the only jockey in the pack who races his horse clockwise around the track. It's faster, he says. Back in mid-December of 1976, when gold was in the $130's, up from its low of $103, someone wrote in and asked what he thought about buying gold. Janeway was the man who predicted in the late 1960's that once gold was severed from the dollar, it would fall from $35 per ounce to $6. He was *the* expert in gold. So he replied: "When you have an asset—like gold—which pays neither interest nor a dividend, you are not investing; you are speculating." The fact that *all* forecasting, *all* investing in terms of a forecast, is speculating, is ignored by Janeway and the other "gold is speculative" experts. When you invest in something that pays you a return you are speculating that the outfit you just loaned your money to won't go bankrupt, that it will continue the dividends, etc. Why do people invest in the stock market, which pays dividends of about 3% to 4% when they can buy bonds paying 12% or Treasury bills paying 14%? Someone buying T-bills since January of 1966, and out of the stock market completely, would be better off today in terms of the preservation of his capital. But the

132

"experts" never mention this. The stock market is a speculative quest for capital gains—a long-shot quest since 1966. This is not to say that the stock market is a loser. Maybe it will rebound. But whenever you are in the stock market (or "in" anything else), you are a speculator.

It should also be pointed out that in times of monetary and political turmoil, he who refuses to take speculative risks is condemning himself to a loss of capital, though perhaps on a slow, paralyzing basis rather than the big loss all at once. If the rate of price inflation is 13%, your 7% 2001 bond or your 9% first trust deed is eroding your capital daily. He who "invests" (meaning he who remains in conventional, acceptable, "prudent" speculations) is lost.

But Janeway was not content to rattle the old "speculation" bones. He never is. He always has to get specific, which is where you can make a bundle by going the opposite way. Therefore, said Eliot: "As far as gold goes, it is a bad time to buy. The late 1976 gold play was a flash in the pan. Gold won't enjoy that kind of move again as long as Russia and South Africa are plagued by their current economic troubles, and dumping their surplus." Well, gold is up, there is still trouble in the USSR, and South Africa is under the worst external pressure in half a century. That's Janeway. His advice appeared in the *Washington Star* (12/16/76).

Gold is just another commodity. This has been very big in recent years. The economists have specialized in this one. It has been considered one of the richest of the anti-gold veins. Now that gold has been severed from the dollar, it has not stayed at the old $35/oz. price. It has gone up and down (as priced in dollars), just like any commodity. Gold is metal, just like copper. So why get so excited about gold? Why make gold into a religion?

Well, they are correct as far as they go. Gold *does* go up and down. Gold *is* a metal. Gold is indeed a commodity. And in times of high price inflation and currency disintegration, the other metals will be just like gold: skyrocketing in price. So why all the fuss about gold?

Here is one very good reason: you can take a British gold sovereign almost anywhere on earth and buy valuable items with it. People make a fuss about gold precisely because people have *always* made a fuss about gold. Moses, in the second chapter of Genesis (2:11), made a fuss about gold. It *is* a commodity. It is *the* commodity. It serves as money because it is portable, durable (nothing destroys it except aqua regia, an acid), divisible (in its pure form, a knife can cut it), and scarce in relation to its weight (high marginal utility per ounce). It is also very lovely to look at. Gold is the Sophia Loren of commodities. I can almost hear William Simon now, looking at Miss Loren and then pointing to a picture of Zazu Pitts and exclaiming, "After all, Sophia Loren's only a woman, like any other woman." All right, Bill, since we're double dating, *you* escort Miss Pitts.

Let's try some other variations. "After all, the Rolls Royce is just another car." "We ought to remember that David Rockefeller is just another banker." "Face it, the Council on Foreign Relations is just another discussion group." "Really, Notre Dame is just another football team." "Kareem Abdul-Jabbar is just another center." "Chairman Mao was just another agrarian reformer." I'm sure you can come up with several of your own. Send them to Bill Simon, Just Another Ex-Monetary Expert, Washington, D. C.

The key element of money is its *continuity over time.* A person will voluntarily exchange scarce economic resources for money only because he expects others to do the same in the future. The fact that a particular monetary unit or form has served as money in the past helps to convince him that it will serve as money in the future. This is one reason why I don't think that the government will revalue the dollar by forcing us to exchange 10 or 20 of our old dollars for one new dollar, a "redback" for 10 or 20 "greenbacks." The reason why people are not suspicious about our declining currency is because they are used to it. They don't know anything else. It has served as money for too long. So old habits are not easily broken. It is only if the old habits are finally broken by monetary chaos, when prices have climbed to astronomical levels, that the government is likely to revalue the currency by knocking off two or three zeroes. As I have said before, it could happen in a national emergency, when the government rations our money back to us, in order to make worthless cash that might be hoarded by the suspicious types (like me) in advance of the Federal freeze on bank accounts and safety deposit boxes. That's why I recommend keeping one or two month's cash reserves outside the bank, but other reserves in silver coins and gold coins. If the government should revalue the currency, it would probably not be any advantage to be holding greenbacks—not in comparison with gold and silver coins, anyway.

Gold offers continuity in exchange, worldwide. Silver coins do in this country. So buy a "bag" ($1,000 face value) of pre-1965 dimes and put your other "speculative" coin money into gold coins. *Get yourself some monetary continuity*, precious metals, that cannot be easily counterfeited by Federal inflationists. If your friends want to trust in the continuity of paper money, let them. I prefer to believe in another, far more ancient and historically reliable continuity, namely, the continuity of fiat money inflations whenever governments depart from precious metal coinage.

Buying gold is unpatriotic. This argument was used on the Greeks just prior to World War II. The Greek government called on its patriotic citizens to turn in their gold coins, accept the government's paper money, and live happily ever after. Greeks, having had considerable experience with democratic governments, hoarded gold anyway. Those few who did act "patriotically" saw everything lost when the Nazis invaded and subsequently stole the gold while debasing the Greek currency. According to one friend of mine, whose uncle was involved in the operation, the U. S. used to fly missions over Greece, dumping high quality counterfeit money over the side of the planes, thereby compounding the monetary crisis. Those who hoarded gold survived far more easily. Moral: "But if any provide not for his own, and specially for those of his own house, he hath denied the faith, and is worse than an infidel" (I Timothy 5:8). Your allegiance is to your family before it is to the bureaucrats and professional confiscators who infest the seats of government.

What *is* unpatriotic is allowing the government to exercise the monopoly of money creation. What *is* unpatriotic is to encourage the debasement of money by permitting the creation of money unbacked (unrestrained) by precious metals. What *is* unpatriotic is to allow the planners to use the control of money as the tool of directing the economy, whether by Keynesian fiscal manipulations (always inflationary) or Friedmanian monetary "stability" (always inflationary). Whether the money supply is pushed up at a Keynesian rate of 8% or Friedman's 5%, the money supply is still compounded, and if you compound any figure at any positive rate over time, it becomes exponential, soaring into the heavens, or, in the case of the purchasing power of money, diving into the gutter. Government planners can no more resist the lure of comprehensive planning through monetary manipulation (debasement) than university economists can resist the lure of unrealistic assumptions.

What *is* patriotic is the preservation of capital. What *is* patriotic is the willingness of men to plan for their own futures, not relying on the confiscatory power of governments to guarantee the futures of all major voting blocs. What *is* patriotic is thrift, intelligent speculation (forecasting), and the setting aside of resources that will facilitate both personal prosperity and the restoration of voluntary trade should price controls and rationing destroy the division of labor and per capita wealth in this country. If a person saves some coins for the future, in the rational expectation that someone else will want to trade resources for some coins, he has not hurt the country; he has only made the coercive plans of the bureaucrats more difficult. *What's good for the country is bad for the bureaucrats.*

You can't eat gold. When you hear this one, you know you're dealing with a person who can't distinguish horse manure from apple butter. There is a good answer for this one: "You can't eat Federal Reserve Notes either." Other things you can't eat: New York City bonds, Penn Central shares, Equity Funding insurance returns, Argentinian annuities, and CD's in the Bankhaus Herstadt in Germany. You can't even eat 1975 WIN [Whip Inflation Now] buttons. But you can buy food with gold.

The government may outlaw gold. The government may also outlaw freedom. This is the reason a person buys gold. It is because bureaucrats and politicians think they have the moral and legal right to interfere with the voluntary decisions of the citizens of any nation that the citizens are wise to invest part of their assets in commodities like gold and silver coins. The government also outlawed gold coins in 1933. Interestingly enough, we can still buy $20 gold pieces (double eagles) in any coin shop. Why? We are fairly certain that the coins in Fort Knox were melted, since some of the gold there (the gold that the Congressional investigating team was shown back in 1975) was admitted to be coin melt. This means that the coins that we can buy in the open market are coins that were *not* turned in back in 1933. It means that the President called for gold in 1933, but gold didn't come when it was called. Not all of it, anyway. Probably not most of it. That was in an era when people trusted Presidents. That was in a period when people believed in the Federal government. Can you imagine the response of those people who have bought gold since 1965? Gold today is bought, not as present money, but as *future money*; not as a present medium of exchange, but as a hedge against government policies. The psychology of gold holding today is completely different.

What if the government should outlaw gold? It could be done by means of the emergency powers held by the President. But to implement these powers, he will also have to implement a whole ocean of Federal regulations—regulations that will require an army of bureaucrats. The very implementation of a comprehensive planning program will make it almost impossible (and very expensive) to implement any single component of that program. They will go after guns, I think, before they go after gold. Then, after their ranks are thinned out a bit, they may decide that those holding gold are also those who hold guns, and frankly, it's easier to write up reports for a living, with the accent on living. In any case, governments have always resorted to banning gold when they have tried to implement total control, and men have always disobeyed.

Anyone who believes that the government might try to ban the ownership of gold has just offered the best argument for buying gold: you can't trust governments.

However, I doubt that the government will make the attempt. First, they have spent a decade to convince us that "gold is just another commodity." If so, then why abolish it? Why alert people to the fact that it is *the* commodity? More important today is the fact that in late October 1977, President Carter signed legislation which included the reintroduction of the right of Americans to make contracts in gold. This had been illegal since 1934. In other words, the final trace of the New Deal's restraints on gold has been abolished. To abolish gold, apart from an executive order, the Congress will have to reverse itself. Congress usually takes a generation to reverse itself, as the gold clause contract legislation indicates. Usually, it refuses to reverse itself; the men are too busy devising new cures to people's problems. So I conclude that Sen. Helms' gold clause legislation has put nails into the bureaucrats' attempts to restrict gold ownership. Emergency powers could pry out these nails, but without very serious economic conditions, I don't think Congress will bother. I don't expect Americans to use this new freedom to make gold clause contracts, at least not for many years, but the freedom is significant nonetheless. It is symbolic of the end of the New Deal gold laws. Freedom is now the political precedent.

There is one aspect of this threat, namely, that government may abolish the ownership of gold, that is significant, at least theoretically. The government may (I believe will) freeze the legal price of gold in the cash (spot) markets and in the futures markets. In other words, I think *all* commodities will be put under the price freeze, including futures prices, at some point. I think it will come in the early 1980's. I could be wrong. Naturally, it will destroy the whole market system of production and distribution. Of course, it will create havoc. Certainly, it is an *insane idea*. That's why I think it's coming.

Ultimately, I think the inflation tax, secured by the legal tender laws, will be coupled with a price freeze. If it is comprehensive, it will have to involve the futures market. The Nixon Administration did not freeze futures last time, and that "mistake" will not be made next time, or at least not through the whole period. If futures prices are left free, there will be a rush from the conventional capital markets into commodities—thereby creating havoc in the government's attempt to keep prices low. Admittedly, I am painting the worst scenario possible. But I am convinced that the slogan of all price controllers in the future will be this: "No more Mr. Nice Guy."

I would still not be a long-term creditor, not with a gold clause, silver clause, or any other kind of clause. The clause must be tied to

U. S. paper money, and U. S. paper money is controlled by U. S. paper politicians. Legal tender is monetary tinder. No long-term credit position can be protected while these words are on our money: "This note is legal tender for all debts, public and private." The long-term debtors will drown the long-term creditors in fiat money, and the number-one long-term debtor is the Federal government.

What I'm saying is this: *legal technicalities like contracts will not hold the juggernaut State.* By all means, use contracts to buy a little protection. Better a gold clause contract than no gold clause contract. Use every device that you can to defend your freedom and your capital. But don't be naive: we are living in an era of *legislated envy.* We are living in an era of judicial lawlessness. We are living in an era which favors the criminal at the expense of the victim. When envy is the ethics of the day, paper contracts will not defend your long-run capital from paper money. Keep your credit position short. A three-year loan to somebody else is extremely long run, justified *only* because of tax considerations (e.g., taking a contract on a piece of property you're selling, with 29% down and the rest to be paid over three years). Even then, I think it's questionable. Pay your taxes, convert the paper money to hard assets, and forget about "passive" income. *Passive income is actively threatened by fiat money.*

If the government outlaws gold, you'll become an outlaw. It's as simple as that. If they outlaw gold, it will be because of their desire to put the whole nation into jail. They will force everybody into the black markets. Selling anything at a price close to a market price will also be illegal. If all voluntary transactions are declared illegal, you might as well keep your gold coins. If you're going to be an outlaw, be a well-heeled one. Gold will then steadily become a black-market money, but as far as I'm concerned, the reason why we buy gold coins is to gain access to a black-market money. Buy now, spend later.

Gold can go down. True. Response: gold can also go up. (You would be amazed at how stupid some of these clichés really are, yet they are written up by the experts.) The propagandists want us to believe that "gold is just another commodity," except that unlike other commodities, gold doesn't go up as often as it goes down. In other words, "gold is just another commodity, except it's a poor investment."

The government may ban the import of South African Kruger-rands. This is supposed to be an argument against buying Kruger-rands. In other words, never buy a commodity which is in heavy demand if the supply is about to be cut off. Implication: high demand, coupled with diminished supply, results in lower prices. Ah, the wonders of applied Keynesian economics! The answer is simple enough: holders of the banned coin will be the recipients of a Federal subsidy, namely, a tariff. The coins will develop a numismatic premium to be added to their gold content value. If you're worried about the possibility of making money, then you can always buy Austrian 100 coronas, Mexican 50 pesos, Hungarian 20 coronas, Mexican 20 pesos, or other "bullion" coins, not to mention U. S. $20 gold pieces and British gold sovereigns.

The government may dump more of its gold. Let's hope so. Gold is getting too expensive for me. I want some bargains. When the Treasury runs out of gold, then the price will go upward once again. There will be one difference. I will have my gold, and the bureaucrats in the Treasury won't, at least not in their official capacity. I'm into gold for the long-haul. If anyone wants to sell me gold at a discount, I'm the long-term beneficiary. Why let the government get the capital gains from a gold price rise? Let them sell it at bargain prices to U. S. citizens, and let them reap the capital gains. Isn't that what we want, gold in *our* hands and not in government's hands? Let them dump to their heart's content. I'll buy some more. Let's face it, where gold is concerned, I can do no better than to cite the immortal lines Burt Lancaster uttered in "Vera Cruz." The "heroine" offers Burt and Gary Cooper a deal: $3 million worth of gold, split 3 ways. "That's a million dollars' worth apiece. That's enough for anyone." To which Burt replies: "Not for me; I'm a pig."

Chapter 17

TESTING THAT "HOT INVESTMENT" OFFER

"There's one born every minute, " said P. T. Barnum of suckers. His knowledge of genetics and demography was limited, but his knowledge of how to attract the gullible was not. Whether or not suckers are born every minute is not statistically demonstrable, but this fact is: as soon as people get some extra money into their hands, they become the lawful prey of the hustlers of the world.

Certain groups are more vulnerable than others. Physicians and dentists have their names and addresses listed in the Yellow Pages. This is almost the equivalent of "Come and get me; I'm loaded!" Professionals spend most of their time with their practice or in leisure activities, recuperating from their practice. This means that they want quick, easy answers to investment problems. Unfortunately for them, and fortunately for the peddlers of "can't miss" investment opportunities, there are very few easy answers to investment problems, and the easy ones that exist always cost too much in time, or long-term waiting, to be desirable to most professionals.

There are always opportunities for profit available. The problem is, however, that there are always *opportunities for losses*. People who don't understand the basis of profits find it difficult to analyze the good opportunities and take them. I would hope that this introduction will at least let people ask the right questions, both of themselves and the salesman, concerning the future potential of a suggested investment.

Profit

Presumably, everyone wants to make a profit. Actually, I don't believe it. There are masochists whose actions indicate that what they seek is a loss, a self-inflicted punishment for living. Gamblers who lose continually are examples of this type of behavior. They are not participants in a market, however. They are participants in a game created by winners for their benefit at the expense of loss-seeking masochists. In a free market, people seek profit, not by creating a high-risk game, but by overcoming *existing* problems. This difference must be understood from the outset: taking (bearing) a risk in a free

140

market is fundamentally different from taking a risk in a zero-sum (winner take all, loser lose all) game. The game creates risk for the sake of risk; in a free market, people bear risk in order to achieve goals that have been created by the actions of outside forces: nature, other people, or the unknown.

The system of economic freedom which permits us the possibility of making a profit simultaneously requires us to risk taking a loss. The *element of risk present in all life* requires men to bear some degree of risk. It is thrust upon us. We act to overcome it. It is the free market, and only the free market, which creates an institutional structure which is able to convince other men, on a voluntary basis, to deal with risk and uncertainty in a manner which directly benefits both themselves and other participants in the market—specifically, those who want to buy services or goods. The market imposes restraints on our actions, through the price mechanism, that are socially beneficial.

We cannot know the future perfectly. We cannot know the present perfectly. Uncertainty is therefore inescapable. Frank H. Knight, in his classic study, *Risk, Uncertainty, and Profit* (1921), argued that risks can be estimated statistically (e.g., how many men in a certain age group will die per 100,000 in any given year), but uncertainty is a completely unknown factor. The goal of any rational economic system is to reduce wasted resources within an uncertain world. In a free market system, waste means any loss borne by the consumer that might have been avoided if producers had possessed better knowledge. The greatest single *economic* benefit provided by the free market (as distinguished from the moral benefits) is its incentive system for the improvement and rapid dissemination of *accurate information.* (The best book on this topic that I have ever read is Henry Manne's *Insider Trading and the Stock Market* [New York: Free Press, 1966]. Anyone who puts a nickel in the stock market owes it to himself to read this book in advance.)

We must be aware of this crucial aspect of the market system before we begin to make investments. The principles of successful investing rest on a willingness to accept the limitations of our knowledge and to act effectively to overcome these limits—in a limited, but profitable, fashion. The person who does not understand what profit is, is at a competitive disadvantage with the man who does understand, other things being equal. (I can say this confidently, since other things never are equal.)

What is the source of all profit? The economists debate this, or used to debate this, and they have come up with some erroneous conclusions. Marx said that all profit stems from the exploitation of human labor by capitalist owners of the means of production. The more exploited laborers there are, the more profits for capitalists (Obviously, the most profitable investment opportunities must be in India and China. Oh. Hmm.) Other answers have been almost as bad. But the two great treatises on profit are Knight's and Joseph Schumpeter's *Theory of Economic Development* (1911). Both of these men concluded that it is the *entrepreneur* who makes a pure profit, but they disagreed about just what it was that the entrepreneur does in order to gain his profit.

The entrepreneur, said Knight, is purely a *forecaster*. He tries to predict the state of the market in the future. He tries to guess the unknowns of the future. First, he must guess consumer demand at particular prices. He must then estimate expected future costs: raw materials, labor, taxes, interest rates, and rent. If expected revenues exceed these expected costs, then the entrepreneur may (if he thinks it is worth it) take steps to meet that expected future demand by consumers. If he is correct in his estimations, then he reaps a *residual*. This residual is his profit. It arises from his ability to forecast the future more effectively than other producers in the market. The consummate entrepreneur, in Knight's analysis, would probably be the *commodities speculator*. If he estimates correctly, he earns a profit; if he doesn't, he makes a loss.

Schumpeter focused on one part of this entrepreneurial function, that of *innovation and organization*. The entrepreneur is the man who finds newer, less costly ways of achieving future goals. He combines the scarce factors of production in unique and hitherto unknown ways in order to meet consumer demand more efficiently (less wastefully). He saves resources, and consumers reward him for his efforts. He reduces waste, thereby releasing scarce economic resources that can be used to meet other consumer demands.

As a comprehensive explanation of entrepreneurship, I prefer Knight's. In his system, the innovator is a specialized forecaster who has guessed that a new combination of resources will better meet consumer demand in the future. Innovation is only relevant within a framework of comprehensive forecasting.

The entrepreneur performs a crucial *social* function. It is one of the real disasters of modern times that those who are successful entrepreneurs fail to understand this role, and they are unable to defend themselves from the envious and ideological attacks on the free market. The entrepreneur owns or controls resources (which may be borrowed), and he attempts to use them in socially beneficial ways—as measured by the demonstrated preferences of consumers. (Of course, if consumers are suicidal, then the entrepreneur's ability to meet consumer demand is not socially beneficial, but this involves a concept of ethical evaluation that is different from—higher than—existing consumer preferences.) The entrepreneur responds to public needs and wants. The buyers can control his actions, but only if they allow the free market to operate without restraint by the State or by thieves and coercers. If they allow other men to enter the markets in search of profits, they thereby increase the number of people who are working for them. The system weeds out the less successful (more wasteful) suppliers. They lose money and therefore control over scarce resources. The more efficient organizers-forecasters steadily gain control of scarce resources, but only so long as they stay efficient. *The market is relentless.* If a person fails to meet its demands, it transfers resources to his competitor. This is what the stock market is all about. This is what lending is all about. The lure of profit and the fear of loss are the public's carrot and stick in the free market. *It is through the profit motive that consumers maintain their sovereignty.*

The Book of Proverbs begins with this injunction: get knowledge. So does the "book" of the free market. The essence of profit is the efficient application of accurate knowledge to the problems of economic production (including distribution).

Knowledge, if it is accurate, inevitably spreads. In fact, the continued ability of a person or firm to produce abnormally high (above-market) returns calls attention to the method of production being implemented. The special knowledge that enables a market leader to outperform his competitors cannot be kept a secret forever. Capital flows into lines of production similar to those pioneered by the high-profit firm. The rate of return on these investments steadily drops. Finally, the leader is forced to innovate again, to find better ways to meet consumer demands in an uncertain future. *The best way to keep a monopoly, therefore, is to compete as though you didn't have one.*

Let us clear up one modern fallacy that is widespread within the highest levels of American business. *The rate of profit is not necessarily related to a company's "share of the market."* There are firms in the electronics industry that are steadily bankrupting themselves by pursuing the demon of "market share," or the percentage of the market. The budding monopolists who are making these decisions are benefiting the consumer in the short run by lowering prices drastically, but it wastes capital in the long run. These firms are like a fireworks display: very bright and very short. The managers bankrupt their firms in an insane quest to control a monopolist's share of the market. Yet a true monopoly, such as the Arm & Hammer baking soda monopoly, returns only average profits anyway. Why bankrupt your firm in order to achieve average long-run profits? *Stay away from firms that pursue a monopolistic share of the market,* unless you are looking for a quick, in-and-out investment profit. Keep it fast, since the company may not be around very long. If they pursue profits, and *as a result of innovation,* they achieve a large share of the market, that's another question.

Successful Investing

Anyone who tells you that he has an investment possibility that can pay you a higher return than you could receive simply by depositing your money in a conventional savings program is saying something very significant. He is really saying that *he has special knowledge of the future which is unknown to, or ignored by, almost all other investors (entrepreneurs) in the market.* This means that he is saying that virtually all other investors *in the world* have ignored this amazing possibility, since foreigners can speculate in American securities and commodities markets. The claim by anyone that he can recommend above-average investment opportunities is nothing less than a claim that he has the ability to forecast the future better than most other competitors.

Should we take someone seriously who makes such a claim? It depends. If, after asking him and ourselves exactly *why* it is that such knowledge should have been denied to or ignored by other investors, and after having received a seemingly intelligent answer, we might be wise to pursue the possibility. After all, people and firms make temporary above-average profits. The same people and the same firms seldom make above-average profits all of the time, however, so find out how long the above-average returns have been going on. If the returns have been *4 to one* or thereabouts over the past *two or three years,* I would be suspicious about jumping in. In fact, the higher the return above normal, the shorter the period of time these returns are likely to continue. The very existence of such returns draws in other investors, reducing the return on the capital invested (the law of diminishing returns). Above-average profits cannot normally be sustained for more than a few years—depending on the time lag in retooling, copying or patent restrictions—in *conventional, easy access investment markets* for capital.

If the person who is telling you this wonderful tale of investment opportunities is telling *you,* ask yourself the obvious: *Why me?* Why is this guy wasting his time on me? He wants a commission, of course, but why not spend time with somebody else? Is this some miracle? Am I the first one he has called? Why did he select my name? If he is operating on a random basis to find buyers, the selling is not very systematic. Did he get my name from a particular mailing list? Why is he setting me up? (This is one reason why it is wise to use a *different middle initial* each time you sign up for anything that is sent through the mails. You can keep a record of which list is being used to sell you something.) If everyone believes him when he tells his story, then the return of my investment will inevitably drop, since my money will be in competition with all the other investors' money. Remember: *it is precisely because most other investors have ignored his claim that has created the possibility of an above-average return on this investment.* On the other hand, if he says that time is running out, that everybody is about to jump on board, that many new buyers will bid up the value of the product and many new investors will rush in to bid up the price of ownership of the shares, you are back to your original question: *Why me?* Why am I the early bird? Why has he failed to convince everyone else so far, but is about to convince them starting tomorrow? If he is selling a commodity, why hasn't everyone already bid up its price? If he is selling ownership in a company, why hasn't every other investor bid up the price of the shares? If you cannot figure out an answer, keep your money in T-bills until something better comes along.

The very essence of a successful speculation is to believe, accurately, that there is some flaw in other people's vision, some seeming defect in the investment, that has kept out your potential competitors. In fact, you probably should have evidence that the salesman's story will not soon be believed. If it is going to be believed the day after tomorrow, then the "why me?" question should be uppermost in your mind. Look at the investment as you would look at a *chain letter:* by what coincidence am I among the earliest to get on board this marvelous chain? Let's face it: we aren't the first. Maybe once in a lifetime, but probably not. And the salesman may use this pitch: a once-in-a-lifetime deal. Well, maybe. But why me?

The person who expects to make an above-average return has got to come to grips with the fact of *uncertainty.* He has to grapple with the dim future, as through a glass which is dark. Ultimately, he must play the hunch, act in faith. Yes or no, invest here or invest there? But as long as a person has a scarce economic resource to invest, he *is* investing. It is receiving some return, even if negative. "No decision" *is* a decision. If you own anything, you are *already* an investor. There is no escape from the full social responsibilities of ownership. The market is relentless. Ownership necessarily requires full responsibility. The future lies ahead, and it is an uncertain future. Whether we like it or not, we must confront it and strive to produce beneficial results from our struggle with it.

Inside Information

The Securities & Exchange Commission has made it illegal for corporate managers to trade with inside information. Manne's book challenges the logic of this restriction, but it does exist. Yet for anyone to claim that he has an investment opportunity that will produce above-average returns, he must ultimately claim to have access to a kind of inside information.

The salesman (even if you are selling yourself on some investment) says he has inside knowledge that for one or more reasons is not being acted on by other market participants. Maybe the information is so technical or obscure that nobody sees it, except you and the salesman. (If it is that obscure, are you sure you and he really understand what you're talking about?) Maybe it is some sort of economic relationship that is operating now but has not operated before, or which others cannot see for some reason. You now have a very good guide: *find out what that reason is.* The key to the investment is not the secret formula or ignored relationship as such; *the key is your understanding of why, for the moment, no one else has seen it.* Or if others have understood it, why they have not *acted* on their information. Is there some unseen risk involved? Do they think there is high risk when there isn't. Who is correct, you or they? *You* have to decide. Since you are dealing with the unknown, or as Knight puts it, with *uncertainty* rather than risk (for which there is some mathematical operating formula), your decision will necessarily be based on *faith.* You have a hunch, a feeling, a faith in this investment.

A good salesman will know how to exploit your feelings and hunches. This is why you must *know yourself in advance,* as well as the markets.

One important restraining factor in the spread of information is the preconceived notions (faiths) of your potential competitors. They interpret the available data inaccurately, you believe, because of their presuppositions about the nature of economics or the universe. *One of the most important of these barriers to accurate knowledge is Keynesian economics.* Another is the almost universally held gospel of the public school textbooks that no depression is possible today, *and* that the government can, eventually, control inflation. This faith is incarnated in the Full Employment Act of 1946, which assigns to Congress the responsibility for formulating and implementing economic policy which will create full employment and stable prices through appropriate fiscal and monetary tools.

When the bulk of investors and consumers believe in such a secular religion, it opens numerous possibilities for *long*-term investing. It means that we can look at what policies are most likely to be imposed by government to deal with the massive problems created by earlier governmental policies. It means that we can make intelligent guesses about the likely effects of such policies. There is an operating barrier to entry in the knowledge markets: *erroneous and widely held ideology*. The graduate schools of all modern universities in every nation have promulgated this ideology in the history departments, business schools, and graduate schools in economics. Thus, the errors are world-wide. The responses of governments, with the exception of Switzerland and possibly West Germany, will be basically the same. This is why we can have some confidence that our unconventional long-term investments will pay off in above-average future returns. Though the markets are world-wide in scope, the errors are also world-wide in scope. The public schools and Keynesian textbooks have created many opportunities for profit. The emperor has no clothes. Buy cloth.

Active Entrepreneurship

The businessman faces many problems in overcoming uncertainty. Someone who invests in the entrepreneur's business also shares in these problems, though indirectly. If an entrepreneur cannot overcome all of these problems, he must know how to minimize them at low cost. His problems include the following:

1. Future consumer demand
2. Present consumer ignorance
3. Consumer resistance and/or suspicion
4. Costs of production (primarily human costs—management)
5. Government restrictions, present and future
6. The entrepreneur's own fears or foolhardiness
7. The lack of capital
8. The speed of information transfer to competitors
9. Lack of knowledge of one's competitors' innovations

Any of these could bankrupt a small entrepreneur, let alone natural disasters, such as floods, droughts, wars, rumors of wars, and rumors of Eliot Janeway's. Rumor is perhaps the most devastating of natural disasters, for when humans get together, nothing is more natural than the spread of rumors, a fact discovered by Richard Nixon. The old slogan, "Buy on the rumor; sell on the news," really works. Sometimes. Or so it's rumored.

When the salesman calls, then, start asking yourself some questions. *First,* why me? *Second,* does the investment offer effortless, passive, above-average returns? How? If the program does offer *effortless* riches ("Just sign on the dotted line....") then at least one of two things will be true. First, we are being asked to bear *heavy uncertainty.* What really *is* effortless is your ability to lose your capital. Second, if there isn't that much uncertainty involved (the future really is that clear), other investors have to *believe* that the investment is uncertain. Their fears are keeping them from accepting the salesman's hot tip. (This helps answer the question, "Why me?" The answer: "Because of them.") Buying gold coins back in 1971 was not very risky, but people thought that it was. Public ignorance, apathy, fear, and Keynesian-based propaganda, not to mention Milton Friedman's propaganda, helped keep competitors out of the gold and silver coin markets. When the inhibitions disappeared, to be replaced by the dream of effortless passive wealth, gold went to $850/oz, and uncertainty reared its ugly head once more. Therefore, keep the *third* question in mind: If this deal is so obvious, as well as effortless, why is someone paying this guy a commission to sell it to me? Why isn't he a low-paid order-taker?

Conclusion

There are always lots of profit and loss opportunities around for the taking. We own assets. The market compels us to bear the responsibilities of ownership. We have no choice. We either lose our assets, increase our assets, or keep them the same. We can bury our talent in the ground, give it to the moneylender and get our interest payment, invest it and get a five-fold return, or a ten-fold return, or lose it. But we have that talent, and we have to do something with it. So when the salesman calls you with his hot tip, try to find out what the *barrier to entry* is. If you think the barrier will be broken later, after you have invested your funds in it to take a position in the market, then you can consider making the investment. Put your money where your faith and knowledge are. But don't invest without searching out the reasons why the investment is a good one, hasn't been spotted by others, and is, ultimately, uncertain.

Chapter 18

BUY AND HOLD...AND USE!

People who have come to grips with the continuing "inflation vs. deflation" debate, and who have decided that it is quite possible for the Federal government to go on creating fiat money, are then faced with the problem of deciding upon a basic investment strategy.

One strategy is known as the "buy and hold" approach. It has been argued by numerous academic economists, especially those associated with the University of Chicago, that the investor cannot, over the long run, successfully forecast short-term price movements in stocks, bonds, and commodities. This is the so-called "random walk" theory of markets. Its supporters argue that the efficiency of organized capital markets is so great that new information—other than insiders' information—concerning future economic events is assimilated by the markets too rapidly for traders to "beat to the draw." In other words, by the time you hear about it, it's way too late. The prices of market shares will reflect the new data before an explanation becomes public knowledge. Therefore, since the capital markets are so efficient, the best investment strategy is to buy and hold a random portfolio, since commission fees (exchange costs) will eventually eat up the random profits that a trader attains. One important study of stock market prices over several decades was made by James Lorie of the University of Chicago, and he concluded that the "buy and hold" strategy would have outperformed any other trading strategy, from the 1920's through the late 1960's.

But everyone who trades, like everyone who gambles, thinks that he has a good shot at beating the market. To buy and hold is an admission of defeat. However, I want to tell you a true story. I once worked in the same organization as a kindly old Ph.D. in economics. He never wrote much, or did much, but at least he was a pleasant chap. He started planning for his retirement back in the 1930's—some cynic once remarked that this was about all he had been thinking about since the 1930's—and he began buying shares of stock. He was once asked how he knew when to sell. "I never did know," he answered, "so I never sold." For forty years he had bought and held. And I assure you, he enjoyed a very comfortable retirement, probably off of dividends alone.

149

Yet this same man, who was a gold standard advocate, had the opportunity to buy some double eagles ($20 gold pieces) back in 1972 at about $85 each. I told him he ought to do it. "What would I do with a bunch of gold coins?" he asked me. "I don't know anything about gold coins." Indeed, he didn't. They now sell (June 1981) for over $700. So you still face the problem: *What,* specifically, should one buy and hold?

It has now become faddish within hard-money newsletter circles to badmouth gold. We are told: "Gold isn't an inflation hedge; it's a chaos hedge." What this apparently means is that anything that is a "true" inflation hedge must appreciate, in terms of dollars, at a steady rate that equals, and preferably exceeds, the officially announced rate of price inflation, whether expressed in the GNP deflator or the CPI increase, or whatever (they never say). In other words, a "true" inflation hedge must be a straight-line hedge; it must never, ever deviate from its upward path. Only if it does this can it be classified as "true" inflation hedge.

But consider what this means. You cannot possibly put your money into any openly traded, mass-marketed investment. All of them fluctuate, and fluctuate violently. By the way, they did in the great inflation in Germany, 1919-23, too. You can't buy shares of anything, or contracts of anything, or rolls of anything as a hedge against inflation. Why not? Because no commodity, no share of stock, no broadly marketed investment appreciates in a straight line.

If a person argues, that "gold isn't an inflation hedge," what he is really saying is this: "I recommended gold as the best inflation hedge in the world in my last book, published just before gold's price collapsed, and gold made me look like an idiot. I'm going to get even with gold. I'm not going to let gold sucker me again. I'm going to recommend all sorts of strategies, and then I'll look very sophisticated, and not just a Johnny One Note. More important, I'll have an excuse when any one or all of my suggestions go sour. Most important, I'll get people dependent on my newsletter for trading suggestions." That's a "true" inflation hedge. "Keep them coming back for more." It works, too.

But if you can't "buy and hold" gold or silver as inflation hedges, then what can you do? *Trade. Speculate. Cut your losses and let your profits run.* Or, in the immortal words of Will Rogers: "Buy yourself a stock, wait for it to go up, and sell it. And if it don't go up, don't buy it." And even more to the point: "Subscribe to my newsletter between rewrites of my *Best Selling Book,* and I'll tell you what to buy and sell." The subscription price keeps climbing: a true inflation hedge.

The trouble is, the guys who write the books that sell well are seldom the guys who make the successful trades in the pits. Traders don't write, and writers don't trade. Not very profitably, anyway.

Which leads me to *North's law of newsletter subscribing:*

There are a lot of sharp guys who can tell you what to buy and when. There are a lot of sharp guys who can tell you what to sell and when. Unfortunately, they are seldom the same guys.

There may be exceptions to this rule. The only ones I know of are those people whose buy and sell system worked almost flawlessly, top and bottom, just before I started subscribing to their newsletters. Or, rather, just before I started putting my money where their advice was.

Or as another cynic explained: "You find out who gave the best advice over the last two years, and you do the opposite of what he recommends over the next two."

What am I getting at? Simply this: *Buy and hold, but don't continue to buy the same thing.* Give the broker his commission money only one-way. Sure, if he calls and says you have to sell, it's about to go belly-up, take his advice. Sell. He shouldn't have to keep calling with this pitch, however. If he does, he is putting you into high-risk crap-shoots. *Stay away from in-and-out trading* unless you are a full-time investor in highly leveraged commodity futures or options contracts.

Does this mean I am a pure random-walker? Don't I think some people can beat the markets continually? Some can. Very, very few. For a while, it may be possible for a number of people to do it, but not forever. If a guy could sense when he *could* and when he *couldn't* beat a commodity, sitting in T-bills or cash during those times when he felt unable to beat the market, then he could get very, very rich. But those who see themselves this clearly are few and far between. Those who can't eventually get margin calls.

What about the average Joe? Specifically, what about you? And what about me? *Don't trade.* Buy and hold, but not the same thing. The commissions will eat up your capital, and the risk will eat up your stomach's lining.

Of course, we letter writers can tell you to trade in your "speculation money." We can tell you to analyze your gold holdings into speculative holdings (to play with) and survival coins. This is good advice, and I've been giving it for many years. There's only one problem: probably 95% of my readers (like me) don't have enough capital to segregate our gold holding so conveniently. If you're like I am, you're hustling like mad just to scrape up enough cash to buy your survival coins, plus all of the other items that price controls and shortages could easily transform into survival items.

The grim reality that most of us face is this: we cannot afford to buy and hold *all* of the items that we need now, or conceivably will need, if the economy crashes, erodes, peters out, or just piddles along.

This is why I have adopted a basic strategy of investing. *I buy for the long haul.* I may fool around with some "penny" gold mining shares once in a while, but even there it's mostly buy and hold. I admire Walter Perschke for telling his *Numisco Letter* readers to unload a few of his previous recommendations, but Walter is a successful trader operating in a specialized market, not a low-commission, high-volume commodities market. And if I were actively trading numismatic coins, I would feel obligated to follow his advice. But even there, I prefer to buy and hold. I am lazy, hesitant to trade, hate to second-guess myself, and hate to pay commissions, even to a nice guy like Perschke. And I am convinced that the prospects for continuing price inflation are so great that I can make money (preserve capital) by holding for the long haul.

Here is a strategy I call "compensated leverage." You buy a producing small farm, or liquid income-producing real estate (home, duplex, triplex), using debt, with the idea of getting completely debt-free for at least one year in seven. You then buy an appreciating asset, meaning a "hard asset" whose price appreciates in terms of depreciating dollars. At some point, probably when you simply want to get off the debt pyramid, you sell your inflation hedges (numismatic coins, stamps, *some* of your bullion gold coins, or some of your debt-encumbered real estate), pay off your debts, and prepare for the inevitable deflation by becoming debt-free. (Remember, I think such a deflation is at least a decade away, and maybe more.) You are trying to gain 100% ownership of "something else"—small farm, duplex, business—by letting mass inflation pay for it—the coins, antiques, etc. You are "making money" by *escaping money* for a period, and then *going back into money*—worthless fiat money—*temporarily,* in order to pay off your dollar-denominated debts.

Do you really "buy and hold"? In some cases, yes. Think of the Indian peasant. He gets payment in silver jewelry from his wife's parents when he marries. He saves these assets for catastrophic emergencies, which includes the birth of six daughters, in order to preserve himself from the unpredictable. This wealth passes from generation to generation, and it has done so for centuries. You hold the assets until you die, or until you pay your daughter's dowry, or until a catastrophe involving life and death arises. Why? Because you are a peasant in an economy with a low division of labor, inefficient markets, and few investment opportunities with comparable safety. You hold until you go. Then your heirs hold. *Quietly.*

Therefore, strange as it may seem, the "buy and hold" strategy works for an economy with *efficient markets* (you can't beat them) and *inefficient markets* (they might beat you). Unless you have a lot of capital, or a lot of courage, or a lot of inside information, you decide what your long-term goals are, and you try to meet them by systematically saving a portion of your income. You invest in a lot of assets, and you don't sell until you're ready to buy "something else," namely, whatever it is you've been saving for.

Your investments serve as an emergency reserve, or at least a solid portion of them ought to. These are such things as bullion silver coins, Krugerrands, and (at least for right now) Treasury bills. Then you need "money to hedges to money" debt-payoff items, such as collectibles. Finally, you need the basic assets of long-term survival (as well as appreciation): some land, some tools, and some food. If you get to this stage, you're doing quite well. You're in a minority of a minority. You can then think about commodity futures trading. And think, and think, and then buy some more ¼-ounce Krugerrands.

Using Your Investment

I am extremely enthusiastic about the idea of buying simple hand tools and garden tools of all kinds. I think the idea of spending $10,000 on an investment in tools is absolutely sound. Are you looking for an inflation hedge, a "true" inflation hedge, a how-to-prosper-in-five-more-editions'-worth-of-monetary-crises hedge? *Buy tools.* Just try to get a set of drop-forged auto repair tools at a 1977 price, let alone a 1968 price. Try to find Case pocket knives at a 1974 price. You want a steadily increasing asset? Buy a tool. Buy a wood-burning stove. Buy an item that is built to last, and lasts in order to build. Buy it now. It won't be cheaper later.

And after you've bought them, learn how to use them.

People seldom sell off complete sets of quality tools at garage sales, auctions, and in the classified ad sections of local newspapers. They always know someone who is willing to pay top dollar. Sure, there are bargains. Yes, if you keep looking, keep studying about tools, keep checking prices and brands, you will, like any full-time entrepreneur, locate some bargains. But your time isn't a zero-cost asset either. You're paying the full freight.

So buy and hold and use. And pass on your assets to your heirs. If you have tools that perform needed tasks, even in today's market, but especially in a market with a reduced division of labor, you have made a wise investment.

Send $1.00 for the *Money Saving Tool Catalogue* put out by

> U. S. General Supply Corp.
> 100 General Place
> Jericho, NY 11753

I would also suggest that you write for the free catalogue, *Hard-to-Find-Tools:*

> Brookstone
> 127 Vose Farm Rd.
> Peterborough, NY 03458

The Whole Earth Catalog series is also a very good place to start researching tools, hobbies, and self-sufficiency. Most bookstores carry at least the latest *Whole Earth Catalog* (Random House).

Chapter 19

DEATH, TAXES, AND BANKS

One of the most common questions I receive during the question-and-answer sessions after one of my speeches is "What do you think about...?" The person then fills in the blank with his latest investment decision. I suspect that what people really want is confirmation of that decision. Without sitting down and discussing each person's goals, financial position, health, years left in the labor force, and other similar issues, it is not easy to give a precise answer to many such questions. Of course, if they ask me what I think about four-year certificates of deposit in the local savings and loan association, the answer is easy. If they ask me about an annuity, it's even easier. But some questions really are difficult to answer. The best we can do, usually, is to set forth a few guidelines that might help in making a sensible evaluation of the future prospects. Here are some of the most frequently asked questions within groups that are fairly well versed in the problems of hedging against government-created disasters.

Keogh or IRA Retirement Plans

The Federal government now provides certain tax breaks for self-employed people who do not have a retirement program through a company. Corporate pension plans are tax-deductible for the corporation, so self-employed people who work in sole proprietorships are now given a somewhat analogous break. Up to 15% of one's annual income, up to a maximum of $15,000, may be socked away in a trustee-managed retirement program, and the money invested can legally be deducted from personal annual income. Similarly, the IRA program allows employees who are not covered by a company pension program to set aside up to $2,000 in this way.

The benefits seem impressive. The tax-deductible nature of these programs allow that old myth, compound interest, to make a person rich on paper. If the compound rate of interest stays at 6% per annum, and economic growth stays at 6% per annum, and your investments keep pace at 6% per annum, and prices stay at 0% per annum (or even fall)—none of which is going to happen, let alone all—then the numbers are most impressive. If a person starts saving $125 per month ($1,500 a year) and receives 6% annual interest compounded monthly, and continues this for 44 years (age 21 to 65), upon retirement he will have a nest egg of $323,033.11. Because the government does not tax the interest return in these retirement accounts, the

155

compounding process goes on without restraint. Some institutions allow *daily* compounding of annual interest.

The banks and other conventional savings institutions are really thumping the IRA tub. Here's an ad that appeared constantly in the *New York Times* in 1977. It pictured a bright, smiling girl who was obviously a lower-level employee in some company. The headline announced: "When I'm 59½, I can retire on more than $290,000 With My IRA." This ad was run by the Dollar Savings Bank in New York. The numbers are there. Of course, the purchasing power of the dollar won't be. This is just the $1,500 maximum IRA account. The numbers are astronomical for the Keogh plans if a person has sufficient income, or sufficient future orientation to save $7,500 a year out of whatever income he has.

When the returns come out of Keogh or IRA accounts upon retirement—assuming the government has not abolished the tax advantages somewhere along the way—they will be taxed as earned income. The capital gains savings do not apply to tax-deferred retirement programs. Therefore, the goal should be speculation. You want the *highest possible annual returns throughout the life of the program,* taking advantage of the tax savings. Then, at the end of the road, a person wants to live off the interest and (somehow) pass along the nest egg to his heirs without having the tax collector gobble up a lifetime of savings. Of course, if the tax collector is gobbling up your income at 50% of earned income anyway, putting off the day of fiscal judgment may be a good strategy. Like Dickens' Mr. Macawber, you can always hope that something (lower taxes) will eventually turn up. To keep your sanity, you should look at all tax-deferral schemes in exactly this way. They are, at best, ways of avoiding inevitable *present* taxes. What you hope is that the inflation tax, or change in the law, or the estate tax, or a combination of the three, will not wipe out your savings, not to mention a bad investment or five along the way.

To "protect" people from their speculative greed, the governemnt establishes guidelines. These are called the "prudent investor rule." The prudent investor rule in a time of price inflation, legislated envy, tax confiscation, and various other disasters created in Washington, is the most imprudent way to invest your funds. The inflation tax will eat up IRA accounts. What I fear about all such accounts is that a few investors will lose their shirts in a "not so prudently operated" account, and the government will step in and require banks and other managers to buy "safe" U. S. debt certificates in order to protect their clients. In other words, I view the tax-deferred retirement programs as *the government's means of tapping the last great pool of private capital savings*. "Everybody into the pool!" shouts the government, and then, when everyone is in, the Congress pulls the plug. To put it bluntly, I don't believe that modern governments ever pass along

long-term tax savings to the middle class. They set up the middle class for the slaughter, generally, by telling the middle class that it's time to confiscate the wealth of the rich. (You notice how poor the Rockefellers have become since the income tax was passed in 1913.)

If some insurance company, savings and loan company, bank, or other "safe and sound" investment program is offered to you as the "safe haven" for your retirement account, hang up the phone. *Never, under any circumstances, put your funds into the hands of an independent, conventional bureaucratic, Keynesian-trained ignoramus who works in the trust department of anything.* If there is one thing on earth that you cannot trust (excluding government promises) it is a trust department. If you can't manage your own retirement program, don't have one. If you can't tell the manager where to put those funds, then get out of your Keogh, pay your taxes, and buy some diamonds, gold coins, or whatever with your after-tax capital. Hide it and forget about it. This leaves fewer records, is more difficult for tax men to find, and generally is the best way to pass along wealth to others—on *your* terms. It's your retirement, and you, not some trust manager, are responsible for your assets. If you delegate authority in this crucial area, you are nothing short of suicidal, tax breaks or not. The trust managers get paid whether or not price inflation hits 20% per annum and your capital disappears into the ocean of fiat money.

Am I saying that no one should ever sign up for a Keogh plan? Not necessarily. I am of the opinion that anyone in a tax bracket under 30% is better off to pay his present taxes and buy "hard assets," leaving as few records as possible. In other words, I think the risk of future confiscation is very great—above 20%, if it were possible to place such boundaries on human action. (It isn't; when I say there is a 30% chance of confiscation, I am saying that I think there *may* be confiscation in the future, but I'm not really *that* confident about my estimate.) However, if the government is getting into your pocket at rates above 30%, then it might pay to go for the tax-deferred plan. If nothing else, the government *may* allow you to take out your money by paying a penalty prior to retirement. If you have been earning 20% on your money by buying and selling, wheeling and dealing, then you might come out ahead, since the profits are not taxable while the money is in the account. But if you are simply planning on "buying and holding until retirement," then you had better be over 50 before entering into a Keogh plan. (For self-managed plans, see p. 192.)

The higher income person should probably incorporate, if he is looking for tax shelter retirement programs. I strongly recommend that anyone considering such a move read chapter 17 of B. Ray Anderson's excellent book, *How to Use Inflation to Beat the IRS* (Harper & Row, 1981). An extremely important aspect of retirement plans is that all assets in these programs are shielded from creditors in case the corporation, including a one-man professional corporation, goes bankrupt. I would recommend that one asset in any large retirement program be a debt-free rental property (single-family dwelling).

For people earning under $150,000 a year, and who want to put 25% (up to about $37,000 as of 1981) into a corporate pension program, the "defined contribution plan" is probably the way to go. Large-income investors may have to go with a "defined benefit program," which allows them to sock away far more than $37,000 a year, but if the fund grows too rapidly—as a result of inflation-hedging —the businessman must reduce his future tax-deductible contributions to the plan. However, he can *borrow* from his plan at market rates of interest, invest the money outside the program, and watch his money multiply, without losing the right to pour more money into the program. This strategy I call "pouring bad money after goods."

You need professional counselling in setting up such plans. Expect to pay at least $1,500 for a professionally designed program, but don't shell out the $5,000 that some lawyer-accountant "entrepreneurs" are presently demanding.

I suggest the following investment program. *First,* 20% of your assets in short-term Treasury bills, if you have sufficient assets (T-bills are bought in units of $10,000, with $5,000 units above the initial $10,000 in any single transaction). These should be three-month maturity bills. If you don't have this kind of money, then buy shares in the strictly T-bill-invested mutual fund:

> Capital Preservation Fund
> 755 Page Mill Rd.
> Palo Alto, CA 94304
> (800) 227-8380
> (800) 982-6150 (Calif.)

The T-bills pay a better rate of return than Capital Preservation Fund, but you can invest initially for as little as $1,000 in CPF, so for the small investor, it is the only way of getting the protection of T-bills and instant liquidity. *Second,* consider putting resource-oriented stocks, or a mutual fund, into the portfolio. (See Appendix C, energy and mining mutual funds.) This might account for another 20% to 30% of the total investment. These are legal for retirement funds, according to the 1981 revision of the tax law code. They are at least related to the actual metals in the ground. If inflation pushes up the price of the assets in the ground, you can at least get increases in the value of your shares. Never forget: when you pull your money out, it will be taxed as earned income; there will be no capital gains rates, unless the law is changed (unlikely).

Third, consider land. You cannot depreciate land, so it belongs in a portfolio that is presently tax-exempt (that is, where rental income can be deferred). You want *depreciable assets* in your *personal* investment portfolio. You might be able to work out the following arrangement (with professional tax counsel): buy a building (depreciable) with your personal money, and the land it's sitting on with your retirement fund money. Then you can pay rent on the land to your retirement account, and these payments are tax deductible to you personally, but not taxed in your retirement fund until you are retired. One possible defect with this approach: it may be difficult to establish which part of the investment is the building and which part is the land. You should get two independent estimates and take the average. Again, consult professional tax counsel. I might recommend 30% to 40% of the fund in land. It depends on whether you're in a growth area. If the area is safe, and the city is 20,000 to 70,000 and growing, then more money here is advisable.

Another variation on this scheme is to own a small farm (or a few acres in a small, debt-free farm). You buy the equipment (depreciable), but put the land in a retirement account. You might be able to use your retirement money to get a "survival" property that has commercial potential. Then buy your home "next door." (Your residence should not be put in the retirement portfolio.) Farm income is taxable, of course, but the farming operation pays rent to the owner of the land, which is your retirement account, and this payment is tax-deductible. Farm income being what it is, the lease payment will eat up a lot of it. This lowers your overall tax burden, at least for the present.

A corporate account should include a *borrowing provision*. You can borrow money from your fund at a market rate of interest (deductible from personal income), and buy whatever you want with your borrowed funds—no trail of paper, and no restrictions by law ("prudent investor rule," changes in the tax code, or whatever). Buy "hard assets"—presently prohibited by the tax code—with the money you borrow from your retirement account.

Consider investing in a "switch fund" that allows you to buy and sell with one phone call, switching from one kind of investment to another. (See Appendix C: telephone switch funds.) Problem: you must have the cooperation of the person who officially supervises your retirement account. Make sure you get advice from your CPA and lawyer before setting up any retirement fund, in order to minimize the management problems.

Finally, if you want no hassles, just buy a high paying money-market fund and forget it. Put 100% of your money in three or four of them, and stop worrying. Most of them will survive, if any of them do. Forget about forecasting; just let the paper money pile up.

Most important: *be ready to cash in your IRA, Keogh, or corporate account, pay the back taxes plus the penalty, and run.* Never lock up an investment psychologically because of tax considerations. Your retirement fund can serve as a sort of emergency reserve for a major crisis. There is nothing sacrosanct about it. *If you aren't willing to cash it in early, don't set it up.*

If a war comes, or the Emergency Banking Regulation Number 1 is imposed, or the IRS changes the rules, or some other disaster hits, your retirement fund could be wiped out. Understand this before you invest. It's a crap-shoot. But if you are guaranteed losses through the income tax bite, then it might pay to consider a Keogh or IRA retirement account. You are gambling, but at least the government is putting up some of the money (by allowing you to escape current income taxes). Certainly, if you now have such a retirement program with a conventional investment house, it's time to change horses in midstream; your horse is standing on top of quicksand.

Safety Deposit Boxes

Should a person put his valuables in a safety deposit box? Frankly, I wouldn't do it. One thing is for certain: I wouldn't put *inheritable* valuables in *my own* safety deposit box. Upon my death, the box is sealed; this is true in most states. (Florida is one exception.) The tax men gather to see what can be picked off. So every family should have its valuables, as well as life insurance policies, the will, burial instructions, and similar death-influenced items in the *wife's* own safety deposit box. Preferably, the box should be in a *separate bank,* paid for by her. If you learn nothing else from this report, remember this. Anyone who still has only one safety deposit box for the entire famly is not taking me seriously on the little, simple things. The wife needs her own safety deposit box. Anything that the husband would prefer to keep away from the tax snoopers should be in her box. Her burial instructions, life insurance (if any), or items she wants to pass on to the children should be in his box. It, too, should be an exclusive box, paid for by him. Why anyone needs a joint box is a mystery to me.

I am forever worried about the implementation of emergency orders in a time of war or other crisis. This is why I prefer *not* to keep monetary or near-monetary assets in a safety deposit box. I think we should think of these boxes as "semi-risky boxes," rather than safety deposit boxes. They do protect you from most fires, most thefts, and most problems that might happen at home. However, they are legal entities, therefore controlled by law, therefore controlled by bureaucrats. Your real safety in life's long-term planning comes from being *invisible* to law, bureaucrats, and documents—at least if the juggernaut State continues to expand over the next 40 years as it has over the last 40.

Safety deposit boxes are *not* automatically insured by banks. You have to buy insurance. This means that you have to list the contents of the box, which is not what you want to do. A solution to this problem is available from the Monetary Protective Group. They sell deposit box insurance which pays up to $50,000 if your box is broken into, or burned. They assume that every claim will be a maximum claim. All that needs to be done is to furnish them publicly available documentation that your box was broken into or in some other way destroyed. For $150 a year, you get the insurance, six issues of *The Personal Security Report*, a copy of a useful booklet on home security, a "midnight gardener" burial device for valuables, and access to a toll-free phone number for advice on personal security. If this makes sense, contact:

> Monetary Protective Group
> One Appletree Square
> Minneapolis, MN 55420

You can buy a "midnight gardener" separately, or you can buy the subscription, the booklet, and the toll-free access number for $36, which is a bargain. But if you store valuables in your safety deposit box, I recommend the insurance. If you put $50,000 worth of stuff in it, your insurance is costing you 3/10 of a percent per annum, which is cheap.

Swiss Bank Accounts

There are reasons for having one, but if you can't afford to deposit over $100,000, I think the reasons are less important. If you think you will eventually flee the country, and you want assets to live on abroad, and you can afford to live on your Swiss bank deposit for at least ten years, then you should have one. If not, then I think there are better deals elsewhere.

If you intend to pursue Swiss banks, bear this in mind. First, it may become illegal for Americans to have off-shore bank accounts, just as it was in Israel for three decades. Second, repatriating your money may eventually prove difficult, especially if war should break out in Europe. Switzerland may be neutral today, but it could fall to the Soviets. This is a risk to be considered. Third, your Swiss bank might fail. This is a long-shot, but it's possible. The fellows at Swiss Credit Bank had a lesson in the risks of investing, as you may remember. In short, if you're talking about survival, buy gold bullion coins, silver coins, and lots of ammunition for your guns. If you're talking about fleeing the country, look into Swiss banking. The best source of information is *Harry Browne's Complete Guide to Swiss Banks* (McGraw Hill, 1976, $10). I recommend a Swiss bank in a tax haven: Bank Leu ("LOY"), Box N3926, Nassau, Bahamas ($5,000 minimum).

There is one reason for using a Swiss bank that should be mentioned. If you are trading gold, silver, or platinum, and you want to avoid getting caught when the U. S. government freezes prices, wages, and commodities some bright Monday morning, then you should probably consider trading on the London market through a Swiss bank. If you buy silver on margin, do it through a Swiss bank. As long as you don't intend to take delivery on the metal, a Swiss bank is probably a good way to maintain secrecy.

If you have some desire to buy an annuity—why, I cannot fathom—you should buy it through a Swiss company, possibly through your bank in Switzerland. If you have need of further information, contact

Assurex, S. A.　　　　　　International Insurance Specialists
P. O. Box 290　　　　　　　P. O. Box 949
8003 Zurich, Switzerland　　1211 Geneva 3, Switzerland

I am not recommending Swiss life insurance. I am talking only about *annuities*. I think your life insurance should be strictly term insurance, payable to your wife in dollars, with the premiums also denominated in dollars. Remember, you have to buy Swiss francs first before you can buy Swiss franc-denominated life insurance, so the premiums go up as the dollar falls.

Life Insurance

As already mentioned, buy term insurance. You die, they pay. Your wife should be the owner. She must pay for the premiums with her own exclusive checking account (not the joint account). The husband should sign a notarized letter saying that he is not the owner of the policy, and that the wife is the owner. I recommend the $100,000 term policy issued by this company:

United Investors Life
#1 Crown Center
Kansas City, MO 64141
(816) 283-4242

If you're 35, you will pay about $220 per year with this policy, and later on you have the option of reducing coverage without cancelling the policy. They also sell a cheaper policy for non-smokers. Your independent insurance agent should be able to buy it for you. If he drags his feet (and he probably will), call the company to locate an agent in your area who sells it.

Three agents who can help you get good policies, in case your local independent agent isn't helpful, are located in Texas.

David Holmes　　　　　　　　George Williams
Life Insurance Truth Society　　Linscomb & Williams
1 Miletus Way　　　　　　　　5909 W. Loop South, #500
Cross Plains, TX 76443　　　　Bellaire, TX 77401
(817) 725-6635　　　　　　　(713) 661-5000

Towers & Associates
Heritage Bank Building, Suite 213
Tyler, TX 75711

Chapter 20

"VALUABLES" DURING HYPER-INFLATION

Investment strategies are very complicated affairs. A *conventional investor* is always concerned about capital gains (as denominated in his national currency) and income (also denominated in paper currency). The *price* he is willing to pay for an asset is, assuming the investor is rational, the present market value of the *expected future income stream, discounted by the expected rate of interest.*

The *unconventional investor* ought to be looking at capital gains and income flow, but he has another dimension to consider: *alternative currencies*. In a time of increasing government intervention, we can expect a flight of capital out of the strictly currency-denominated investments into the "alternative money"-denominated investments.

It is incredibly difficult for conventional investors to rethink their attitudes toward money. Everything they are familiar with in the conventional markets is related to the domestic monetary unit. Yet it is risky to lock one's future income stream into currency-related investments. The currency units of the world are not to be trusted. They are government monopolies, and shrewd men do not trust government monopolies.

Even unconventional investors find themselves slipping back into the thought patterns of conventional investors. I am constantly amazed in my discussions with hard asset-oriented people at the extent to which they have remained infected with the "traditional wisdom" of conventional investing.

Let me offer an example. I talk with people who have invested substantial proportions of their assets into gold coins. They will then measure the extent of their financial wisdom by the appreciation of the dollar price of gold. Yet these same people would not be willing to sell their gold at today's price. They expect further appreciation. Fine, but *why use the dollar as the measuring device?* Isn't the dollar exactly what gold buyers are trying to escape? Isn't the total unreliability of the dollar the heart of their investment philosophy? Yet they persist in thinking of the value of gold in terms of its dollar-denominated price.

Shouldn't we consider, instead, the *collapse of the dollar* in terms of its *gold-denominated price?* Shouldn't we be thinking in terms of one-five hundredth of an ounce of gold, compared with the former

163

value of one-thirty fifth of an ounce?

It is far easier—meaning far more conventional—to measure gold's value by the quotation in dollars. But this consideration should be acknowledged in advance by the unconventional investor as a kind of shorthand. Naturally, it is valid to quote so many dollars per ounce, but a person who is trying to flee from dollars should *never* make basic investment decisions in terms of *gold and dollars* as such. He must rethink his philosophy. He should be thinking in terms of *gold and dollars and something else.*

"Something Else"

I am not trying to be cute. I am trying to crystallize your thoughts. I am trying to get you to think through the implications of your own philosophy of investing. It really does matter what you think about your assets. You have to decide just what it is you're trying to accomplish with your capital.

Gold and dollars and something else: here is the necessary formula for capital preservation. The dollar is money, meaning an acceptable medium of exchange. "Medium" means intermediary. You sell goods for dollars because you think someone else will, in the future, sell *you* goods for dollars. *You are not after dollars; you are after goods and services.* Dollars are simply a shorthand for economic calculation—a shorthand without which all modern economies would collapse, since the division of labor requires an acceptable medium of exchange, and fiat currencies provide these accounting standards in the world today. You may prefer to measure your capital gains in terms of dollars, but the more inflationary the economy becomes, the more erroneous your shorthand calculations will become. You should always keep some idea of the purchasing power of the dollar in the back of your mind when you start calculating your capital gains.

If you consider your profits in gold, they should be hard asset-denominated profits, adjusted by the capital gains tax losses that you may be paying. If you convert from gold to dollars to assets, you will lose part of your profits when you pay the tax. If you pay the tax, and intend to continue paying it, then you should always discount your profits mentally, so as not to paralyze yourself when it comes time to sell out (see "Banana Peel Investing"). The conversion from gold to dollars to something else involves a loss. If you tithe, it involves a further reduction in assets. Never forget this.

All right, what are the implications of the "gold to dollars to something else" formula? Most important, you have to answer this question:

"What do I intend to do with those future dollars?"

You would be astounded to learn that the majority of gold coin investors have never really thought this through. They are stuck in the mental straightjacket of conventional investment categories. And by "they," I mean *you*.

When do you intend to sell your gold? When the dollar-denominated price reaches what level? If you have never considered this question, you are in trouble. To answer it, you should consider the following factors:

1. How fast does gold hit this dollar-denominated price? (Will it push even higher?)
2. What are the prospects for war at that time?
3. What is my income for that year? (tax considerations)
4. What can I do with the money at that time?
5. What is the future of the dollar at that time?
6. Is it still legal to buy and sell gold without leaving records?
7. Are the same economic policies that created price inflation still in effect?
8. Has gold become an alternative currency unit on markets that I deal with? (Black markets)

People invest in gold for conventional reasons, of course. They buy gold futures contracts, never intending to take delivery of the actual physical gold bars. They put gold away for a few years instead of opening a bank account. They use gold as collateral in some sort of loan transaction. But I am not talking about the semi-conventional uses of gold. I am talking about unconventional investing.

What do you intend to do with the gold coins? *Sell* them for dollars? *Barter* with them? Those are the *only* choices (other than sell them for some foreign currency). You are after future goods and services, agreed? But *how do you intend to buy them?* With gold or paper money? This is the heart of the "gold to dollars to something else" equation. Will it really be an equation? Will the entries on all sides stay fairly constant? Will gold = paper money = goods during the time frame of the conversion process?

If you are acting rationally, you will not sell your gold for money unless you trust the stability of the dollar's purchasing power during the conversion period. The sale of gold means that *your faith in the dollar,* at least temporarily, *has been restored.* You want "something else." Are you more likely to be able to buy it by holding gold or paper money? Which is money for you? Which is your "medium" of exchange? In short, what are you predicting about *other people's* assessment concerning gold and dollars in the future, namely, at the point when you convert to "something else"?

Remember, you're *not* after money—a medium of exchange. You're after the things that the medium of exchange will purchase *when you decide to buy.*

The best way to keep from getting hypnotized by gold, buffaloed by gold, dizzied by gold, and ultimately dumped by gold, is to keep in mind that gold is a potential medium of exchange. As conditions change, the usefulness of gold as a medium of exchange will vary. You are after "something else." You must time your actions to enable you to get the greatest quantity of "something else" with your gold or paper dollars.

Some Myths of the German Inflation

There are endless stories about how much gold would buy during the worst months of the great hyperinflation in Germany in 1922-23. More and more, I am beginning to doubt them. Unless I can get primary source documentation, I have a tendency to dismiss them as myths. Why? Because other data, both theoretical and historical, point in the opposite direction.

We believe that our modern productivity stems from the division of labor on a free market. Yet we also know that the destruction of reliable money inhibits the division of labor. *Bad money drives out good markets* (North's revision of Gresham's law).

When money is no longer reliable, people have great difficulty making accurate assessments of the value of capital or any other economic resource. When information costs rise, the economy is crippled more and more. Yet it is money, within the framework of an unhampered price system, which is the most stupendous conveyor of information ever developed by man. Profits and losses are measured in terms of money. Destroy the relative stability of money, and you destroy economic calculation. (For an interesting and useful discussion of the accounting implications of this fact, see the book, *Economic Calculation Under Inflation,* published by the Liberty Press, 7440 N. Shadeland, Indianapolis, IN 46250: $8.95)

Why, then, should we believe that *in general,* the person with gold coins was able to buy *important* goods—important in the conditions of 1923—with gold? If the destruction of the market was the inevitable result of mass inflation, why should we think that mere pieces of yellow metal were sufficient to overcome all the terrible losses of efficiency associated with the breakdown of a modern market economy? Is gold magic? Are gold bugs the new magicians? Or is the heart of our prosperity the existence of unhampered markets and personal freedom?

Let me refer to a most remarkable book, *When Money Dies,* by Adam Fergusson. It was published in London in 1975 by the little-known firm of William Kimber & Co. It sold for five and a quarter pounds. It is a non-technical study of the great inflations of Germany,

Austria, and Hungary in 1923. You can probably still order it from *Blackwell's,* Broad Street, Oxford, England, a firm I have dealt with successfully for many years.

Fergusson cites a letter from Sir Joseph Addison, the Chargé d'Affaires in Berlin for Britain, dated September 11, 1923:

> Unknown heights have now been reached. The floating debt increased this morning by 160,000 milliard [billion] marks. Efforts to calculate in something else are vain: it all comes back to paper marks. The shops are demanding pounds, francs, Danish crowns and any other foreign currency you may care to enumerate, and then take half an hour ascertaining how many thousand millions they require in paper marks: hence an increase of prices quite beyond the fall in the mark. Except for things like tram fares, we are now charged for most articles a few hundred millions more than the same would cost at present exchange rates in London. It is natural, for the shopkeeper discounts a further fall. He has become unaccustomed to thinking in simple figures, so it is thought that forty or sixty shillings must be nothing without millions at the end of them. The Adlon Hotel charges the equivalent of 4 pounds or 5 pounds for a bottle of wine...(pp. 176-77).

Fergusson adds in a footnote concerning the price of wine in Berlin: "Ten or twelve times the London price: a bottle of good claret at the Savoy Hotel in 1923 cost about 10 shillings." Ten shillings made half a pound sterling.

What this means is that for the average purchase, the average man would have been far better off *living in London* with his pile of gold coins or stable foreign currencies. The London markets had not been disrupted by several years of horrible inflation. It was the *freedom of the market* and the *stability of money* in London that made daily living *less* expensive, even in terms of gold, than Berlin.

I am reminded of the story related by Prof. Donald Kemmerer concerning his father's interviews of Germans for his famous studies of the German inflation. (His father was Prof. Edwin Kemmerer of Princeton.) He asked the same question of many Germans: "What could you have done to make things better for yourself in spite of the inflation than things would have been had there been no inflation?" The answer was always the same: "Nothing." Sure, food storage would have helped, or some dollars, or some gold, but ultimately, almost *everyone* lost.

Naturally, some sharp bargainers were able to make those spectacular trades that we read about, though perhaps they were not that spectacular. There are always successful entrepreneurs who have the right asset to trade when another person is desperate. I am talking here about *average people* in their *daily exchanges.* It was here that men lost more by the disintegration of money than they made by their ownership of gold or dollars (which was the universal measuring device for the mark—the dollar-mark exchange rate was announced daily and then hourly).

The people who did better than most were the peasants. They had *food* to sell, and they were favored by the *below-market interest rate loans* of paper marks that were made possible by the huge outpouring of marks by the German central bank. (On the final day of the infla-tion in November of 1923, the call loan rate for money on the stock exchange was 10,950% per annum, while the central bank was still charging 90%.)

What was observed in all three of the defeated nations should stand as a warning to all of us: the steady transfer of *formerly* valuable assets to the peasants. And once the crisis ended, those formerly valuable assets became valuable once again. Consider the diary entry of Jan. 1, 1919 by Anna Eisenmenger, a widow of a former middle class husband in Vienna. If we expect the worst of the various scenarios, we should look at these words, not the nonsensical hopes of the more utopian goldbug newsletters, as the most likely results of mass inflation:

> Even the most respectable of Austrian citizens now breaks the law, unless he is prepared to starve for the sake of obeying it.... The fact that the future is so uncertain has led to stagnation in industry and public works, and swelling numbers of unemployed supported by the State...yet it is impossible to get domestic servants or indeed any sort of workers....
>
> Heightened class-consciousness is daily being instilled into the manual workers by the Socialist government, and, in heads bewildered by catchwords, leads to an enormously exaggerated estimate of the value of manual labour. Only in this way could it come about that the wages of manual workers are now far higher than the salaries of intellectual workers. Even our otherwise honest old house-porter is demanding such extravagant sums for performing little jobs that I prefer to do the heavier and more unpleasant household work myself....
>
> I survey my remaining 1,000-kronen notes mistrustfully, lying by the side of the pack of unredeemed food cards in the writing table drawer. Will they not perhaps share the fate of the food cards if the State fails to keep the promise made on the inscrip-turation of every note? The State still accepts its own money for the scanty provisions it offers us. The private tradesman already refuses to sell his precious wares for money and demands something of real value in exchange. The wife of a doctor whom I

know recently exchanged her beautiful piano for a sack of wheat flour. I, too, have exchanged my husband's gold watch for four sacks of potatoes, which will at all events carry us through the winter. . . . When the farmer's eyes rested on the grand piano at which Erni [her blinded son] was seated improvising, he took me aside and said: 'My wife has been wanting one of those things for a long time. If you'll give it to me, you shall have all you want for three months'. . . .

There was a steady stream of pianos, furniture, family heirlooms, gold watches, jewelry, and gold coins *toward the farms,* and a stream of food flowing the other way. We are talking about the breakdown of the national division of labor. We are talking about the disintegration of money and the markets that money had made possible. *It was food, not gold, that was king.*

What does the term "valuables" mean? Gold, silver, jewelry, precious stones? Why do we call them "precious"? In short, what are "valuables"? It depends upon *external circumstances* and the *evaluations* of buyers and sellers concerning these circumstances. Forget about "intrinsic value"; start thinking about market value. Consider the words of Judith Listowel, a Hungarian:

My relations and friends were too stupid. They didn't understand what inflation meant. They didn't rush to get rid of their money (that was what the Jews and the Germans did). All my relations thought it would stop the next week—and they went on thinking so.

They woke up very late. They started selling their valuables because they couldn't buy food—the china from the mantelpiece, the furniture, the silver. That made them think—it made them think when the price of a set of old silver spoons went up from 20,000 to 40,000 crown in a matter of a week or two. And if you had to sell a valuable writing desk for money which was worth only half as much a week later, of course there was ill-feeling.

It was resented when Jews bought these things. The Jewish women would turn up at parties or at *the dansants* when we were all broke, wearing silver fox furs—three at a time for ostentation—and diamonds which they had bought from our relations for a song—or what, when they saw them again, had become a song. My relations didn't know the value of anything. They were stupid. Our solicitors were no better. My mother's bank manager gave her appalling advice—he didn't know what he was talking about either.

She was no anti-semite. Indeed, she was a liberal who was shocked at the rising anti-semitism that was produced by the inflation. But one stupid display seems to lead to another, and then back again. This ought to be a warning to anyone who has assets in a time of crisis. Keep them hidden, and don't be arrogant.

The Jews had been badly treated in Hungary since the 1860s, and were not received socially for many years. Nine out of ten bore grudges, and when the opportunity of impressing the arrogant gentiles arrived at last, who was to blame them for taking it? When they made a success of inflation, they were hated. When they were ostentatious about it, they were hated even more. It may have been stupid of them, and of course the wiser Jews, especially the older ones, were greatly upset, and remonstrated with the younger, because they foresaw the antagonism their behavior would create....

Ultimately, there were no winners. Hitler proved that well enough.

One Possible Strategy

With this as the background, I come to the main point. What do you intend to do with your "media" of exchange? What will you do with your gold coins? Will you barter on a narrow, inefficient, possibly illegal market? Or will you sell gold for paper money? Will you hold through the inflation, the controls, and then sell in a deflation or recovery period? Or will you try to sell out at the top, meaning the *bottom* of the dollar's slide? You had better decide soon.

To illustrate a most important use of fiat money—the repayment of debt which is denominated in paper money—I return to Fergusson's narrative.

Herr Hans-George von der Osten, who had formerly flown with Baron von Richthoven's Flying Circus and was later for a short time Goering's ADC until he shot the Reichmarschall's favorite stag, recollects that in February 1922, with a loan from a friendly banker, he bought an estate neighboring his own property in Pomerania for 4 million marks (then equivalent to about 4,500 pounds). He paid the debt in the autumn with the sale of less than half the crop of one of his potato fields. In June of the same year, when prices were shooting up ahead of the mark, he bought 100 tons of maize from a dealer for 8 million marks (then about 5,000 pounds). A week later, before it was even delivered, he sold the whole load back to the same dealer for double the amount, making 8 million marks without raising a finger. 'With this sum', he said, 'I furnished the mansion house of my new estate with antique furniture, bought three guns, six suits, and three of the most expensive pairs of shoes in Berlin—and then spent eight days on the town.'

This was simple commerce: the only thing to do with cash by that time was to turn it into something else as quickly as possible. To save was folly.

Von der Osten was a piker. Had he waited one year, he could have paid off the debt on his estate with the proceeds from the sale of one potato or one egg. He could never have bought the shoes, antiques, and other goodies with the paper money generated from the sale of one potato, however.

What would have been the best strategy? He should have bought the antiques, guns, shoes, and so forth by borrowing even more on his farm from a private lender or a commercial bank, and then paid off the debt a year later with that single potato. Meanwhile, he could have bartered his potato crop for even more furniture.

Conclusion

When a society creates an economic environment where such profits and losses as these are possible, it has pursued immoral monetary policies. We have to face squarely the realities of confiscation through mass inflation. We have to understand how the system operates and how to defend ourselves against it. People who look at money income, instead of "goods and services income," are generally destroyed by inflation. This, unfortunately, involves millions of people.

Prices rise because people bid up prices by means of fiat money. Everybody falls behind—almost everybody—because of the disruptions in exchange and production produced by the insecurity and instability of money and contracts. The fact that it was cheaper to live on gold in London than in Berlin in 1923 testifies to the devastating effects on productivity that monetary inflation can produce. Real income falls for almost everyone because real production falls. Mass inflation produces inefficiencies that reduce the purchasing power of money even more than the mere increase of monetary units. Thus, at the end of mass inflation, prices rise even faster than the percentage increase of money. Not only is demand (as measured in money) increasing, but supplies are decreasing (lower productivity). Prices skyrocket. Increasing quantities of money raise prices, and decreasing supplies of goods and services also raise prices. The economy gets "the double whammy."

What I want you to understand is this: pieces of yellow metal are helpful in mass inflation, but they are not cure-alls. We need durable goods during such times. We need them, first, to guarantee ourselves a steady stream of goods, since we remove ourselves from full dependency on the market supply system. Second, we need goods in order to keep us from having to sell our gold, silver, and heirlooms in order to eat and survive. On the far side of the disaster, we will still have our metal capital and our heirlooms. We don't have to dump our silver and gold coins at a discount in relation to food, simply because we will not be buying food during the crisis.

Anyone who thinks the list of goods needed by a family is minimal needs to read Appendix A of this book, which I have reproduced by permission from Joel Skousen's book, *Survival Home Manual.* This list is huge. It will shake most people to the core. We are too dependent upon a market supply system that can be disrupted by mass inflation, price controls, terrorism, and war.

Your gold, in short, should not be aimed at getting rich in mass inflation. It should be used as a survival reserve, as a form of capital that will be valuable on the far side of a disaster, and as a means of gaining access to paper money that can then be used to pay off debt and pay taxes. But gold is not to be thought of as a means of buying up valuable items—valuable during a crisis, anyway. It may be used for buying up items that won't be that valuable during a crisis (pianos, old paintings, antiques, etc.), but which may appreciate after the crisis is over. But for such purposes, food and basic necessities will be much more useful than gold.

Chapter 21

COMPENSATED LEVERAGE

Long-term debt is one of the disasters of the twentieth century. The availability of easy credit, such as 20-year, 30-year, and now even 40-year mortgages, all guaranteed by taxpayers through the FDIC, FSLIC, and the Federal Reserve System's printing presses, has converted the thinking of men to the logic of permanent debt. For some reason, men almost always think of themselves as long-term debtors, which makes them easily susceptible to the lure of "a little inflation" per annum, in order to relieve them of their debt burden. They vote in terms of the psychology of debt, that is, how to skin those so foolish as to have become long-term creditors denominated in fiat dollars. Yet the grim reality is that *most of the productive people of any society have become long-term creditors*, though for some reason they never understand the implications of this fact. They own rights to future payments in dollars (Federal Reserve Notes): annuities, cash-value life insurance policies, bonds, mortgages, pensions, and various social security programs.

When I say that people do not understand their position as long-term creditors, I mean that they do not recognize these investments as long-term credit investments. If they did, they would not be so ready to commit their capital to such sure-fire losers. I have pointed out the danger of such investments for years, as have other hard-money newsletter writers, yet when I speak with people concerning their present assets, they are proud to point out to me how much they have "saved," they think. They have, in fact, *given away* capital assets to the inflation monster. Show me the person who says "I can't buy gold; I need income," and I'll show you a person who has not understood the nature of loaning present dollars in exchange for future depreciated dollars.

We have seen the transformation of earlier American investment practices, which were based on short-term credit (except for corporate bonds), into the psychology of long-term theft. We have shown people the marvels of repaying with future depreciated dollars their present debt obligations. We have made the theft process of mass inflation acceptable, step by step, as we have redefined "a little inflation" as

173

2%, then 4%, then 6% per annum—always knowing that the present rate of price inflation is higher than the "acceptable" rate. We have shown two generations of Americans that debt pays—at the expense of ignorant long-term creditors.

The Bible affirms that the debtor is servant to the lender (Proverbs 22:7), and that it is best to be totally debt-free (Romans 13:8). Debt is for emergencies, and it should be limited to six years, maximum (Deuteronomy 15:1-6). The economy of the Bible assumes that there should be no inflation of the currency—honest weights and measures—and that long-term debts tempt whole populations to violate the prohibition against debased coinage (Isaiah 1:22). In such a non-inflationary economy, the borrower is indeed servant to the lender. Long-term debt, however, offers the debtors a way to escape, a way to make the creditors the captives: monetary inflation. The purchaser of an irrevocable annuity, for example, is easily the captured, not the captor. (And, I might add, irrevocable annuities are the favorite traps issued by churches, seminaries, and other usury-peddling religious hustlers to the gullible members, all in the name of Christian stewardship.)

This being the case, I do not recommend long-term credit positions. But since I do not recommend that people offer others long-term credit, I do not recommend that people accept long-term credit, thereby becoming long-term debtors. My rule is clear: *stay out of debt, except in an emergency, and then accept no debt that cannot be paid off within six years. Every man should live totally debt-free one year in seven, minimum.* This lets us keep the lure of "theft through inflation" at arm's length, and preferably farther. It also places on us acknowledged limits on what we can successfully forecast about future economic conditions. As the Psalmist said, "The wicked borroweth and payeth not again" (Psalm 37:21a). We should not shrug off massive personal indebtedness, which puts us at great risk of defaulting on the loan. Do not accept debt burdens that you do not think you can reasonably pay off within six years. And take this debt burden only because you are convinced that we face an impending emergency.

This is not your run-of-the-mill investment advice from those who accept the grim reality of long-term inflation. But those who advocate massive personal indebtedness are really saying one of three things. *First,* we can perfectly predict the future, and we know that deflation cannot come, and that we will not, in our own individual positions, be whipsawed by the loss of job or income in a temporary recession. *Second,* even if we are uncertain about the future possibility of deflation, we can always declare bankruptcy and start over. *Third,* we might as well gamble on inevitable inflation, despite the precedent that successful "skinning of the creditors" sets for future generations. Since I accept none of these premises, I cannot in good conscience recommend long-term debt, even in a time of inflation. It may well be profitable in the short run. It may make it possible for a few people to make fortunes on other people's money. But it is not the way I think you build up an alternative culture of the disintegrating secular culture in which we find ourselves trapped. If we cannot offer decent alternatives now, what will we say if and when leadership is offered to us after the present economy fragments? *Our goal is long-term social reconstruction, not quickie profits through endless debt pyramiding.* We are also trying to avoid personal bankruptcy.

Emergency Debt

We need capital. We need it to provide *leisure* in the future, a prerequisite for taking leadership. We need it to provide *protection for our families*. We need it to *finance voluntary charities*. We need it to increase our ability *to master our environment through the division of labor*. Thus, in a time of rapid, escalating price inflation and social disruptions, we need to increase the size of our capital holdings.

What do I mean by "capital"? First and foremost, I mean *intellectual and moral capital*. I believe in this form of capital because it is highly *mobile*—and because it cannot easily be *taxed*. Borrowing to provide an education is eminently sensible, if the training provided is really likely to be useful to the recipient. (Borrowing to get a Ph.D. in sociology is not so smart, in other words.)

Then there is one's *home*. This is the item that most of us have indebted ourselves long-term to buy. If a home is in a safe town, or if you are buying it for appreciation to enable you to buy a small-town house or small farm, then it seems legitimate. Rent controls will reduce our mobility. Price controls will make home construction risky, as construction materials will become scarce under the controls. The thought of being without a home in the future disruptions is unpleasant. A home is a legitimate investment, when it is suited to present and expected future needs of one's calling. High debt for social status should be avoided, especially when the envious start dropping by with torches.

Tools of all kinds are legitimate to buy on credit if there is no other way. These should be selected with an eye to the future. What kinds of tasks will be necessary in a period of reduced output, shrinking markets, social turmoil, and a reduced division of labor? These are the tools to buy now.

Gold and silver coins are legitimate capital investments. They should probably be purchased outright, however. These are to be held close to you in case of a panic. They are mobile. They are your long-term survival hedges.

We could go through several pages like this, but you get the point. It is best to pay cash. *If you absolutely have to own something, pay cash* (and probably leave few records). If you think you will need something, but you could survive without it, consider borrowing to buy it. If you don't want something repossessed, pay cash. If you don't want something confiscated, leave few records. For example, I would buy handguns with cash payments. I would not buy them with a credit card. But if I had to, I might buy handguns by taking out a signature loan at a bank, or a second mortgage.

One reason for borrowing on 90-day credit now is the establishment of a credit record that enables you to borrow more later on. Buy on credit now, even if you do not like debt, because *in an emergency you will want to borrow to the hilt*. I will give one important example. If price controls are imposed, you will have a few weeks to buy items on the shelves. You may only have a few weeks. You will have to make emergency purchases of goods that may have to last you for several years. Credit may be imperative under such circumstances. So you borrow now, always keeping money in reserve, and repay on time. *Get your borrowing limit built up in advance.* If you have an American Express "green" card, apply for a "gold" card: it allows you instant credit of $2,000.

To discipline yourself, always be sure that you borrow only for production assets like tools, or for consumer goods that are durable and possible candidates for shortages in the near future. Be sure you have money on reserve, or liquid assets on reserve, or 99% sure income within three months, to pay off the debt. You are only establishing an *emergency credit reserve*—an established credit rating—not financing a buying jag.

Just remember December 8, 1941, the day after Pearl Harbor. On that day, the smart man started buying tires, spare parts, silk stockings for his wife (or the black market), a new car, tools, household appliances, and whatever else he could beg or borrow. It was then or never. On that day, it paid to have unused credit reserves.

A price and wage freeze will be a replay of Pearl Harbor. Praise the Lord and pass the MasterCard.

Escaping Fiat Money

Don't swallow paper. That's my chief investing motto. Liberals much prefer "you can't eat gold," but mine makes more sense. Don't become the final recipient of fiat money. In other words, *don't become a long-term creditor.*

Let me offer a familiar example. Someone sells a piece of real estate. The only way he could sell it was to accept a note, such as a first mortgage, second mortgage, or whatever. What should he do? He has three sane choices. *First,* discount the note for cash. Others may be stupid enough to want to become long-term creditors. *Second,* trade the note for more real estate. *Third,* go out and buy another piece of property on debt terms similar to those involved in the original sale. If you don't want to take the first two approaches, then don't sell the property for more than a six-year note, assuming you have decided not to become a long-term (over six years) creditor. But whatever you do, *don't swallow paper.* Better to serve as a funnel for paper money: you get paid by your debtor, and you immediately pass on the depreciating fiat money to your creditor. You wind up with the appreciating real estate, not the depreciating paper money.

This leads us back to another of my formulas for economic survival: *gold and dollars and "something else."* You are ultimately after "something else." It's true, you can't eat gold. You also can't eat paper dollars. You're after something else. The question is this: *Which is the most efficient, least expensive way to enable you to get ownership of something else?*

When gold goes to $800 or higher, are you thrilled? If you're in the commodities markets, this needs no answer, since you're after dollars anyway, in the short run. But if you're holding gold for long-term appreciation, you should be horrified. Gold at $800 means we're that much closer to gold at $1500, and gold at $1500 means international currency panic, trade war, possibly international war, price controls, shortages, and all the other "solutions" to long-term monetary inflation. When I see gold shoot from $600 to $800 in a few weeks, I get a sick feeling. Is time running out? Gold is not like General Motors stock. You should not be ecstatic when gold goes up, since this means that the dollar—and with it, the world's reserve currency-based trading system—is going down.

I'm speaking here of *gold held as a survival asset.* I can think of one set of circumstances in which a rise on gold's dollar-denominated price might thrill me. If I were heavily indebted on a small farm, on which I intended to ride out any domestic crisis, and I found myself able to sell off a few gold coins, buy paper money, and *pay off my debt on the farm,* then the rise of gold's price would not be a direct threat to me. In such circumstances, I have allowed the panic in the gold markets to pay off my farm—to buy it outright.

In other words, I have escaped dollars. But I have escaped dollars more efficiently than merely by purchasing gold coins and holding them for appreciation, since "appreciation" is usually defined as dollar-denominated price appreciation. But if other hard goods—food, tools, housing, etc—are also rising in price rapidly, then the gold is less useful to me in my ultimate goal, namely, escaping paper money. *This is the meaning of leverage.* I wind up with more appreciating assets—gold, land, tools, etc.—than I would otherwise have been able to accumulate in a fixed period of time. Why? Because I have accepted the burden of paper-money denominated debt. Instead of relying on my annual income to finance my purchases, which means a frantic pursuit of rapidly appreciating items, I can rely on my *forecasting skills* to finance these purchases. In short, I have become an entrepreneur—a speculator or forecaster. Why not use these talents? Why rely exclusively on my wage-earning abilities to finance the emergency items that I need, or think I will need?

One answer why not is this one: I may guess wrong. I may forecast gold's rise in price, and deflation may hit, and I will find myself in debt without adequate reserves to pay it off. This is quite possible. It should warn us against massive personal indebtedness. Debt is a burden. But so is mass inflation with price controls. Here is our awful problem: *How to escape the greater burden?*

I recommend using *compensated leverage techniques* to enable us to accumulate survival capital more rapidly. Here is the basic approach. You buy an asset that is important to you, but *not* absolutely imperative. This may be a home, a farm, a set of tools, land, income-producing real estate, a business, or education. You finance it with borrowed money. Then you buy another asset which you expect to appreciate before your six years have ended. This is purchased outright. If the mass inflation hits, you sell off a portion of your back-up assets, "buy" money, and pay off the debt.

For example, you decide to buy a farm worth at today's prices $100,000. You should then borrow as much of the purchase price as possible—say, 80%. You then buy a back-up asset, such as $30,000 in gold coins. Your goal is to sell off the coins in the midst of, or close to the end of, a period of heavy price inflation, retaining perhaps half of your coins in the deal, while buying the farm outright. You will have to calculate just how high the gold would have to go to enable you to accomplish this. You will have to decide whether you want a smaller farm or more gold if you don't think gold will rise high enough to make this transaction possible.

If your area of expertise is real estate, and if the thought of national rent controls doesn't bother you, then you might use your real estate pyramid instead of gold. But if you ride the pyramid higher and higher, you should set a date for liquidation of a portion of the empire in order to gain access to fiat money that will pay off the existing debt.

What you want is a *debt-free empire,* reduced through timely, principled sales of a portion of that empire, just prior to a deflationary currency reform, or at the end of your six years of debt, whichever comes first.

You are not trying to achieve the impossible with borrowed money. *Every debt pyramid eventually topples.* You must *not* adopt the philosophy of former multi-millionaire James Ling, whose empire toppled in the credit crunch of 1969-70: "This process can go on forever. Go in a company, buy it like we did Okonite, recoup your cash, and start redeploying again, constantly, over and over. There's no end to this." That's what the man said (*Newsweek,* Jan. 23, 1967). He also said: "I once heard a man brag about not having any long-term debt. That isn't a realistic attitude. On balance, it's always better to go to the money market." (*Fortune,* Jan., 1967). Results, as measured by L-T-V stock performance:

> 1962: $15 per share (1962 purchasing power)
> 1968: $169 per share
> 1970: $10 per share (1970 purchasing power)

Conclusion

Take some debt, if that's the only way you know how to get control of needed survival assets now. Take the debt with a stock of appreciating liquid assets to back up at least one-third of the total debt. Hope for an appreciation, in dollars, sufficient to enable you to: 1) pay off the debt; 2) pay capital gains taxes on the profits earned by the asset; 3) have some fraction of your original holdings of the asset still in your possession. I would use *diamonds, rare coins, income-producing real estate, antiques, art objects, collectors items,* and other rapidly appreciating investments to serve as the compensation for my leverage. I would prefer to sell off these more speculative assets to gain access to the debt-liquidating paper money, rather than survival assets like Krugerrands, silver coins, or other directly barterable hard assets. You can live without antiques, art objects, and rare coins; you may find it too risky to sell off your "survival assets." Decide which portion of your assets should be used for compensated leverage, and which will be sold only in a total emergency (like that last .357 magnum round). You can keep records for those items that you eventually intend to sell for paper money. I buy speculative *"penny gold" shares* for this purpose. Contact Jerry Pogue for more information: (800) 426-1608. *Paper shares to paper money to debt liquidation.* I hope it works. Remember: this is an *anti-inflation* strategy. It should not be expected to work in times of recession, stable money, or deflation.

Chapter 22

TURKEY SHOOTS

"It's as plain as the nose on your face." It doesn't take Cyrano de Bergerac to figure out that polite people should avoid these words. Nobody likes to hear that something important is right under his nose. The trouble is, that's just exactly where important things are likely to turn up.

It's a question of perspective. Or maybe it's timing. Then again, it's really a matter of experience. On the other hand, it's knowing the right questions to ask. Or a combination of the above. But the fact remains, *when people get too close to a subject, they have an amazing ability to ignore the obvious.* And the obvious resents being ignored. It strikes back in the most annoying and loss-producing ways.

Take for example a recent theory of stock market investing. The *Wall Street Journal* has written several articles about an investor who does extremely well, year after year, by adhering to a very simple investment assumption: *You can't make money investing in losers.* His whole strategy is to develop predictive techniques that enable him to spot future losers. Obviously—there it is again—if everyone went looking for losers to avoid, the system would break down, since the market would discount the new information so rapidly that he couldn't reap his entrepreneurial profit. His forecasts would be less successful. Still, everyone is looking for those big winners, leaving the field of identifying the losers pretty much empty. It reminds me of that old story about the professor who attended the college beauty contest and spotted a young man who was intensely rating the girls. "Trying to pick a winner, young man?" he asked. "No, sir. I'm trying to spot a loser, so I can tell her how gorgeous she is. That gives me an inside track when it comes time to cheer her up after the contest." Everyone *knows* that you can't win with losers. So why is it that everyone leaves the field open to someone who simply makes money by eliminating the losers from his portfolio? It's as easy to profit from knowledge about losers as it is to profit from winners. But if you started an investment newsletter called, say, *Spot the Losers,* you would have trouble getting it marketed.

When people start dumping a stock or commodity, it's called profit-

180

taking. Why not loss-avoiding? Somehow, people in the investment markets are lured by the glitter of profits, gains, increases to boggle the mind of Uncle Harry at the next family reunion.

There is an exception to this rule, however. If an item really isn't worth much, but someone gets it even cheaper, he brags. I can remember the response of a lady on a Caribbean cruise. I had just bought a rather attractive sea shell for $3. A lady came up and asked me how much I had paid. I told her. "That's a shame," she said. " I bought mine from one of those boys at the pier, and I only paid a dollar." She was quite proud of herself. And I, having been over-charged, was despondent. Of course the trip down there had cost her about $1,500 or so, while I had come with Howard Ruff's lecture team, and it had cost me an hour lecture. In any case, the sea shells were cheap compared to the cost of the cruise. But it was that percentage—200%—that made the difference. We can all understand a bargain like that. (The capper came when another lady—who was loaded down with trinkets—commented on how my shell was chipped, which I would never have noticed, not being a skilled shell man. The real winners were the *kids* unloading the junk on us, and the *owners of the cruise line,* but everyone was comparing notes with each other to find out who had got the real "bargains." The natives are returning the favor that was shown to them by our European ancestors to their ancestors several centuries ago: unloading the trinkets on the dum-mies. The lady who had commented on my chipped shell later won first prize in the ship's masquerade contest by hanging all the trinkets around her neck and shoulders and writing "sucker" across her forehead. Everyone recognized the sagacity of her observation.)

We have to recognize our weaknesses. If we are less alert to *loss-avoidance* than profit potential, then we have to overcompensate to protect ourselves. We have to look at those avenues of loss avoidance more carefully, since that's where the average guy, and even the sophisticated investor, neglects his homework. (Now that I think about it, maybe it's only the sophisticated investor who is prone to neglect loss-avoidance. Maybe the average guy knows better.)

Where Will You Sell It?

There are a lot of pitchmen out there who are ready and willing to unload an overpriced turkey on you for a fat commission. Let me pass along to you *North's law of investment turkeys:*

> *The fatness of the turkey is in direct proportion to the fatness of the commission.*

Clever, right? If I'm lucky, Allen Otten will quote it in a forth-coming *Wall Street Journal* column. The trouble is, it's true. The reason why the commission has to be fat is because the item does not have a ready resale market. That means that the investor is buying the sizzle, not the steak. The salesman is fattening up the pigeon with lots of talk about the huge profit potential in this "once-in-a-lifetime deal." He talks about all the potential, diverting the pigeon's eyes from the grim reality.

The buyer should be very wary of fancy brochures, especially color brochures. He should be wary about free dinners, and free trips to Desert Paradise, Arizona. The odds are, Desert Paradise, AZ, was more recently known as Prairie Dog, AZ, and soon will be known as Dry Heaves, AZ. You wouldn't believe that fifty years after the swamp sales boom of Florida collapsed in a wave of scandals, that the same swamp land could be sold to unsuspecting buyers in New York, but it can (and is). Why don't people figure out that free dinners touting real estate in Florida, New Mexico, and Arizona are a threat to their solvency? (I suspect that it's very hard to sell the same sort of land that is located in Nevada. Nevada is synonymous with gambling, and gambling is what the free dinner is all about.)

I used to do telephone consulting for Howard Ruff. I kept getting calls from people who wanted to know what to do about the land they bought in [Florida, Arizona, New Mexico, or the Bahamas]. I usually had to tell them to regard the money as a sort of unaccredited educational program's tuition fee. The school of hard knocks has just graduated another searcher after wisdom.

How can you protect yourself? Here's a rule of thumb so incredibly simple that it has sat there unnoticed, right under that proboscis of yours, for years. This tip could be worth tens of thousands to you. Oddly enough, it's something that won't make me famous in the newsletter industry, and I won't be able to use it in signing up new subscribers. Why not? Because it's a *defensive investment tip*—you know, loss-avoidance. And loss-avoidance doesn't have much sizzle. But it can serve you as a shield in the future, and I can guarantee you that you'll never forget it. Here goes:

> *Find out how much it will cost you to sell it.*

That's it. No muss, some fuss, and real protection. If you can come even close to answering this question before you sign the dotted noose, you will have a very good idea of what the item is really worth to you.

Let me give you a very specific example. Say that you're looking at *a piece of recreation property,* i.e., dirt, rocks, and a few trees. This young man in the suede shoes is telling you that you have to buy today, that the price is going up soon, that this is, so to speak, the last train out. You should take the following defensive procedure before you sign anything. *First,* get to a phone book. *Second,* turn to the yellow pages under "Real Estate." *Third,* call at least three local realty offices and hit them with the following story. You're thinking about selling some land in the new Ecstacy Acres development. At this point, there will be a wild burst of laughter, some coughing, and the words, "I'll bet you are!" *Fourth,* you ask him what price per acre you could expect to get for the property you're considering. What you want to know is the amount of the discount—*the price spread*—between what the suede shoe boy is asking and what the general public is paying. *That's how much it will cost you to sell it.* Get at least two opinions.

It is my opinion that in any real estate deal involving undeveloped land, if the price spread is greater than 20%, it's not worth your time. In other words, if you have to take a *discount of 20% or more* when you turn around to sell, you are buying sizzle. You have to take the discount because, simply, you're not much of a salesman. You don't have the money to invest in full-color brochures and free steak dinners. You don't have gleaming teeth. You don't even have a pair of suede shoes. And when the potential buyer sees *you,* he'll start looking more closely at the land. Good-bye instant profit.

The reason why you should avoid most high-commission purchases is that you need *liquidity* in times like these. That means you want to be able to *sell fast* without having to offer a *discount,* or spend too much on *advertising,* or *improving* the property, and without having to offer some salesman a *fat commission.* You need to buy something, in other words, that has a *wide, developed, open market,* with a public exchange like a stock market or commodities market. You need lots of buyers and sellers, *unless* you are the man with special knowledge of the product, the local market, or future conditions. In other words, *if you aren't the fellow with the suede shoes, stay away from the "golden opportunity."*

Another example of this kind of investment turkey is the "instant collector's item, limited edition." It's limited mainly by the cost of running full-color ads. They have run out of presidents, great moments in sports, and state flowers on genuine china doorknobs. We're now down to the wives of vice presidents and replicas of key United Nations votes on issues of concern to the Third World—all faithfully reproduced on silk flags, suitable for framing. But this set is "one of a kind." You only need to agree to buy one per month until sometime after the Second Coming in order to complete your set (and the terms of the contract).

Where will you sell it?

A simple question, really. Who is out there who will want a complete

set (let alone a partial set) of Dwight D. Eisenhower water color fac-
similes engraved on two dozen miniature brass spittoons? You must
say these words to yourself:

"How can I be sure that a bigger fool than I will show up, cash in
hand, to take this one-of-a kind investment off my hands?" This is
not to say that a bigger fool approach to investing never works. It
does. You can buy shares of stock in companies that specialize in the
production of items aimed directly at the biggest fools imaginable.
They frequently use the subtle appeal, "You'll make a mint!" You
may, but only if you buy their stock, not their reproductions. (And if
they run out of fools, or fools run out of money—you know about
fools and their money—then maybe you won't make a mint with the
stock.)

But It's An Investment

Then why are you walking on it?

This is another variation of the "great reason to buy" pitch. The
salesman, having spotted his mark, tells you that not only is this one
of the last ones available, but it's also useable right now. You know,
like a Persian rug. Or a new Mercedes. Something you really want
because it fulfills a lifetime dream, or your sense of beauty, or your
determination to impress Uncle Harry. But it's overpriced, and you
know it. Worse, Uncle Harry will know it. "Another toy, eh, Billy?
You never could resist a toy. Why, I remember that rocking horse you
wanted, the one that lasted two weeks...." So you take along the
salesman's pitch, "but it's a great investment." The function of the
pitch, basically, is to give you something extra to take along with
you—an excuse for stupidity, poor planning, inefficient shopping, or
just plain basic lust. It soothes the conscience. It justifies nonsense.
"An investment, of course." And since you never intend to sell it,
you'll never really have to test the validity of the theory. You'll never
have to test your "investment" in the market.

If it's an investment, then at what price do you intend to sell it?
What is your investment strategy? If you don't intend to sell it, then
how can you be sure it's really an investment?

All right, a true antique may really be an investment. It may be a
capital asset in time of an emergency. It may be a desirable item to
pass along to the favored child. *But it's an investment in the strict
sense only if you are familiar with the secondary market for the item.*
It's your knowledge of the secondary market for the item, not the item
as such, that makes it an investment.

I'm sure Harrah's auto collection is worth tens of millions of
dollars. His antique cars are really one-of-a-kind. They are individually

irreplaceable in some cases. But before he died, I noticed something significant: he didn't drive them to work. He didn't take week-end jaunts to Elko in them. They were investments. He treated them as such.

I used to get calls from physicians who wanted to buy a twin-engine plane. I was invariably told that it's just an investment. And, by the way, it's deductible. "Would you buy it if you didn't like to fly, and you could still make money with it by hiring a part-time pilot?" I asked. "Well, when you put it that way, no," was the usual reply. It really isn't an investment. It's a toy. It's a tax-deductible toy. That's fine, but why contact me for advice? I give *investment* advice. (By the way, if you're ever asked to take a flight in a private plane by a physician-pilot, regard it as the equivalent as an offer to take a drive with an ordained minister. Doctors think they're too smart to crash, and ministers think they're too holy. Few ministers believe in predestination, but they often drive as though they did.)

"But I Need the Income"

This is one of my favorites. This is the one that kept Milton Friedman and Eliot Janeway from buying gold—no income. If it doesn't pay a dividend, it isn't an investment. It's speculation. So they say.

Let's talk about income. First of all, as far as passive income is concerned, there isn't any. Not in an economy experiencing 10% price inflation. You may get 11% on your money, but you're taxed off the top, and what's left over doesn't keep pace with price inflation. In short, *there is no passive income; there are only various stages of capital consumption.* It's only a question of how fast you want to consume your capital.

If I buy an item, sell it a year later, and make 100% on my money, have I received income? As far as I can tell, I have. It wasn't passive. I had to make a decision to sell. I had to part company with the item. But I did certainly come out ahead.

What people want today, especially retired people, is passive income. They want to make a one-time decision and then sit back and enjoy life, *income assured, decisions deferred, capital preserved.* This is retirement thinking. It's *suicidal.*

Yes, many of them know that passive income is a myth. They also know they can't afford to retire. But they turn their backs and their capital on what they know, choosing instead a short-term fantasy world. They *want* to retire. They *want* passive income. They want it, and they're going to have it, and nothing I can tell them, including facts they already know, will dissuade them.

Why do retired people need income? You think I'm nuts. Not at all.

What I try to point out is this: *they don't need money income.* They need the items that dollars *presently* buy. They will continue to need such items. Then why tie one's hopes to money? Why not buy what you need in advance?

A person may have $50,000 investment capital. Why not take $25,000 of it and buy those durable goods that he or she expects to consume over the next five or ten years, and store them? Why not buy all the light bulbs, kitchen utensils, consumer durables, paper products, frozen beef, frozen food, dehydrated food, new clothes or fabrics, sewing machine, thread, and so forth? *Buy and store.* If a person needs more space, then he can rent a mini-warehouse. Pay a year in advance (ask for a 10% discount, of course). Mini-warehouse space isn't that expensive. There is the theft problem, but inflation is a more certain form of theft.

If the rising prices of everything exceed the return on conventional investments, then *why don't people just sell their conventional investments and buy the goods?*

Isn't this obvious? Then why don't more people start buying this way? Why don't senior citizens form co-ops and buy goods in bulk at sharp discounts? Why don't they abandon their CD's, utility stocks, 8% municipals, and all the rest? Why don't they buy what they want, in bulk, in advance, on sale? Why don't they buy their future income by buying future consumption items? Why do they trust in the purchasing power of a monetary unit that is wholly untrustworthy? What is patently obvious has escaped them.

Sure, it's a hassle to shop now in bulk. It involves foresight. It involves *active* investing. Too many Americans are used to the idea of a guaranteed future, where everything they want will be available for money, including money that will be in demand. People have been lured into *passive thinking.* Their investing reflects their thinking. If a person is going to speculate—that is, deal with the uncertain future—it's a safer bet to *speculate against money and for goods.*

Conventional wisdom in investing is geared to *passivity toward monetary fluctuations.* Since 1965, that kind of thinking has been loss-producing. We want to take something for granted in our equations, and money has been our chosen stable factor. But our government's policies have been opposed to stable money. The familiar monetary unit is a thing of the past. We must all be active speculators. We must speculate in the knowledge that *trustworthy money is a thing of the past.* Passivity toward monetary affairs in not benign neglect; it is loss-producing. The government is *actively inflating.* We must be *actively evading.*

Conclusion

If you want to avoid turkeys, start with the dollar.

Chapter 23

WHICH TAX TO PAY AND WHEN TO PAY IT

One of the points I have tried to stress in earlier chapters is this: we live in the era of government-imposed wealth redistribution. Two centuries from now, they may describe our age as the age of secular humanism, or the atomic age, or the era of total warfare, or the century of the tyrannies. But it would hardly be an exaggeration if they describe it as the *age of confiscation*.

What we have witnessed is the expansion of the modern confiscatory State. When the First World War began, the total national debt of the United States was in the one billion dollar range; specifically, as of June 30, 1916, it was $1.225 billion. A year later it had doubled to $2.975 billion. In mid-1918, it was $12.4 billion, and on June 30, 1919, it was $25.5 billion. The 1920's saw a steady reduction of this debt, down to $16.8 billion in 1931, but Hoover began a program of large deficits (by earlier peacetime standards), increasing Federal debt to $19.4 billion, enabling Roosevelt in the 1932 election to label Hoover the biggest spender in history. In mid-1941, the debt was up to a bit under $50 billion, and a year later it was $72.4 billion. In 1945 it hit $258 billion, and it stayed in the $250-270 billion range until Kennedy came into power.

When we consider the fact that in 1916, the Federal government collected a grand total of $782,535,000 in taxes of all kinds, we can begin to grasp the magnitude of what modern statism has cost us. The Federal government cannot operate for a single day on that income. (Of course, the dollar bought a lot more in 1916.) The fact is, the expansion of Federal power has paralleled the expansion of Federal taxation. The same has been true of state and local taxation. We have seen the transformation of the public's willingness to resist taxes. Only in the last few years has anything like a widespread tax resistance movement come into prominence. It took 60 years.

The tax revolt is bound to be limited to a minority of Americans. Few of us are able to escape Milton Friedman's invention, the withholding tax. (That's right; it was Friedman who promoted this form of tax collection in the early 1940's, when he was a government employee. He said it would make it easier to collect taxes. He was absolutely correct.) We have little choice. We pay. The government automatically overwithholds, so as to force us to file each year for our refunds, and also to get the use of our money, interest-free, for a year, and also to keep us happy at being given back Federal money each year. Meanwhile, the purchasing power of the dollar has dropped another 10% or so.

How many people are really going to drop out? How many are going to file "5th Amendment" tax forms? Not many. But as I point out in chapter 7 of my book on price controls, when the government goes to the second stage of the tax escalation program—to monetary inflation—the public finds out how to resist legally by buying inflation hedges. Inflation, not being seen as a form of taxation, becomes fair game for *inflation-hedging,* which really is a form of tax rebellion.

Stage three of the tax escalation, price controls, calls forth *black markets.* These "alternative zones of supply" are also tax resistance entities. Then comes stage four, rationing. And the response is *barter,* the feudalization of the economy, which destroys the government's ability to collect taxes efficiently, since money no longer talks in the economy, and it is basic to Federal tax collection that they collect taxes denominated in Federal currency. It is very difficult to collect taxes "in kind," meaning goods and services, except at the local level.

In fact, *mass inflation eventually destroys the government's ability to collect taxes.* At first, the inflation of incomes (nominal, dollar-denominated incomes) pushes everyone into higher tax brackets. The tyranny of the graduated income tax lures governments into inflation, in order to "soak the middle class." California's Gov. Jerry Brown can say in all honesty that he has not raised taxes in California since he came into office. True enough; he has simply sat back and watched Washington's inflation push everyone into higher income tax brackets in California. The graduated income tax almost guarantees mass inflation, as the Federal government seeks to collect more and more taxes from us. And what can we do, say that the trap we set for the rich (or the trap our grandparents set back in 1913) was immoral? But now *we* are "the rich" who are getting soaked. The envy trap has caught us all, throughout the world. Envy, plus inflation, is totally destructive.

However, all is not lost. Eventually the government gets its reward. The currency unit begins to fall in value too fast. In Germany, Austria, and Hungary after the war, the inflation eventually paralyzed the civil service. When the monetary unit was falling by 50% per week, the taxpayers merely had to delay the payment of their taxes for a month or so, and they effectively wiped out their real tax obligations. Then, government being what it is, there were delays in the handling of the money. By the time the civil servants got their pay—relatively fixed pay—the currency had fallen another 75% or more since the time it was actually collected. You can imagine what happened to the income of the civil servants. And as you imagine it, project your image into the 1990's. Now I ask you, isn't that a delicious vision? All those IRS people getting their declining salaries. All those other paper-pushers eating their paper. Wonderful!

In short, almost no one escapes. When the tax traps are laid by one group or one generation, everyone eventually suffers. That's why no "new, improved" tax should be passed unless it removes older ones totally. Even a "good" tax, when piled on top of all the bad ones, is a disaster. Tax reform is a myth. Its function is always to set more traps.

What I predict is a steady erosion of the monetary unit until the day when the government finds that it no longer can operate in terms of its own money. Then will come a day of reckoning. Will some President impose the *Emergency Banking Regulation Number One*? (See chapter 5 of my price controls book.) Will they freeze all bank accounts and *ration our money back to us,* as this regulation threatens, according to a local committee's assessment of what kind of income each of us deserves? Or will there be a currency reform, when some zeroes are erased from the currency? Or will the free market simply impose a new currency on government: gold, silver, or whatever?

We have to make predictions along these lines. If we don't, then we will be skinned. We have to make forecasts about the kind of confiscation we will face in five years, ten years, or two decades.

Speculation

The meaning of "speculation" is simple enough: *forecasting.* We make predictions about the future, and then we plan for them as efficiently as we can. We try to achieve our goals with a minimum expenditure of scarce economic resources. In other words, we guess. Then we spend. And at the end, we hope that we have guessed and spent right. If so, we have more capital at our disposal than our competitors.

But if speculation is simply forecasting, what about the supposed distinction between *speculation* and *investing?* Actually, it's more of a conventional distinction than an economic one. An investment, say the experts, is one which gives you steady income. A speculation is all capital gains. You make it or break it on your guess. However useful this distinction may be for simple decisions, it's basically incorrect. How do you know that a particular investment will pay you a fixed return? Sure, it may pay you a fixed dollar return. But so what? What if the purchasing power of the dollar falls? The important question is the question of *real income.* How much will you be able to buy with the income you receive? You have to make guesses.

Naturally, some investments give you less to worry about in the short run. You know more about a T-bill return than you do about the price of gold in the immediate future. But with your *greater knowledge of the economic future,* your *potential returns go down.* You decide to reduce your risk, and so the market pays you less. You decide to forego dealing with the truly uncertain aspects of the future, but you forego profits, too. *Profits come from a successful forecast of the uncertain future.*

Thus described, an *investment* is a somewhat more secure speculation. You know more of the expected future return than you do with a pure speculation. You bear less risk, less uncertainty. But you pay for this escape from risk and uncertainty by accepting a lower profit margin.

It is my contention, as well as the contention of Prof. Hans Sennholz, that *we are entering the era of the speculator.* Why? Because government policies of wealth confiscation are beginning to disrupt the free markets to such an extent that we are vastly increasing the range of uncertainty. Remember, it's the free market, with its lure of profit, that encourages uncertainty-bearers to enter the market and deal with the future. But if you take away the profit motive, they won't do it, or they won't do it as well. Profit and loss weed out the poor speculators and reward the successful ones, which places more and more capital into the hands of those who have successfully met the demands of the consumers with the least expenditure of resources. Take away profit and loss (as you do in socialism of all brands), and *you guarantee an increase in uncertainty.* The day-to-day economic events get more difficult to deal with. Disruptions become more extensive. Shortages appear, and capitalists don't rush in as fast as before to deal with them. We enter the *shortage economy.* Only the so-called "black markets" relieve these shortages on a semi-systematic basis.

Then why is the coming era the era of the speculator? Sennholz doesn't mean that everyone will become a legal, licensed, officially approved speculator. He means that those who want to make profits will be *forced* to become speculators. Those who seek to escape the terrible burdens of the government-imposed, tax-destroyed, official, legal "markets"—which are not really markets at all, but are simply centers for redistributing confiscated goods—will be forced to bear the risks of participating in underground, possibly illegal markets. Or if they are in the legal markets, they will have to see where there are some openings in the armor of regulations, some potential for profit. But this means a potential for losses.

People who like security and vote for socialism in the hope of attaining security are thereby destroying the means of economic security, namely, the free market system. People do like security. They do like to know that their newspaper will be delivered on time, that there will be milk on the supermarket shelves when they go in to buy some, that the dollar will command respect when they try to spend one. But socialism and inflation are destroying these hopes. We are going to wipe out the economic futures of many of those who cling to security. On the other hand, we are going to see millions of Americans forced into high-risk markets by the pressure of economic shortages. They will be forced to bear uncertainty to an extent that would have been unnecessary in a free market. When they produce losses—and you know they will—they will be furious, enraged.

Stay out of their way when the collapse takes away their dreams. Stay out of the way of those whose commitment to security also has led them into destruction. The middle classes will become ugly, envious. The security-chasers and the unsuccessful speculators will not appreciate their more successful competitors. *This means you!* Keep your assets concealed.

What Kind of Confiscation?

Which is the killer tax? Which is the one that threatens your future most? Which is the one to avoid paying at all costs? Or better, which ones?

Here is my warning: *you must pay some taxes some of the time.* The tax rebel pays the *risk tax,* the threat of jail and lost income (or life) during his stay. The tax cheater faces fines and harassment by the IRS. People worry about this. The worry can kill you, if you're a true worrier. Most people aren't cut out to pay this kind of tax.

Is *income taxation* the tax to avoid? Well, at least it's predictable. If you pay it, *you can buy anonymity.* If you want to, you can start drawing out more and more cash, week by week, from your bank account. You do so quietly, so as not to attract suspicion. You build up cash assets, not for the sake of cash reserves, but as a working capital for *invisible purchases.* You go to used goods markets, auctions, swap meets, and other outlets that work with cash. *You hide your money, legally, since you paid the tax on it.* If you keep receipts, you do so only to prove that you didn't make the purchase with money that was skimmed illegally from your business. You keep the receipts separately from the goods, hidden, to present on request *at your discretion.*

If you pay the income tax, then use a growing portion of your after-tax income to buy *invisible assets.* You are buying anonymity. This is something worth paying for. Don't move heaven and earth to avoid paying the income tax, if by doing so, your after-tax income leaves endless records.

What do I have in mind? Well, take the Keogh or IRA retirement plans. They leave records. In most cases, you cannot instruct the trustee to buy and sell what you want. A few outfits *will* take your advice; for example:

First Citizens Bank & Trust P. O. Box 3028 Greenville, SC 29602	Security National Bank 1 Security Plaza Kansas City, KS 66177 (Glenn McCarty)
Lincoln Trust P. O. Box 5831, T. A. Denver, CO 80216	First State Bank of Oregon 121 S. W. 6th Portland, OR 97201

You put *record-leaving assets* into a plan like this, such as numismatic coins, diamonds, and non-depreciable, fully paid-up land (if you want such an investment). If you can get tax benefits from any investment, don't put it in your Keogh plan. What you want in the plan—assuming you want the plan at all—is any asset that you expect to appreciate over the next decade which of necessity leaves records (i.e., you intend to resell it into a market that leaves records), and which cannot give you tax benefits without the Keogh or IRA "protection."

When you pull these assets out, unfortunately, they are taxed at full earned income tax rates, averaged over 10 years (given the present tax rules, which can always be changed). If you make huge paper profits, you wind up right back in the high income tax brackets that you're trying to avoid today. On the other hand, if you don't make huge paper profits, then *you have paid the inflation tax. That is a far worse tax to pay than the income tax.*

What about the *capital gains* tax? If there is a "good" tax to pay, it's this one. At least you get reduced rates. And you can defer selling until it's a more opportune time to sell. Perhaps you can use section 1031 of the Internal Revenue Code and get a tax-deferred exchange of real property in order to put off the day of reckoning.

But this tax has a hidden trap. If we are entering the era of the speculator, then *the most important asset anyone has is the psychological, legal, and market ability to move capital assets into new markets and out of dying ones.*

What if you're in the commodity futures market, and the government imposes an emergency executive order to freeze all commodity prices? You have just lost your market ability to escape. What if the government shuts down your market, if only because too many people are escaping the inflation tax on a particular free market? You have lost your mobility. What if the fear of capital gains taxes freezes your capital in a market that is being strangled by Federal regulations, or price controls, or whatever? You have lost your capital, not to the capital gains tax collector, but rather to your *fear* of paying the capital gains tax collector. In the era of the speculator, it's probably cheaper to pay the capital gains tax, or even the income tax (if the fear of income tax is about to lock you into a bad investment while you're waiting a year to "escape" into a capital gains tax bracket).

Mobility, mobility, and mobility: move fast, little sheep, or get sheared.

Conclusions

Decide right now which taxes you're willing to pay. Then try to do your best to decide when you want to pay them. Then start structuring your investments to meet your tax goals.

For example, you may think you'll live long enough to survive *mass inflation* (a tax to avoid) and the controls-induced *shortage tax* (the tax, above all, to avoid). You think that in 1990, or 1995, or whenever the destruction of the dollar ends, and a new currency is introduced, that prices will fall. Not comparative values, but only dollar prices. This will drop your income and your estate's dollar value into far lower brackets. At that time you can die peacefully, knowing that you've escaped the estate tax collector and the capital gains tax collector. Fine and dandy. But if you're pyramided into a real estate scheme that goes bankrupt when deflation finally hits, then you have just paid the wrong tax. The capital is gone. So what should you do? Here's a strategy I've outlined before, but it bears repeating:

1. Buy leveraged real estate (tax benefits: depreciation and deductions for interest payments)
2. Use equity to borrow more money to buy more property
3. Exchange it, don't sell it for cash (defer capital gains taxes)
4. Decide when to sell off half or one-third of it
5. Pay your capital gains taxes
6. Pay off all loans on the property remaining
7. Go into the deflation period with a debt-free empire

This means that you must pay the Federal piper once, but not again (if you time your escape properly). You pay the lowest tax possible, the capital gains tax, having avoided the income tax, the inflation tax, and (possibly) part of the shortage tax. You have let inflation pay for your post-inflation capital.

When you use debt to allow inflation to work for you, you're taking very high risks. This is one reason why I don't like long-term debt (over 6 years). One thing is certain: *give the other guy the last 20%*. Get off the debt pyramid a year too early rather than staying on a week too long. Musical chairs is very risky, and almost nobody beats both the inflation mania *and* the deflationary reaction. Don't be greedy. You want to preserve capital, not risk it all on one huge crap-shoot.

Remember the words of tax expert, Larry Abraham: *every tax code has loopholes.* However, every good tax shelter *must* have two features: 1) reasonable prospects for an economic return, apart from the tax consequences; and 2) natural inflation-hedging aspects. If both are not present, *pay your taxes and hide the leftovers.* Now is the time to decide which taxes to pay and when to pay them.

As I have mentioned earlier, very good estate planning book is B. Ray Anderson's *How You Can Use Inflation to Beat the IRS* (Warner Books, 1981; $6.95). Buy it. Read it. Set up your estate accordingly. Be sure your tax counsellors—lawyer and CPA—have read this book, agree with it, and know how to implement its strategies. You need to read it in order to ask them the proper estate planning questions.

Chapter 24

THE THREAT OF FAMINE

Mediaeval history, therefore, is an impressive demonstration that by wrong policies governments can reduce mankind to want and can bring civilization to the verge of extinction. Policies which deprive the farmer of independence in the use of land, which restrict cultivation or destroy what has been produced, are farming for famine, and the same can be said of debasing the currency....

E. Parmalee Prentice
Hunger and History (1939)

Famine has been a big topic of discussion since the mid-1960's, but especially since 1968, when the counter-culture first heard about the population boom. I can remember giving a lecture to over a thousand undergraduates, primarily freshmen, in 1967, in which I discussed the agricultural revolution of the 18th and 19th centuries. I reminded them of the horrors faced by Ireland in the late 1840's, when the potato crop failed. Boredom. Zero response. Not a "hot topic" in 1967. The next year, it was time to distribute free contraceptives to the world. Fads, like freshmen, suddenly appear, stay around for a few years, and then graduate into the hard world of reality, to be forgotten or to grow up. (You would be amazed, I suspect, to read some of the books by Prof. Alvin Hansen, the man who taught Samuelson his Keynesianism, which came out in the 1930's. He was extremely concerned over population growth. There wasn't any, it seemed. This was leading the Western industrial nations into economic stagnation and decline. The government simply had to do something to stimulate demand to compensate for the stagnating population. And so it goes with Keynesians. If it ain't one thing, it's another.)

The population boom, coupled with the ecology crisis, mixed in with the technological imperative, topped off with a dash of inevitable capitalist contradiction, clearly spelled disaster. Anyone could see it. In 1968. So the "back to the soil" movement hit—a kind of modern-day Russian *Narodnik* fad, when the sons and daughters of the upper class urban intellectuals returned to the rural regions to spread the gospel of socialist freedom. Only this time, it was not to convert the peasants, with their $50,000 tractors and combines, to urban rationality. It was to escape armageddon. (How ya gonna keep 'em off of the farm, after they've seen "Soylent Green"?)

Are their instincts correct? Is armageddon coming? The radical students were reading the Paddocks' *Famine, 1975* (1968) and getting hysterical. The conservatives, this time a few steps ahead, returned to their well-thumbed copies of Van Gorder's *Ill Fares the Land* (1966) in search of evidence to see whether the Communists were somehow pre-empting conservative prophecies. The level of argumentation in most of these books was, at best, erratic. But they had all been preceded by the really great book on famine, Prentice's *Hunger and History,* published by Harper & Bros. in 1939 and reprinted by conservative Caxton Press in 1951. Sadly, it is now out of print. Its message is clear: famine was common to most earlier eras of man's history, is still taking place today in backward nations, and can happen again. Citing a study by Cornelius Walford, he lists the four primary causes of famine in man's history, and weather, you will note, is not on the list:

1. The prevention of cultivation or the willful destruction of crops (including war);
2. Defective agriculture caused by communistic control of land;
3. Government interference by regulation or taxation;
4. Currency restrictions, including debasing the coinage.

His warning should be memorized by all candidates for employment by the Department of Agriculture as part of their Civil Service exam: "And all through those millennia of suffering, man was ready and able to move ahead. He had the intelligence that he has now. What he needed was freedom to use that intelligence. When governmental restraints were removed, when the right to enjoy private property was established and protection given from confiscation, from invasion of personal rights, and from excessive taxation, all the rest came very quickly. Human history is not merely the tale of 2300 years of pause and 39 years of activity. It was first and foremost the tale on the one hand of 2300 years of various ways of living in which man was never fully his own master, and, on the other hand, 39 years of freedom." When the agricultural-industrial revolution hit the West in the second half of the 18th century, it created a unique historical phenomenon: two centuries without a famine in Western Europe (during peacetime). There was only one ghastly exception: Ireland.

Ireland was not an industrialized or industrializing nation. It was not a free nation. It was not a future-oriented, self-consciously optimistic nation. It *was* a one-crop nation. Furthermore, it had been subjected to famines, on and off, for a century prior to the 1845 disaster. On 16 separate occasions between 1800 and 1845, local and even national crop failures had caused terrible pain. "Thus," writes Cecil Wood Smith in her detailed history of the famine, "the unreliability of the potato was an accepted fact in Ireland, ranking with the vagaries of the weather, and in 1845 the possibility of yet another failure caused no particular alarm" (*The Great Hunger,* 1962, p. 38). What happened was a famine so fantastic that literally millions starved, and other millions emigrated. It lasted for years. There has been no sustained increase in population in Ireland since the end of the famine, so shocking was it to those people. They had been lulled by recurring disasters into imagining that another one was just "famine as usual." It was not taken seriously. Complacency eroded their ability to take action and diversify their crops. Men are creatures of habit, and sometimes habit can kill you.

The Subsidies with Strings Attached

We know how the weather follows socialist nations and plays havoc with them. We are amused by the endless *Pravda* forecasts of a bumper crop of Soviet wheat, and we are upset when they buy grain from us when the bumper gets smashed on the way to the Kremlin. The fact is simple: bad weather is the farmer's age-old foe, but a free agriculture allows for flexibility needed to rebound. A free society places a premium on entrepreneurship—successful forecasting and planning—which in turn encourages some men to plan for one crisis, some men another, and some for perfect weather. Some win, some lose, but the nation eats. Agriculture is decentralized.

Nevertheless, we must never think that the existence of a free market agricultural system guarantees good harvests if other sectors of the society are not free. We may point to the New Deal, as many have, and say that free agriculture lost its most precious heritage in the 1930's. That would be a mistake, I think. The origin of agriculture's most pressing problem was not the New Deal. The origin of the Achilles' heel of American agriculture came in 1862, the year the Federal government established the Department of Agriculture. In the same year, Sen. Justin Morrill convinced his colleagues to pass the Morrill Act, which gave each state the right to claim 30,000 acres of Federal land for each Senator and Representative, if the land would be sold and the money used for the construction of land-grant colleges— agricultural and mechanical colleges. The same bill had been introduced by Morrill in 1857, and President Buchanan had vetoed it. Now, for the first time in American history, the Federal government had entered the field of higher education with a direct subsidy. (Obviously, West Point had come earlier, but that involved buying military talent to be used by the national government.) Morrill's other act, the tariff of 1861, was passed after the South had left the Union; it reversed a generation of low tariffs and economic freedom. The Civil War was the turning point on the American road to socialism; the New Deal was merely the beginning of the straightaway.

The land-grant colleges, by setting a precedent for Federal subsidies to education, were bad enough. But the content of the course work in agriculture has led, decade by decade, to the erosion of America's soil. Agricultural advancement was turned over to the B.A.'s, then M.A.'s, and finally the Ph.D.'s in agricultural research. They have accomplished for agriculture what the Ph.D.'s in every other state-subsidized academic discipline have accomplished: disaster with footnotes. Additional appropriations were made in 1890 and 1907. The Hatch Act of 1887 provided funds for experiment stations, and thereby shifted some of the emphasis to research in preference to teaching.

The Department of Agriculture, through its county agricultural agents, its data gathering, and its short courses in modern farming, established a tradition of "good" socialistic benefits that gave its operations legitimacy. Then came the New Deal, when the leadership was taken over by the most extreme leftists of the New Deal, including the infamous "Ware cell," made up of such luminaries as Harry Dexter White, Alger Hiss, Laughlin Currie, and others. Its Secretary was Henry Wallace and his advisor was Rexford Guy Tugwell. The precedents had been set; the rest was simply a matter of time and ideology. We no longer have truly free agriculture.

Sir Albert Howard's great books, *The Soil and Health* and *Agricultural Testament,* both of which should be read by anyone seriously interested in buying rural property, chronicle what has happened to agricultural research by state-subsidized, tenured, self-certified, Ph.D.-laden experts. By relying on hybrid seeds, commercial fertilizers, and the mining of the soil, they have led the modern world into an incredibly precarious position. The land is a living thing, and its power to maintain a balance under man's careful control has now been seriously weakened. Trees that required spraying once a year in the 1930's in the San Joaquin Valley in California now require half a dozen sprayings to keep the bugs away. And with each spraying, Cesar Chavez can claim that the farm laborers need his union to protect them from unscrupulous agribusiness farmers. (The smart ones in the fields have chosen pesticides and the tender mercies of the Teamsters Union in preference to Chavez's union, in election after election.) American agriculture has become totally dependent upon chemical fertilizers and imported nitrates to survive commercially. The quadrupling of prices in 1974 of nitrate exports from North Africa paralleled the quadrupling of oil prices. The West *has* to pay. (The trouble with Washington is that the immense quantity of fertilizer that it sends us is fake, like everything else in town. It smells awful, but it won't grow anything.)

I have never seen a textbook in American history that had a single bad word to say about the Morrill Act of 1862. I have never seen a bad word written about the educational services of the Department of Agriculture. Van Gorder's book praises tariffs, praises the county agriculture agent, praises agricultural data-gathering by the Feds. Then he criticizes the drift into socialism. Amazing, isn't it? The string attached to Federal agricultural subsidies was very long; it has now become a tightrope.

The Hybrid Disaster

Breed a donkey with a horse and you get a mule. A mule works hard for a while, but it proves to be sterile. Farmers over the millennia have understood that the strength of the mule should not be viewed as a good reason for saving money by killing off their donkeys and horses. We should be thankful that when the first mules were born, the discovery was not made in the animal husbandry department of an American land-grant college. They would have recommended shooting horses and donkeys.

Unfortunately, the development of hybrid grains has been one of the most ballyhooed products of university research. Back in the early 1960's, the Federal planners were shouting the praises of the "green revolution" that was going to feed the world. As always, there was (to quote W. C. Fields) an Ethiopian in the fuel supply. The new, high-protein, high-yield hybrids required lots and lots of fertilizer, and the poverty-stricken foreign farmers who were supposed to benefit from these crops were unable to afford them. A few backward nations did adopt these revolutionary seeds. Then came the oil cartel and the nitrate cartel. There went the green revolution.

Modern agriculture is, like all other industries, highly dependent on technology, capital, and educational advancement. But by creating a system of state universities, the tenure system, faith in academic certification, and Federal agricultural agencies to disseminate this information, we have created a *monopoly of information*. The university professors and USDA researchers are not entrepreneurs; they are subsidized and protected bureaucrats. They control access to most of the media. Prior to 1965, they had an overwhelming monopoly, and it was only the *total* distrust which grew out of the counter-culture and peace movements, coupled with an older, more traditional distrust of the experts by conservatives and organic gardening "cultists," that has offered any alternatives. Why should we expect socialistic, tenured agricultural education to be any less narrow, any less biased, any less resentful of outsiders and "amateurs," any more willing to compromise, and most of all, any more willing to depart from the methodology of the Ph.D dissertation, than any other educational monopoly? Why should agricultural research be any more immune to the lure of grants, advancement, and consulting fees from huge multinational firms? Why should we expect the big agribusiness donors to political campaigns, which involves the oil firms that produce petrochemical fertilizers, to put up with anti-commercial fertilizer experimenters in the USDA?

The problem is not that socialist research is totally uncreative. The problem is the specialized approach involved in all research guilds, for when this is combined with tenure, subsidies, and licensure (B.A., M.A., Ph.D), it creates one-way tracks to disaster. Such a disaster is the hybrid seed. The press mentions the problem occasionally. The *Los Angeles Times* ran a front-page special interest feature on June 4, 1974, which spells out the problem. It was never mentioned again, so far as I know. The story is indeed scary. There is an international erosion of genetic material going on in the plant world.

Seeds of Destruction

For as long as man has walked the earth, plant life has flourished. Species produce innumerable variations, each with its own weaknesses and strengths. Consider apples. At the turn of the century there were 6,000 different American varieties. But with the extension of mono-crop, mono-seed agriculture, apples now have only about 100 varieties.

So what? We can do without all those varieties, right? Wrong. In the endless competition between each variety and its natural enemies—insects, blights, disease—there is a constant give and take. Scientists are only now coming to grasp the implications of this fact for modern, specialized agriculture. Plants and diseases in their natural state develop resistance against an invader or a host's resistance. A blight may hit one variety, almost destroying it. But the invader is never entirely successful. The survivors breed descendants that resist whatever new strength the invader had. Sooner or later *any* variety can be hit and decimated, but it goes on. Give and take persists. Meanwhile, there are other varieties to eat.

Except with hybrids. Scientists have discovered what the organic gardening people have said for decades: all hybrids are risky. They do not always reproduce. Even when they do, modern agricultural methods dictate that a whole new batch of seeds be ordered each year. Farmers do not plant with seeds produced, year after year, on their land, in their region. A new hybrid may be introduced on a national scale, become popular, and replace the other varieties in different regions. These are the seeds of destruction.

In 1970, a disease called T cytoplasm finally found the vulnerable spot in American high-yield hybrid corn. "We were sitting around fat, dumb, and happy," reports Dr. William Caldwell, a geneticist of the USDA. "The hybrids were producing well and all of a sudden the disease hit. We didn't believe it could happen, but it did." Indeed it did: by the end of the season, 15% of the nation's corn crop was lost. In some regions of the South, it was 50%. (Another example was the durum wheat crop of 1963-64. A virulent new rust destroyed 75% of the crop.) What if it happens again? "In 1970 I knew we would make it because there was a year's supply of corn in reserve," said Dr. H. O. Graumann, director of agricultural research at the USDA. "We just don't have that cushion now." Furthermore, it now appears that hybrids are far more subject to plant diseases than non-hybrids.

In previous crises, we simply ordered new seed crops from *underdeveloped nations* that had not adopted our commercial techniques of mono-variety seeds. These primitive regions served the West as living storage banks of resistant genetic material—alternatives in a time of crisis. Now they are almost gone. For example, Afghanistan served for decades as a storage bank for wild wheat. In the 1960's a drought hit that tiny nation, and American famine relief agencies went into action. The United States shipped tons of emergency flour to them. Realizing that they had no need to worry about starvation, the Afghanistan farmers promptly ground their own wheat into flour, confident that they could get fresh seeds from the U.S. They could and did. So much for *that* wheat genetic tank. Robbed by the unthinking foreign aid experts.

India and Pakistan have adopted Western wheats since 1965. According to the report (it seems unbelievable, frankly), in 1965, there were 25 acres, total, in both countries that were devoted to Western wheat. It is now 25 million acres. In Ceylon, 90% of the rice crop is planted in three or four varieties, supplanting literally thousands of local varieties.

The USDA has a germ plasm bank of 100,000 plant varieties in Ft. Collins, Colorado. Some critics have stated that its collection is unsystematic and haphazard, which I can certainly believe. The budget has not increased since 1958 for this project. And if a blight should hit a key crop, and the USDA had the only known alternative genetic strain—well, I leave it to your imagination what the possibilities are for Federal planning and distribution of this particular capital good.

Even more pessimistic is the position of this country as far as the origin of its seeds. With the exception of the cranberry, the artichoke, and the blueberry, every other American food crop has its base somewhere else in the world. "Thus the United States, with the largest food production of any nation, is extremely vulnerable to an epidemic attack on a food crop for which it may have no stocks to breed resistance." Our only joy may be that in some future crisis, nobody else has any alternatives, either.

Part of the problem is the fault of the free market. The market is no better than the decisions of the consumers. If men want one kind of corn, with tidy looking single rows, that is what they will pay for, and this is what farmers will supply. The overconcentration of population in urban centers—made possible by state-financed highways and other forms of transportation, made possible by below-market priced public utilities, made possible by welfare checks that keep people in the area that they were working in when they (or their grandfather) lost their job—has led to crops selected in terms of ease of packaging, durability and long life in shipping, and visual appeal. It is possible that the free market might have led to our present crisis anyway, but without state agricultural colleges, Federal agricultural information, tenured experts in nutrition, and foreign aid to the underdeveloped world conducted on a State-to-State basis (rather than by an individual-to-individual or church-to-church basis), it would not have happened so rapidly. There would be more alternatives around.

Conclusion

A farm is a good investment. A farm that avoids the use of hybrid seeds, only one variety of non-hybrid seeds, pesticides, chemical fertilizers, and imported nitrate fertilizers, is more likely to be productive in a crisis. A local crop produced by locally developed seeds that have stayed competitive with their natural enemies: this should be the goal. Diversify. Avoid mono-crop agriculture. Plan for the crisis market that is likely to come, not the commercial one expected next year. As with all other investments today, avoid the phrase: business as usual. We have had our warning with the corn blight of 1970. Let us not ignore it, the way the Irish ignored their warnings. They, too, were a mono-crop nation. Do not eat your planting seeds; have a reserve. We have to do better than the USDA or we may starve.

"Give us this day our daily bread" is not an idle prayer for children. We may be reminded of this fact within our lifetimes—or deathtimes. For a free brochure on buying and planting non-hybrid seeds, write "Seeds," P. O. Box 6421, Tyler, TX 75711.

Chapter 25

OVERSPECIALIZATION

We are living in a time of increasing nihilism. The thirst for destruction is a religious phenomenon. Henry Miller, the self-proclaimed obscene author, years ago called for "the time of the assassins"—a time of tearing down—and we may be seeing his hope coming true. We are not facing merely extortionists today; we are seeing what may be the cutting wedge of a new round of terror, waged by men who appreciate terror for its own sake. If they are after money, it is money that will buy more terror. Unlike the Mafia, these new assassins are not after money as such. In short, they can be neither bought off nor reasoned with. They are the ultimate domestic danger. If they should be temporarily successful, they would bring on martial law, with all the accompanying loss of freedom, wealth, and efficiency that military and semi-military regimes necessarily involve.

The Western world is incredibly interdependent economically. The extensive division of labor internationally is the source of our massive productivity. But consider: Could you, through your own skills, keep yourself and your family alive? Could you survive apart from this division of labor? Most of us, if we are honest, would have to answer no. (And the person who answers yes may not be figuring on the arrival of his in-laws, cousins, and neighbors, not to mention the tax collector, to absorb his productivity.) The economy is like a huge machine; it may be able to run with a few of its parts malfunctioning, but there comes a point when it breaks down. Or to use Miss Rand's analogy, Atlas shrugs (or is put into jail for violating an EPA ordinance).

The smooth operation of this machine rests upon certain fundamental assumptions and practices: respect for contracts, stable or slowly moving prices, social peace, insurable (predictable) limits on disruptions, low tariffs, and the absence of innumerable government controls on production and trade. But we are steadily seeing the erosion of all of these supporting factors. We are seeing the construction of a so-called risk-free society, in which every person, from the Penn Central executives (but not stock and bond holders) and the Franklin National Bank executives (but not the stock holders) to the endless welfare recipients, is told that he is basically safe from his own miscalculations. Those who are willing to bear the risks and pay their own freight, are now saddled with everyone else's risks and freight. *The risk-free society almost certainly guarantees collective disaster.* We can insure against theft; we can't insure against life. Not without dying, anyway.

If these underpinnings are destroyed—self-reliance, honesty, stable money, etc.—then we would be utterly foolish to expect the fruits of the division of labor to continue. They won't. We will see the steady erosion of our economic opportunities, which means the erosion of our wealth. Now, however, we face an even greater danger: not just a steady erosion, but a revolutionary break. The ultimate discontinuous event in an industrialized society, I should think, is the detonation of a nuclear device in a major city. The disruption is unthinkable. So we don't think about it. But the effect would be economic paralysis, not just in the threatened (or former) city, but in every city, every job, every case in which men had relied heavily on the money, the information, or the production of that major city. Remember: ninety-five percent of Americans are urban and suburban dwellers (although for the *first time in U. S. history,* the demographic shift back to rural areas started in the early 1970's).

The Alternatives: We are headed in the direction of breakdown. If monetary inflation continues, as I am certain it will, the whole fabric of trade will be threatened. Price and wage controls will be reimposed. Down goes the division of labor. Down go the long-term capital markets. Down goes personal productivity and therefore personal wealth. Up go real prices (black market prices), including all those "luxury" items not under price controls: jewelry, gold and silver coins, art objects, antiques, used goods, and "junk." These will be the only markets performing even reasonably well—the place where intelligent men's capital will be located. (And the more crucial these markets are for supplying people's most important economic needs, the more likely the participants in these markets will be labeled "unpatriotic." Now is the time for intelligent investors to decide for themselves what the word "patriotism" ought to mean. One's psychological stability may depend upon it. Does patriotism mean uncompromising allegiance to fundamental American principles, or does it mean allegiance to the messianic political State? It would be easy to say that what's good for me is automatically good for the country, but very few of us really can defend ourselves from criticism—self-criticism, criticism from our children, criticism from our neighbors—by an appeal to pure anarchism. Most conservatives *do* think of themselves as patriotic. What do *we* mean by the term?

Warning: don't try to figure this out *after* the crisis on some ad hoc basis! Act in terms of principle—informed principle—*now*.)

If monetary stability should reappear, however, there will be a recession, followed by a depression the likes of which we can barely imagine. Any talk about a "rapid recovery" from a year or two of monetary stability is whistling in the graveyard. There are so many government controls (to "protect" us from depression), so many regulations, trade union controls, government-protected cartels, minimum wage laws, capital controls, and so on, almost endlessly, that monetary stability will not save us from disaster. Monetary stability, in the face of earlier predictions and actual corporate plans for more monetary inflation, will break the companies that planned for monetary inflation. What is needed is fully flexible prices and flexible labor and capital markets. What is needed, in short, is *economic freedom*. But that is precisely what we have lost for the last forty or sixty years. There will be cries for more aid from the government, more controls of vested interests, more Federal action. The philosophy of government intervention is today a religion throughout the world. Men will turn to their favorite idols even when the idols are collapsing. Men are pragmatists; they will not be forced into a new religion until there are no more possible or even hypothetical avenues of escape from further economic disaster. More public service, more government money to housing, agriculture, education, etc. More, more, more: mostly more money. They will inflate. That is their only option, *given* the fact that *the cure for depression is two-fold:* stable (or declining quantity of) money *and* full economic freedom and price flexibility. They will not give us the latter.

There are no *politically* acceptable cures for inflation. To cure inflation we would have to suffer a massive depression *and* return to economic freedom to pull ourselves out of it. There is no way we can have the necessary economic freedom unless there is a radical shift in public opinion. That shift is not evident anywhere on earth. Every special-interest group will claim its patriotic right to protection, its constitutionally guaranteed right to survive. Business as usual—meaning government intervention—will be seen as true patriotism. The medieval guilds did not give in to the modern capitalist free market without a centuries-long political struggle. Neither will today's medieval guilds. When you see the National Education Association call for a return to private education and competitive wages, as well as the abolition of teacher licensing, then you will know that the psychology of the messianic State has been broken. Then, *and only then,* can the policies of monetary restraint and balanced budgets work to bring us back into a more stable economic environment.

There is only one way we can guarantee a stable economy: permit individual freedom ("instability") of choice. Without this, no panacea, no magic formula, no econometric model, no political program, no return to gold, no abolition of the Federal Reserve System, can be expected to produce anything except a depression, followed by political repression and reinflation. The problem is in the hearts and minds of citizens, not simply in some temporary, easily fixed gimmick in the economy.

Don't confuse symptoms with causes. The *symptoms* of our unenviable plight are manifold: fractional reserve banking, legal tender laws (the *real* monetary problem), monetary expansion by the Federal Reserve System, the monetization of debt, trade union controls that are guaranteed by Federal legislation, tariffs, the regulatory commissions, and so forth. The *causes* are far deeper: the faith in government as a director of the economy, the faith in government as a competent and moral redistributor of people's wealth, the confidence in econometric models (this confidence, by the way, is beginning to wane), the rejection of the idea of personal responsibility for one's economic actions, the antagonism to the right of profit. You cannot "tinker" away the causes. *The causes are moral and intellectual.*

Intelligent investing absolutely demands intelligent assessing of cause and effect. Don't be misled. Don't swallow "conservative" panaceas any more than "liberal" panaceas. Panaceas are only making us sicker. They keep our attention focused on the periphera of economic life. There is no magic wand. There are no magicians. There are a lot of self-proclaimed magicians, and from time to time, their magic tricks work. But any investment scheme that is not grounded on a realistic assessment of the true conditions of the world is guaranteed to fail. The problem, to quote Shakespeare, is not in the stars. The problem is in ourselves.

Markets: The *technical* foundation of our wealth is the whole system of economic institutions that have been constructed on the *moral* foundation of our freedom to choose. These institutions are our markets: for labor, for capital, for property (including intellectual property). Markets constructed in terms of one set of conditions—the conditions of economic freedom—cannot possibly function efficiently if these conditions are changed. But if they do not continue to function efficiently, our wealth will inevitably be eroded. Should they break down rapidly, the loss of wealth will be extremely rapid. This is always the threat to specialized production. When the conditions change for the worse, i.e., when government intervention increases and personal freedom decreases, or when revolutionaries blow up power stations, then the former specialization is found to be *overspecialized* under the new conditions. As Adam Smith pointed out so long ago, specialization is limited by the extent of the market. Economic controls reduce the extent of the free market. So does violence. Therefore, economic controls and violence reduce specialization's profitable role. There has to be *retrenchment*. That's what 1929-39 was all about from an economic point of view: retrenchment in the face of overspecialization. It reduces one's wealth. It destroys one's expectation of increasing opportunities. And, most importantly, *thwarted expectations* are the stuff of *revolutions*.

We are witnessing the steady compromising of international and domestic markets. Mass inflation, coupled with politically inescapable price ceilings, will break them; monetary stability or contraction, coupled with politically inescapable price and wage floors, will break them. *There is no way out: the division of labor will fall, and productivity will fall.* Long-term credit markets, right now, are being broken by price inflation expectations. Yet the presence of these markets has helped to create the mass production which all of us enjoy, and even more important, all of us *expect as a matter of course*. Ortega y Gasset's *Revolt of the Masses* long ago characterized our mass culture as one based on a shared delusion: that civilization is somehow automatic, rather than a thin veneer over potential barbarism. So it is with most of us: we assume that long-term capital is automatic, and that the fruits of mass production can be maintained in the face of radical economic and social change.

The prospects for gold: The prospects for gold are bad. They are only better than everything else. If you don't think this way, you're bound to be disappointed. Your pieces of yellow metal offer advantages over pieces of green paper, but they are no substitute for lost freedom or lost monetary stability. The metal always has a market, but sometimes the market may be illegal, or rigged locally (lack of information), or heavily controlled by the government. Not everyone recognizes the value of gold, which means that the market can be narrow, especially when a breakdown makes communications and transportation expensive. What gold offers, above almost anything else, is continuity. Ten years from now, gold will be valuable. Maybe it won't be as valuable as it is today, but it will retain a good chunk of its value. It might be worth more in terms of purchasing power. Gold doesn't offer miracles; it offers the longest track of success record in man's financial history. That should be worth something to you. But don't overestimate it. It performs well in inflationary and military crises, but we would all be better off without gold and the crises.

The happy talk of "profits" with gold at $1000 per ounce are misleading daydreams. When gold climbs above $1000 per ounce, you are no longer measuring the appreciation of your capital; you are watching the destruction of confidence in a whole civilization—a civilization constructed in terms of honest governments, honored contracts, and limited indebtedness. You are charting the destruction of the division of labor.

I have no doubt that a few gold coins will buy lots of big, shiny, gas-guzzling automobiles in days of mass inflation. But the reason gold will buy them is because they are a luxury no one can afford any longer. Their value falls because they are no longer seen as useful to a majority of buyers (or even the formerly wealthy minority). I have no doubt that a few gold coins will buy several rental properties in downtown Detroit. Big deal. Who would want such property? But I have doubts about the "gold to productive, safe, comfortable farm land" ratio. It will be a lot better than the "paper money to productive, safe, comfortable farm land" ratio, but don't be naive. Urban Germans did not buy off endless numbers of productive farms in 1923 with a couple of British gold sovereigns; they bought food and paid their taxes and rent. They survived. But they could not buy up all the farms. Farmers were not stupid. What would they do with the gold coins? Move into Berlin and rent an apartment? Would you have sold a farm under such conditions? Again, don't be naive. Economic naiveté is not profitable.

The institutions that have provided us with our historically unprecedented wealth will not be functioning efficiently under the conditions that are usually prophesied by those who promise a golden age for those who own gold. Had nations never inflated, had gold been the voluntary coin of the realm (if that is what people want), had there never been legal tender laws, had economic freedom been preserved first and foremost in men's hearts, then we would now be experiencing the highest possible "gold to consumer goods" ratio. That ratio would be far higher than any "gold to consumer goods" ratio imposed today (and by imposed, I mean imposed by voluntarily acting economic actors, i.e., *market*-imposed), even if such an imposition were politically possible. We cannot erase a half a century of monetary insanity. That insanity has reduced our freedom and our wealth. We are not able to return at zero cost to a wholly new world of freedom. We cannot buy back economic paradise with a bag full of double eagles.

Black markets are not efficient. They are more efficient than government-controlled markets, but they are less efficient than free markets. Remember Prof. Ben Rogge's warning: if any economic escape hatch proves to be popular with large numbers of citizens, governments will seek to control access to that escape hatch. We are not going to see contracts written in terms of gold; at least, we are not going to see them upheld in the courts. Paper money will still be legal tender. Gold will be a valuable commodity, and a good black market exchange medium, but it will not be the legal "coin of the realm." Therefore, do *not* expect your wealth to increase simply by the mere possession of gold coins. Expect it to decline less disastrously than the wealth of those who have not bothered to collect some coins. There will be no handy supermarket dispensing shelves full of mass-produced wealth, simply because there will be no universally accep-table monetary unit, no courts willing to defend private property rights, no confidence that the authorities can protect store owners and suppliers against theft and revolutionary violence. The structure of *mass production* rests on *institutional confidence,* and this is precisely what is being broken by the same forces that are driving up the "paper money to gold" ratio. If gold continues to go up, then confidence in the prevailing institutional arrangements will go down. That will destroy the productivity of our markets.

Strategy: One short-run approach (six years or less) is a policy of *compensated leverage.*It is possible to assume a debt for the purchase of land, tools, supplies, and education, on the assumption that you will convert a portion of your present assets—gold coins, silver coins, gold mining shares, art objects, etc.—into paper money, and then use the added paper money to pay off your debts. This enables you to buy at today's prices. Assets that will be productive in terms of a reduced division of labor will be expensive, even in terms of coins, in five or eight years. You would probably be better off to use some of your pro-ductive assets today to put a down payment on another asset that will be vastly more productive in the future.

The best hedge against inflation, depression, revolution, and mar-tial law is the same: a forthright, courageous, and content commit-ment to principle. Roger Babson's wonderful little book, *If Inflation Comes* (1937), still available in used bookstores and in Good Will stores, put it best: "Most important of all, one should use his time and money to prevent inflation before it comes and store up health and courage to carry one through beyond the period of stabilization." Things may look pessimistic for the coming thirty years, but in the long run, the Keynesians are all dead; God, and the work of the people of God—the remnant—continue. We, or our grandchildren, will win this battle. We may not see it, but that should not reduce the pleasure of doing our work today. We are *lock-pickers,* jiggling at the lock; if we can't get it open, we can train up those who will replace us. Even-tually, the door will be opened. Let us be realistic about the future: it will be hard and bright, like a precious stone.

Chapter 26

TERRORISM

Development of atomic explosives that could be carried in backpacks has prompted the Federal Bureau of Investigation to devise contingency plans to evacuate major cities and impose "modified martial law" in case of nuclear threats by terrorists.

U. S. News & World Report
(June 4, 1979)

One of the concomitants of political disintegration, at least in the last two centuries, has been the increase of terrorism. Small groups of dedicated, ideologically committed nihilists strike out at the symbols and leaders of a particular nation. Sometimes, these acts are part of an overall co-ordinated plan, such as Germany saw in the 1930's, when bands of Communists and Nazis competed against each other in the creation of social unrest. But in other cases, terrorist activity is the product of a purely destructive, anarchistic impulse. The terrorists are not seeking to destroy a particular society in order to replace it with a new structure. Instead, they are dedicated to the idea that all political order is anathema. Everything must be destroyed, simply for the sake of destruction. This is envy incarnate.

The Marxists have always been ambivalent concerning the uses of terrorism. They have always been aware that the revolutionary anarchists threaten the power of an expanded socialist State. Friedrich Engels, the co-founder of Communism, and the man who subsidized Karl Marx throughout the latter's career, ridiculed the anarchists in an 1874 essay, "On Authority." A revolution requires power, meaning centralized power. You cannot do without a State until the revolution is fully consummated. Thus, the Communists have been willing to use the anarchists, but they have never been willing to admit that sporadic terrorism, as such, has any long-term benefits for the prophesied revolution. Lenin made this clear in his book, *Left-Wing Communism, an Infantile Disorder*. Terrorism only has meaning within a framework of planned revolutionary violence, Communists teach.

The modern terrorist organizations, like the Red Brigades of Italy, have nothing but contempt for the official Communist parties. The fact that they would execute Aldo Moro, the socialist politician who forged the compromise that allowed the Communists into the cabinet,

210

alongside the Christian Democrats, is indicative of the thinking of the new nihilists. They think of the Communists as stodgy remnants of an earlier era. They think they are not revolutionary enough.

What are the goals of the terrorists? I wonder if they know. What must be understood by anyone who wishes to make sense of their rhetoric is that the ideal of social justice is only the backdrop for their real commitment, namely, revolution. Revolution is its own goal, its own justification. We are dealing with *the religion of revolution,* an ancient faith which preceeds the world of Classical Greece. It represents a return to the chaos cults of the ancient (and present-day primitive) world. These cults believed that regeneration, both personally and culturally, could come only through the *systematic ritual violation of all standards,* and some of these groups wanted to extend the chaos beyond mere ritual. Some of the residual signs of this ancient faith are Mardi Gras, carnival, and New Year. But most important is the religion of terrorism. These people really believe in the benefits of total social conflagration. Terror is the means of achieving this goal.

There is another feature of terrorism that is curious and absolutely fundamental. This is the belief that State repression can be beneficial to the cause of the terrorists. Remember, these people really believe in the rhetoric of "true" democracy, meaning the idea that "the people" must be won to the cause of revolution. If a particular government has the support of the voters, then it must be because the voters are confused. They must be alienated from their commitment to the present social and economic order. Their confidence in their rulers must be shaken. How better to accomplish this than a two-step program: 1) convince people that the State cannot protect the rich and powerful from violence; and 2) let the people taste the wrath of the State when the government destroys civil liberties. This will produce the sought-for "alienation" of the people from the present civil order. The result, they believe, will be the coming of a Stateless world.

Let it be pointed out from the beginning that Marx himself had ideas similar to this one. In his much-neglected "Address of the Central Committee to the Communist League" (1850), written shortly after the universal failure of the various revolutions fomented by groups of international revolutionaries, Marx offered the following strategy to his followers. It was a *strategy of provocation,* designed to keep the bourgeois rulers at the throats of the people. Marx wanted repression by the victorious bourgeois class over the "feudal" remnants of the pre-1848 period.

> Above all things, the workers must counteract, as much as is at all possible, during the conflict and immediately after the struggle, the bourgeois endeavors to allay the storm, and must compel the

democrats to carry out their present terrorist phases. Their actions must be so aimed as to prevent the direct revolutionary excitement from being suppressed again immediately after the victory. On the contrary, they must keep it alive as long as possible. Far from opposing so-called excesses, instances of popular revenge against hated individuals or public buildings that are associated only with hateful recollections, such instances must not only be tolerated but the leadership of them taken in hand.... Alongside of the new official governments they [the workers] must establish simultaneously their own revolutionary workers' governments, whether in the form of municipal committees and municipal councils or in the form of workers' clubs or workers' committees, so that the bourgeois-democratic governments not only immediately lose the support of the workers but from the outset see themselves supervised and threatened by authorities which are backed by the whole mass of the workers. In a word, from the first moment of victory, mistrust must be directed no longer against the conquered reactionary party, but against the workers' previous allies, against the party that wishes to exploit the common victory for itself alone.

This is a two-fold program. First, keep the violence against the old symbols and leaders alive. This strengthens the power of the workers' enemies, the democrats, but only temporarily. The second phase, the creation of workers' councils—the alternative governmental structure—is prepared by the Communists in order to threaten the power of the victorious democrats. Hatred first against the reactionaries, then hatred against the democrats. But the first stage strengthens the hands of the bourgeois parties. In short, you expand the terrorism of your political enemies in order to create a kind of "workers' consciousness."

The terrorists, however, take it a step farther. They are willing to take the brunt of the State's terror, while the Communists prefer to let the old reactionaries suffer at the hands of the State. However, a fusion of goals (Communist and terrorist) can be achieved: the Communists are perfectly willing to see the terrorists become the victims of bourgeois reaction. The sadism of the Communists combines with the masochism of the terrorists. The goal of both is to create a sense of despair and alienation among the workers, so that they will turn against the institutions of bourgeois society. It doesn't hurt the Soviets if the terror gangs create havoc among the Western democracies, even though the first victims of Soviet "justice" would be the terrorists themselves—a fact they seem to understand.

If all this sounds crazy, that's because it is. The ideology of revolution is mad. The strictly totalitarian and authoritarian states are not the ones that suffer at the hands of the terrorists. It is the weaker democracies, hamstrung by civil liberties, that cannot seem to deal with the terrorists. When repression *really* comes, the terrorists never, ever survive.

Italy

If any democracy is weak, it is Italy's. Here is the ultimate confusion: a Roman Catholic country that has the strongest Communist party in the West, a nation that never seems to be able to form a government, yet whose bureaucracy bumbles along nonetheless. Here is a nation of secret societies, dominated in some regions by the Mafia. Who could miss an easy target like Italy? Certainly not the Red Brigades.

How bad is it in Italy? Very bad. Incredibly bad. A grim article appeared in chic *New York,* the successful magazine which frequently becomes a kind of cultural wedge for the next wave of avant-garde nuttiness. Anthony Haden-Guest wrote about "The New Immigrants," who are mainly the Italian rich. These people have seen their world collapse in the last decade. *La Dolce Vita* is as long gone as Anita Ekberg's figure; she expanded, while the "sweet life" contracted. It is absolutely unbelievable.

There are three competing groups of kidnappers in Italy: the Sicilians (who are in it purely for the ransoms), the free lancers (who sometimes sell a captive several times to other "entrepreneurial groups," with the ransom rising each time), and the politicals. The politicals are the most feared. The Sicilians are regarded as gentlemen, the free lancers as amateurs, and the politicals as killers.

In 1978, a T. V. interview was conducted with an Italian lady named Carla. Her story did become a best-seller in France, but no Italian publisher wanted to touch it. She was kidnapped because she was the only person remotely related to the family that owns Fiat who didn't have her own bodyguard (her son married the daughter of Fiat's director). The kidnappers had combed the pictures in the paper of the wedding, trying to find the vulnerable person. She was held for over a month, until her ex-husband came up with the money (the intended ransom payers didn't pay). They treated her roughly, but she did survive.

Parties are limited to less than half a dozen guests, when a decade ago hundreds would be invited. Says one wealthy lady: "Your psychology changes. You don't go out anymore. If I *do* go out, I will never wear furs. I will wear something you don't see. And jewels are *finished.* I know that one day all my friends will have gone. To Paris, London, South America, New York. And I will be all alone." The exodus has already begun. Italy is averaging one kidnapping per week.

"The richer the driver, the more inconspicuous the car," writes Haden-Guest. No one wants to put on a display of wealth. They are armed. They buy bodyguards (at $1,000 a month). In their own land, the rich are going into seclusion. The radicals are systematically uprooting the rich. The Sicilians help out, too.

What is happening? The primary cause is the previous intellectual radicalization and secularization of Italian thought and culture. The State-supported schools, whether democratic, fascist, or radical, have undermined the older faith in traditional institutions. Hagen-Guest reports this incredible story. As you read it, consider the implications for Western Europe as a whole:

> Recently, I spoke to an acquaintance who had just been to a dinner party in an Italian embassy in the Middle East. During the meal, a young woman on the embassy staff announced her un-qualified support for the kidnapping of Aldo Moro. Were she on Italian soil, she added, she would be tempted to join the Red Brigades herself.
>
> After dinner, the writer expressed his surprise to the Ambassador. "Oh," the ambassador said, "we have quite a little Kremlin here."
>
> He could not, he observed, use the embassy code room.
>
> Secret stuff went by ordinary mail.
>
> What about the "NATO secrets"?
>
> The writer laughed, "What NATO secrets?" he said.

Our Collapsing Intelligence Network

In the fall of 1977, hearings were held before the Subcommittee on Criminal Laws and Procedures of the U. S. Senate's Committee on the Judiciary. Senator Orrin Hatch conducted the hearings, backed up by Strom Thurmond. Committee member Edward Kennedy was con-spicuous by his absence. I have gone through three volumes of the testimony, but Volume I gives the basic story. The story is simple, and the title of the published hearings conveys it: "The Erosion of Law Enforcement Intelligence—Capabilities—Public Security."

The key to all law enforcement, contrary to Starsky, Hutch, Mannix, and Bulldog Drummond, is the *informant*. In short, "I Led Three Lives" was closer to the truth than anything else. Without the infor-mant, intelligence-gathering dies. He may be a rival crook, or a patriotic citizen, or someone out for a reward, or an envious relative, or whatever, but without him, the authorities operate in the dark. And according to the testimony, the Freedom of Information Act of 1974 and the Privacy Act are successfully drying up informant-related data.

Mistakes have been made in the transmission of FOI-unlocked materials, and informants have been identified. For example, certain revolutionary groups will require all members to write in and ask if a file is kept on them. One of them—the informant—will receive written confirmation that he doesn't have a file on record (unless another informant has submitted information, or unless the FBI creates a dummy file). Presto: the group has identified the informant. (Testimony of former Deputy Attorney General Laurence H. Silberman.)

When the Freedom of Information Act was passed, Congress was told by experts that it would cost about $50,000 per year for the entire Federal bureaucracy to comply. (Of course, Congress was also told in 1970 that Amtrak would turn a profit in three years.) The FBI now spends $13 *million* a year, not counting litigation costs, and not counting the loss of time of 50 trained agents, plus 325 other full-time workers. Also, Silberman said that 200 additional agents had to be called in to handle the backlog.

Now, says Silberman, local and international law enforcement agencies are refusing to send information to the FBI concerning suspected criminals and revolutionaries. They fear exposure for their informants. Also, the Privacy Act threatens them, should inaccurate information be transmitted, or data that may be private under the terms of the law, and therefore illegal to transmit. Says Silberman:

> Without informants, criminal law enforcement is impossible. Former associates in the Bureau have told me that informants have been literally frightened by the knowledge that under Freedom of Information Act/Privacy Act requests these risks do occur. As a result, there have been several occasions where informants have requested the Bureau to destroy everything in the file which relates to them. Indeed, their activity in providing information of law enforcement importance has been chilled. I can't blame them.

Stuart Knight, Director of the Secret Service, whose organizaton is assigned the task of protecting the President's life, admitted that local law enforcement agencies no longer have much information in their files, and they can't transmit data to his organization. The collapse of information is so staggering that certain cities have in effect been blacked out.

> Senator HATCH. Have you ever recommended that the President not visit certain cities?
>
> Mr. KNIGHT. Yes; we have, but I prefer not to name the cities (Vol. I, p. 35).

I don't think I need to spell out the implications of this, but when the President's bodyguards are uncertain about their ability to protect the President in certain American cities because of the lack of intelligence information, things are not in good shape. Knight's people have estimated that the fall-off in incoming information is close to 60%, and that the quality of this information is also down sharply. He estimates that an *overall decline of 75%* is likely. This same figure was offered by Glen King, the Executive Director of the International Association of Chiefs of Police. Between 50% and 75% of the total intelligence-gathering capabilities of local police departments has simply disappeared since 1974 (p. 48).

The article in *New York* refers to a document which I have not been able to track down yet, *FBI Domestic Intelligence Operations: An Uncertain Future.* It has only recently been de-classified, and the author says it "makes poignant reading." In my own discussions with retired FBI agents, I have learned of the general demoralization of the pre-L. Patrick Gray agents, and the unwillingness of the present agents to risk retroactive court trials (which they must finance personally on a bureaucrat's income). It is easier to file routine reports, draw your paycheck, and let the bombs fall where they may. If you think the FBI hasn't lost its former prestige, can you name its present director?

How Soon?

The U.S.A. isn't Italy. We have a large middle class, and the very wealthy are not well known, nor are they so systematically the victims of envy in this country. There is far less impetus for revolutionary violence. Also, the failure of terrorism in the 1960's to accomplish anything has reduced the appeal of terrorism. But it is obvious that a few suicidal terrorists can cause havoc with the social fabric, once people lose confidence in their institutions to defend them. An entire social class is terrified in Italy. The social fabric is in tatters, yet there are only a handful of full-time terrorists. They have great leverage, once men's confidence in their institutions fades. *Terrorism flourishes in the midst of a spiritual crisis.* That crisis is not inspected at U.S. borders and sent back to Italy, France, or Colombia.

U.S. News & World Report (May 22, 1978) reports the opinion of one American expert in terrorist tactics. He says that "the most likely strategy would be to attack power grids, knock out vital computer centers and even shoot down commercial airliners." Walter Laqueur, one of the foremost authorities on world terrorism, reports that a shift took place in terrorist circles after the 1967 death of Che Guevara in Bolivia. "A decision was made by revolutionaries to transform the struggle from guerilla warfare in the countryside to terrorism in the cities. The idea of mobilizing the people and establishing liberated areas was abandoned in favor of small terrorist bands operating in urban areas where they had a better chance of survival and of achieving maximum publicity.''

What if the Soviet Union supplied a low-power nuclear weapon or two to some terrorist group—a nice, dirty bomb that might be believed possible for a terrorist with an M.A. in physics to construct? A *New York Times* story (March 23, 1978) revealed that a 22-year old former Harvard student with only one year of college physics designed a *series* of nuclear weapons that two government bomb makers indicated were highly credible designs. He drew them up using only publicly available information. There is enough missing high-grade uranium and plutonium (MUF, material unaccounted for) to make a "theft" story believable. The Soviets could simply watch American cities paralyzed with terror in the face of a domestic terrorism threat (after the terrorists exploded a bomb where they said they would). What is the risk to the USSR?

There are good reasons apart from terrorism to start looking for rural property. But to ignore terrorism as a real threat to the urban division of labor is naive. The threat is real, and the breakdown of the FBI makes it that much more real.

Stay tuned for the ever-popular series, "I Led One Life," the continuing story of a government official who had the chance to infiltrate the Weather Underground, and instead requested a transfer to Butte, Montana.

Conclusion

Terrorism, like crime, is not a new phenomenon. It appears whenever the religion of revolution becomes strong enough to challenge the institutions of a society whose people are losing faith in the religion which built that society. A fine book on the origins of Western revolutionary thought is James Billington's *Fire in the Minds of Men* (Basic Books, 1980).

We cannot hedge against every possible disaster, but we can reduce our vulnerability. Small-town life (at least 100 miles from any missle silo or SAC base) is less vulnerable. Give it some serious thought.

Chapter 27

HEAD FOR OUR HILLS

As I never cease repeating, men do not agree with each other. This is as true for the tightest-knit monastic community as it is of the pluralistic culture we refer to as the West. There is always room for disagreement. The advantages of disagreement in economic affairs should be obvious, but they seldom are. First and foremost, there is the doctrine of human freedom. Because men are free to think what they please, they exercise their callings, including their intellectual callings, in different ways. The doctrine of freedom informs us that no single human agency is omniscient. If we believe this, then no one has perfect or exhaustive knowledge. If Jesus Christ was not ashamed to admit that even He did not know the timing of the final day (Mt. 24:36), then why should we expect that anyone should have perfect knowledge? The old rule of the Book of Proverbs is a fine one: "Where no counsel is, the people fall: but in the multitude of counsellors there is safety" (Pr. 11:14).

The reason why people pay high subscription rates for newsletters is to gain access to a specialized form of counsel. The price of the subscriptions is high because the market is narrow. Actually, the economist would call the market *inelastic* (meaning relatively unresponsive to price changes). Lower the subscription rate, and not that many new people will buy it; raise it, and you won't lose that many subscribers. So the prices stay high. The customer is buying very specialized information, i.e., a smaller market. Indeed, some buyers of the very expensive letters prefer it this way: their competitors are screened out by the high prices, or so they think.

There are problems with this narrowness, however. Sometimes the reader thinks that one man's opinion is a substitute for his own thought and responsibility. The better the writer's predictions, the greater is this tendency to evade responsibility on the part of the readership. This is why newsletter cults develop. It makes it nice for the editor when subscriptions need to be renewed, but it places an immense burden on him, assuming that he cares about his readers' futures. The writer also faces a problem of overconfidence: his readers like what he says, and the narrow audience tends to applaud louder.

218

The skeptics have dropped their subscriptions long ago. Writers and readers lose their perspective, expecially after a long series of successes. Pride goeth before the fall.

One of the problems of being, say, a Harry Schultz or a Harry Browne, is that in the earlier stages of the bull market for gold, it was relatively easy, by following basic economic principles, to predict the *general* movement of prices, including gold's price. I did it, too. It was no big deal. The only reason we were right and the media wrong was because the thinking of a Mises or a Roepke, which most of us borrowed, was completely foreign to the popular press. Besides, pragmatism rules in the investment world, and who was going to listen to a bunch of old-fashioned economists like Mises and Jacques Rueff? In other words, when mere economic principle was sufficient to predict the general shape of the long-run economic future, some otherwise average thinkers made big reputations among a minority of readers.

But now the game is much, much harder. The pragmatists are far more alert to gold. The obvious gains are in the past; the movement of gold and silver from artificially depressed prices into the free market has forced upon the newsletter writers and seminar givers a new set of problems, mostly associated with *timing*. Now we must guess what buyers and sellers will do in the short run. We can make good guesses about the long run, perhaps, but these guesses are not good enough for those who play the short-run, leveraged markets. The traders must now face the facts of life: the skills used by the gold bugs of 1965-80—long-run forecasting of the economically obvious—are not the same as the skills of the speculator. Today, however, the successful gold bugs have larger audiences as a direct result of their former successes. When it's easy to predict the future, but no one is doing so, then by definition only a few people will listen to the prophet. (If it's easy to predict, and lots of people do so, then five minutes later, literally, the market adjusts to the known future, discounted to the present, and the game gets tough again.) Then, after the prophet has exhausted the possibilities of the obvious, he gets his large audience, and the newcomers expect his later prophecies to be just as good as the earliers ones. The more people who follow the prophet's advice, the tougher it is for him to perceive entrepreneurial possibilities, since he is now in competition with his own followers. This is why it is most unlikely that chart-watching will turn long-term profits: too many people start using the system, and it won't work any more. Anyone who has a working *system* is not apt to be writing a newsletter; he is more apt to be a floor trader on some exchange, or an expensive expert hired by some floor trader. He keeps his mouth shut, except when buying or selling on the exchange's floor.

The Prophet Speaks—Biweekly

Prophets have a problem in the newsletter business. Like the *Wall Street Journal*'s "Heard on the Street" column, space has to be filled. For the stand-up comic, each routine has to be funny; for the newsletter writer, each issue has to contain secret new facts which nobody else has figured out yet. This leads to a very serious problem: *gimmick reporting*. There is an increase of the bizarre. The prophet starts making very weird suggestions. The more chaotic the economic events, which is certainly the case these days, the less restrained the prophecies. Worse, the less resistance on the part of the reader. Fear distorts people's ability to make accurate judgments. Yet now is the time to make the judgments count. There is no clear answer to the most important question: How long until the apocalypse? There can be no single answer. In a pluralistic society, with differing skills, assets, and geographical locations involved, the question has to be: How long until *my* apocalypse?

Let me illustrate my point. In the newsletter field, Harry Schultz is one leader, at least in the gold-bug camp. His subscription price reflects this position of supremacy. Harry is a man without a country. (So is Harry Browne, psychologically.) He lives out of a post office box. His income, his success, his fame, and his subscription list are not dependent upon his residence. This is true for several of the apocalyptic letter writers. Their commitment is primarily to their typewriters, and their typewriters are portable. This fact is central to the psychological character of the apocalyptic newsletter business. The world of the newsletter writer may be very different from the world of the newsletter reader, especially with respect to long-term personal goals and responsibilities.

Not everyone can be a newsletter writer. (If everyone could do it, subscription prices would collapse—a horrifying thought!) But people tend to give a lot of weight to what their favorite letter says. The weakness of the establishment press is that they all talk to each other at parties in New York or Washington, and they all read each other's columns in the *New York Times* or *The Washington Post*. The problem with apocalyptic newsletter writers is that they talk only to people who give gold seminars. Nobody can escape this problem. Let the readers beware.

The talk finally began to shift to personal survival in these letters in 1974. But what kind of survival are we talking about? Harry Schultz wrote in letter #328 (Nov., 1974) that people should be buying long-life foods for storage sufficient for one year, a rural retreat, separate power and water facilities, gold and silver coins, skills at being self-sufficient, and books on growing food. Fine. But then comes phase two: have bank accounts in several countries. At this point, he is talking to the very, very rich who live only to preserve monetary capital, or else he is talking to people who like to sit around and daydream a lot. Accounts in foreign paper money assets are useful in a major crisis for only one thing: *emigration*. And it takes a pile of money in any account to finance life in a new country.

Emigration

Emigration is easier for a man who lives out of a P. O. box. But what about readers who act on what he says, but who are not prepared psychologically to count the costs of living abroad? Consider the Costa Rica Exodus syndrome. A nice place, I have no doubt, if you speak Spanish fluently and are a Costa Rican. Here is a nation with less geographical area than San Bernardino County in California, with a rate of price inflation of around 20% per annum, bounded on the south by Panama—Panama—and on the north by Nicaragua. It is to this "haven of safety" that conservative, monolingual Americans are expected to flee. Who or what is to protect Costa Rica if the United States should no longer be in a position to help small Central American nations against Communist infiltration and guerrilla activities? The American who makes a permanent move to Costa Rica will live in a ghetto, highly visible and highly vulnerable, for the rest of his life, probably without access to many newspapers or magazines (once the international economy goes tariff crazy and completely inflation crazy), thousands of miles from children and grandchildren, without influence politically or culturally, and without the hope of having influence in the long run. A man's labors will be for the survival of his physical capital and body, nothing more. This is psychological suicide. Jews escaping the Nazis, Nazis escaping the Red Army, and Vesco escaping the law may conceivably have been sensible in heading for Costa Rica, but it seems a bit silly for newsletters aimed at Americans to devote more than a paragraph or two to the question. [I wrote these words in early 1975, long before Nicaragua fell to the revolutionaries.]

I am told that there is a phenomenon called "island fever" which hits mainlanders who spend more than a year in Hawaii. They feel compelled to leave their isolated world occasionally and come to visit the states. Islanders can survive, but not emigrants from the states. The psychological costs of adjustment are too high. Think of the costs in a foreign nation, where the language, laws, customs, weights and measures, hopes, and first principles are different from everything in a person's history. Men can tolerate the radical discontinuity of economic disruptions far more easily than they can deal with cultural shock in a foreign land.

There are too many newsletter writers who regard some bit of foreign soil as if it were some mammoth Sun City retirement village—Leisure World in German or Spanish. While Negroes in America are trying to earn their way into the suburbs, the rich are thinking about emigrating to the ghettos—pleasant ghettos, perhaps, but ghettos nonetheless. Show me a man who has spent his life building up his capital by subduing his portion of God's world, and I will show you a man who had better not cart himself off to Sun City unless he has a good job there. With fringe benefits. Bored men are dying men; and unproductive men, if they used to be productive, are bored.

The Concept of Personal Capital

There is an unfortunate tendency to regard capital as that which can be measured by entries in a ledger. The most important capital is personal, and it involves moral standing, intellect, respect in the community, and commitment to basic principle. There are millionaires who are devoid of personal capital. When a person uproots himself, he loses a portion of this capital. This is one of the costs of urbanization: there are no well-known men ("elders") who stand as beacons of principle. Life is too mobile, transfers are too common, and no one knows his next-door neighbor. We find that urban life, while bringing the blessings associated with anonymity, upward mobility, and high income, also loses the social cement which rural life—more personal life—provides. When the external agents of social control, such as the police and the schools, begin to lose authority, there is nothing left to hold urban communities together except brute power. This is one reason for planning an escape route. But the man who abandons the city for a foreign ghetto in which he has small chance of exercising his personal capital has traded one set of benefits without getting much more in return than personal survival.

Retreat should be optimistic. It should be based on the idea that one's *total* capital, but above all personal capital, must be protected for later use. The man in the small town who has an established reputation and perhaps a thriving business should stay where he is; his leadership will be more effectively exercised locally than in some unfamiliar community. Better to die with your boots on than to die in some version of a Sun City recreation hall. (Unless, of course, you were earning a living by painting the hall.) Better to be buried in Cucamonga than in Costa Rica.

The Threat of War

We are often told that those who grew up in the 1950's grew up "under a mushroom-shaped cloud." Well, I grew up in the Fabulous

Fifties (which weren't), and if there was one problem that did not bother my generation it was The Bomb. No one paid much attention to it at all. We assumed that nobody was crazy enough to start a nuclear war. Today, on the other hand, there is a growing sense of concern over the possibility that a real nuclear exchange is possible. It is talked about in Washington, in newsletters, in books (e.g., R. E. McMaster's *Cycles of War*).

How can any of us be sure? What we do know is that the aging leaders of the Kremlin—the last of Stalin's associates in genocide—will be departing to their much-deserved eternal rewards over the next few years. Who will replace them? Middle-level bureaucrats equally committed to stabilizing the system? Military men ready to make their careers by achieving victories in foreign policy? Will the internal pressures require a war to soften up the Russian public? An external threat? Will our flight from the Panama Canal signal our position as an easy pushover? If we are afraid of Torrijos, can we challenge the Soviet Union?

The Soviets are afraid of the Chinese, for good reason. They don't want a two-front war. What if they see a means of backing us down, creating the "Findlandization" of Western Europe? This would allow them to concentrate more forces on the Chinese border. Will we back down? That's their number-one gamble. Panama makes that gamble less risky.

I'm not sure how important the Panama Canal was (is) economically. Had it been my decision, I would have auctioned it off to the highest *private* bidder a long time ago, with our rights of intervention in wartime retained. My attitude toward the Canal was like my attitude toward TVA: sell it. But as a symbol of American power, it was a dangerous thing to give away—indeed, pay them to take it off our hands—because it was given up under duress. It is now *a symbol of our unwillingness to fight,* which is the best sign for a bully that we are easy pickings.

The possibility of nuclear war increases when the costs of production are reduced for numerous smaller nations. This seems to be what is taking place today. We are, in effect, manufacturing the technology which will produce the equivalent of the Saturday night special in nuclear weaponry. When this technology spreads, as it will, the risk of some kind of escalation increases. These weapons won't go away, unless some sort of technology of neutralization is developed, which is certainly conceivable, but as yet is unavailable. If, for example, a laser beam device could be devised that would keep the warheads from going off, and the beam could be put into operation from a satellite, then there would be a way to keep the bombs at bay. But as yet, no such device is ready, at least not on our side of the Iron Curtain.

The Soviets do not have as concentrated a population and industrial base as we do. According to a dismal study produced by the Boeing Company, *Industrial Survival and Recovery After Nuclear Attack* (Nov. 18, 1976), "The U. S. retaliatory arsenal, even if devoted entirely to industrial target destruction, could cover no more than 2% to 3% of the Soviet Union and no more than a few thousand aim points. Hence, industrial installations in the USSR will survive if they are dispersed over more area or aim points than the U. S. can cover. Since its implementation in 1932, the Soviet civil defense program has established effective procedures for industrial dispersal" (p. 15). Simple, foxhole-like shelters could protect the lives of 99% of the Soviet population (p. 7). Yet this is exactly what the Soviets are actively constructing. Of course, not every Soviet citizen could get to a shelter. But in another Boeing study, *Effect of Evacuation and Sheltering on Potential Fatalities from a Nuclear Exchange* (Aug. 15, 1977), we find this estimate: "If the Soviet Union evacuates and shelters their population per their published plans, its losses in a full-scale nuclear war with the United States would be about 4 percent, or 10 million people, about half of their World War II losses" (p. 30). This should be possible in 1985.

Of course, a three-day exodus (walking) from the major cities of the USSR would be the tip-off of a coming crisis. We could go on full alert. *But if we gave them three days, they would have us trapped.* As much as half our population would die in the first nuclear exchange, assuming the Soviets went for our cities. (I suspect they would first hit our military installations.) Perhaps the only response we could make, three days after the evacuation was begun, would be a threat to use cobalt-tipped missiles, meaning permanent (for many generations) destruction of the habitable cities of Russia. But without this, they could rebuild far easier than we could.

The Russians are a captive people. They could be ordered to evacuate. On the other hand, the Soviet leaders may be fearful of what war would do to their ability to control this captive population. I don't know which way the present-day leaders would go. China's presence on the borders would be a major restraining factor. It would be a very risky bluff, if it really was a bluff, to evacuate all the major cities. But once evacuated, the Soviets would have tremendous leverage. I think we would give up Western Europe to Soviet hegemony. Western Europe would become a series of satellite nations.

Urban Crises

Another fear is a combination of terrorism, shortages induced by controls, disruptions of public utilities (both terrorist-induced and controls-induced), and the government's response, martial law. There is no way today that the FBI can monitor the radical revolutionary groups. The Freedom of Information Act has eliminated the crucial figure, the informer. The attacks on the Bureau have done their work: the bureaucrats are finally acting like bureaucrats. No younger agent will soon risk his neck. It's easier to fill out reports than find out what's really going on. There will be *terrorism*. Count on it. Random, seemingly unstoppable terrorism is frightful, and it will allow the State to tighten its grip on society—probably one of the major goals of the terrorists. And what if the USSR were to supply one of these groups with a couple of pseudo-home-made nuclear weapons? What if the Soviets made it look as though they were not involved? What if one group were to announce a detonation somewhere, and then, after it had proved its point, announced such a future explosion in the following locations: New York City, Washington, D.C., London, England, and Zurich? Bombs in these four locations could bring down the West. Most of the West's communications are located in these cities. So is the West's gold. The threat could permanently disrupt the cities. Who would live there? Who would work there? The threat could paralyze the West. The actual explosion might bring no threat of retaliation to the Soviets. We are conditioned to believe that the smarter M.A. in physics could build such a bomb, and the Federal records indicate that there is enough plutonium missing to allow the construction of such a bomb. (See the article in *New York* [Nov. 26, 1979]: "Nuclear Nightmare: America's Worst Fears Come True.")

When any of these events, or events like them, start disrupting urban life, there will be new interest in safer rural areas. This is one reason to start planning a move now. It takes time and study to begin; it takes a willingness to pay the psychological and financial price. It will be more costly later, especially as counties start erecting "no-growth" restrictions against outsiders. One bomb scare could make it very difficult to move.

The boys at the Trilateral Commission, like most of their predecessors at the Council on Foreign Relations, have ignored Soviet tactics. The old-line liberals like Paul Nitze (who served under JFK and LBJ) are now really frightened. I agree with them. If you would like a graphic demonstration of the problem, get a group together for a showing of the film, "The SALT Syndrome." It's available in a 16mm format. You can rent it for $35 from

American Security Council
Boston, Virginia 22713

I really think it would do people a lot of good to see this film. Yes, it's biased. But it's not so biased as to be completely irrelevant. It tells enough of the truth—as much as honest men can ferret out of the Federal data banks—to drive home the reality of what I have summarized earlier in this chapter.

Still, you don't have to believe in war to outline a grim picture of most of our cities. The thin veneer of civilization is just that: *thin*. We are too interdependent. We are too specialized. A monetary crisis could force the government into steps that are little short of tyranny. (See my chapter, "Blueprint for Tyranny," in *How You Can Profit from the Coming Price Controls,* 1980 edition.) You will want to be out of their way if it happens.

I want to reprint an essay that was published in the *International Wealth Protection Letter* (second October issue, 1975). It outlines my basic approach to retreats. I have not changed my views:

Retreats: Communal, Private, or What?

For obvious reasons, those individuals who turn to gold and silver for wealth protection also are likely to consider other "fringe" means of preserving their assets. Few of the gold-oriented newsletter writers have ignored the possibilities of social turmoil, martial law, price controls, rationing, and all other potential crises that would seem to confront the United States. For this reason, people who read gold newsletters have been exposed to the idea of retreats. Is it a good idea to invest a portion of one's assets in an alternative life style, which every retreat scheme necessarily is?

As a hedge against roaring bureaucratization, there is no doubt in my own mind that a *retreat property,* especially one which can serve as a rental unit, is a good hedge. A person can get tax deductions for the interest paid on such a venture (this is the one thing that governments are willing to subsidize that might conceivably be a sensible investment in an age of mass inflation: debt). Furthermore, it allows tax deductions for any repairs or used furniture installed in the rental unit. There are problems, of course: vandalism, taxes, paperwork, tenants who refuse to move out when armageddon is due, etc. But for people with limited resources, this is one way to buy a retreat property.

Another approach is to find *rural employment* that brings urban income. Mail-order businesses, so long as the U. S. Postal "Service" doesn't collapse, are one possibility. Get out to your property and begin fixing it up for the long haul. Buy what you need *before* price controls force mass-produced products right off the legal market. Begin to get used to a new form of living early. Find out who your local law enforcement people are and start getting friendly. Get a reputation for being an asset in the community; you may need local friends later.

But the question always arises: Should we buy our property outright or go in with others to reduce costs? If you think you need several hundred acres, but you don't have the capital, can the load be shared? *The division of labor is important, especially during an economic crisis.* Wouldn't it be a good idea to have others of a similar persuasion, but [with] different skills, available locally? For the protection of one's property, isn't total isolation and self-sufficiency impractical?

All of these ideas are valid. But there is one consideration that should be kept in mind: *the principle of private ownership.* One of the reasons why we are in the world-wide governmental mess we are in, is because the principle of private ownership has been repealed by the politicians. Why should freedom-loving individuals compound the already entrenched political principle of communal ownership? The key problem, technically speaking, of any socialist commonwealth, as Prof. von Mises pointed out back in 1920, is that it has no ability to calculate economic value. Without a free price mechanism based on private ownership, especially of capital goods, the socialist planners cannot allocate scarce economic resources efficiently. This is as true of the commune as it is of the socialist State, at least in principle. Only because there are outside free markets can commune leaders find out what a resource is worth. But if price controls distort external markets, how will the commune know what something is worth? Can the directors peer into men's minds and compare interpersonal assessments of utility?

The Pilgrims were forced to introduce the common storehouse in Plymouth Colony; the merchants of England who had put up the capital insisted on this arrangement. It led, inevitably, to the demand for scarce resources being greater than the supply. Families balked at being required to place their hard-earned assets in a common warehouse. Output fell and starvation threatened the little colony. Gov. Bradford was practical enough to drop the whole project despite the word from England. Immediately, the scarcity problem was solved. Production increased, and the little colony was able to pay off its debts, although it took a generation. Almost an identical series of events took place in Jamestown in this same period. . . .

When groups of like-minded individuals go into common ownership arrangements, they soon learn how unlike-minded they are. Who is to police the common pasture? Who gets to run how many animals on it? Who gets access to what firewood? How are costs to be assessed? Who deals with which local bureaucrats? Who speaks for the group, both to the outside world and to the commune's members? What if someone wants to sell out? What if the communal property is not yet paid off? *Can* any individual sell out? The old rule of the market must be understood: if a man cannot *disown* property at his discretion, then he does not truly own it. Who assesses the commune's property taxes? On what basis? How are the original parcels to be apportioned? How can the group keep the Securities and Exchange Commission out of the picture? The ownership of "shares" brings them into the picture, legally though not morally. If the incorporation of the commune involves buying a piece of the commune, then the SEC declares jurisdiction. . . .

It is far better to select a general area in which to locate, and then each family can move in leisurely, or move out leisurely, without internal group hassles or external suspicion concerning "them hippies" or "them Birchers." Not everyone will assess the imminence of the apocalypse in the same way at the same time. If the principle of private ownership is maintained, but group co-operation is seen as the long-run goal, then the best of two worlds becomes possible. Everyone pulls his own weight in his own field; more acres are plowed, under these conditions. [end of original article]

Outside Target Areas

I discussed retreating with Prof. Han Sennholz in 1978. He told me a very interesting story. He had known a German gentleman in the late 1940's who had been a teacher of philosophy in a German gymnasium in the early 1930's. (The gymnasium in Europe is comparable in rigor to one of our colleges, usually; in the 1930's, they were rigorous indeed academically.) When Hitler was appointed Chancellor in March of 1933, the man knew what could be expected. He immediately requested that he be allowed to switch to mathematics (uncontroversial) from philosophy. This request was granted. Then he began looking for a rural school to teach in. He found one a few years later. He moved before the war to a rural town in southern Germany. He bought a home, some land, some farm animals, and tools. He settled down. He emerged from the war unscathed, with his capital intact. Essen, the city he had left, had been a great industrial center. It was in ruins in 1945. The man's good fortune held out: he was only a few miles from the newly created East German border—on the West German side. He had suffered a loss of income and prestige in the 1930's; he lived better than most in the 1940's. More important, he lived.

Another point: if there should be war, colleges will probably be used as refugee centers, or hospitals, on a temporary basis. Sennholz lives in a small town 60 miles north of Pittsburgh. Where will people go after they are removed from the hospital, so-called? Probably into the larger homes of local residents. Sennholz saw this happen in Germany after the war. The authorities literally forced these homeless people (partially due to rent controls) onto private families. They came in with tape measures and decided how much space a family could "spare."

Moral: you get advantages living near a college, such as lectures, films, sports events, and stable income in the town (student and faculty money). But you take a real risk should nuclear war ever become a hideous reality. Be aware of the costs and benefits in advance. Also, you might try buying a small farm house, with a second close by—for visitors, relatives, caretakers, or just plain refugees. At least you keep them at arm's length. It would also be an insurance policy against fire in the main home in days when homes will be difficult or impossible to rebuild. A used mobile home would be a good investment.

All of this may sound ridiculous. If crises never come, it no doubt will turn out to be ridiculous in retrospect, except to those who find that they truly enjoy the quieter life of a small town or rural area close to a small town. No doubt it looked ridiculous to that instructor's colleagues when he left the full security of that gymnasium in Essen. And then there's the story of that nutty guy, Lot, who gave up swinging Sodom and headed for the hills. So if *you* decide to go, tell your wife not to look back, or if she does, carry along a barrel. Salt is a good commodity for barter in a crisis.

Chapter 28

RELOCATING

One of the most important resources I have as a newsletter writer is the knowledge in many different areas that my readers possess. As my list has grown larger, this resource has begun to pay even higher economic returns. I am now in a position to provide far better information than I could have offered three years ago, simply because my subscription list is ten times larger. If anything, I have neglected to tap this crucial resource. I have not been creative enough to get my readers involved. If I can find more and better ways to do this, I am confident that *Remnant Review* will improve. In a very real sense, each subscriber has potential access to the knowledge of others. All I have to do is to tap the right reservoirs of data.

As I travel across the country giving lectures, meeting with new people, and seeing parts of the country that I haven't seen before, I am increasingly impressed with the wide variety of environments that offer important advantages as possible retreat, retirement, and relocation centers. While I think there are a few places that are better than the others, I am impressed by the fact that there is no region of the continental U. S. that is totally devoid of relatively safe places, short of all-out nuclear war. I have made it a point to stay in touch with people I have met who live in these regions, so that I can keep my subscribers appraised of some of the opportunities.

Most of you know that I am pessimistic with respect to the economy in general, the military strength (or absence thereof) of the United States, and the possibilities for domestic violence posed by a banking or monetary breakdown. I have said, over and over, it will probably pay a man to begin rethinking his personal geographical situation. It will pay him not to remain vulnerable to the risks that most heavily urbanized regions necessarily bring.

This is the toughest advice to swallow for the vast majority of readers. They may be willing to buy some gold coins, or invest in short-term T-bills. They may be willing to buy a year's supply of food for each member of the family (rare, by the way). But when you challenge a man's geography, you challenge his whole life style, including (usually) his occupation. It is no longer simply a question of rethinking one's priorities in life. There is where few people will follow good advice. It costs too much.

Nevertheless, a few people are willing and able to move. Mostly, this means retired people. Sometimes it means younger people who are just starting out in life, although few of them subscribe to financial newsletters. But some people are at least willing to entertain suggestions. That's what this chapter is all about.

You should give very careful consideration to your present vulnerability. Nothing motivates a person to move better than coming to the realization that he's sitting on top of a time bomb.

Where Would I Go?

Because of my age and religious committments, there are certain places that I would prefer as a primary residence. You may not agree. But I'll go through several areas that I think might be suitable for you. I'll also tell you where you can find similar advice from other people who have looked carefully at these problems.

There are several features of a community that I want that may not appeal to you. One is a private school, preferably Christian, but unquestionably private, for my children. I will not send them into the humanistic, tax-supported compulsory school system. I would teach them at home before I would send them to a government school. One way you can offer home instruction to your children is to contact:

> Home Study Program
> Christian Liberty Academy
> 203 E. Camp McDonald Rd.
> Prospect Heights, IL 60070
> (312) 394-9220

The school offers a nice layer of bureaucracy between you and the local school board, since it licenses you to create your own school. This may not stand up everywhere, but at least it's something. They can offer you suggestions for beginning such a school.

I also want a community in which there is some sense of solidarity, or if this is lacking, then at least a subgroup within the community that offers this. You cannot reasonably make it alone. Also, it is unwise to rely on any one figure to serve as the focus of a community. If he dies, or runs off with somebody's wife or daughter, the community effort may disintegrate.

It's my contention that the problems of radioactive fallout are far less than the problems of immoral, ruthless, or envious neighbors. Fallout goes away after a week. The neighbors don't.

I like moderate climates. Admittedly, a fierce climate, such as in northern North Dakota and northern Minnesota, will keep away your everyday, run-of-the-mill looter, but I'm a creature of at least moderate comfort. But never forget that there is a real tradeoff: a bad climate (or better yet, a region with an overrated bad climate) may be better than 2,000 rounds of .45 ammo.

I want access to water, either underground, or better yet, from adequate rainfall. I will put up with humidity to guarantee a green environment.

With these preferences of mine in mind, let's look at some pretty good spots.

West Coast

Starting from California and going north (which is what any sane man in southern California should do), you can consider the following areas: 1) the old gold mining region of Highway 49; 2) the area around Redding; 3) the area around Eureka—all in California. Crossing the border into Oregon, coming up from Eureka, go straight north to Brookings or inland toward Medford. I've got this thing about volcanoes, so I'd prefer to be west of them. I'd go all the way up Highway 5 to Bellingham, Washington, and then turn due north to Lynden, where I used to live. This is not to say that there are no points in between; there are. But if you're going to all the trouble of moving into a safer area, why settle for less?

In the old gold mining country, there are some decent areas. One town that is a bit expensive, but which has a conservative Protestant church (the Orthodox Presbyterian Church) is *Sonora*. The trouble with the town is that its schools are not that good. Its population is 7,000. Employment opportunities aren't too good. The climate is moderate. Less than 30 minutes away is Angel's Camp, where the Chalcedon organization is located. They are in the process of getting a Christian school going. An exceptionally good research library is available to interested scholars at Chalcedon. For more information about Sonora, contact Rev. Roger Wagner, 21948 Crystal Falls Dr., West, Sonora, CA 95370.

The town of *Anderson* is not somewhere you would normally pass through. It's about 10 miles south of Redding. At the Northstate School is an exceptionally gifted teacher, Rev. C. W. Powell. The school's tuition is quite low, the community is small (lower middle class), and there is a decent church, which Rev. Powell pastors. But the main advantage is the high quality education available for children, K through 12. For more information, contact Rev. Powell, c/o Northstate School, 1195 N. Balls Ferry Rd., Anderson, CA 96007.

The California and southern Oregon coastline is beautiful,

relatively safe (especially from radioactive fallout), and somewhat depressed economically, due to their dependence upon logging, which faces real trouble. The school problem is a real one. The area around *Eureka* at least has the facilities of Humboldt State, which makes some kinds of academic and cultural activities available. For people who are looking for a small town yet who don't want to go "cold turkey" culturally, a college campus in the area will ease the transition. You get the benefits of urban culture without being in a city. If the school is not too large, you reduce the traditional town vs. gown conflicts that have plagued universities since about the 11th century. Farther up the coast is *Brookings,* and halfway up the Oregon coast is the quiet little oceanside town of *Florence.* I think these are good retirement areas.

At the very northwest corner of the U. S. is a unique little town, *Lynden, Washington.* It's about 3,500 in size, within walking distance of the Canadian border. Because of its overwhelmingly Dutch population, it is clean, efficient, and even a bit picturesque. Its climate is a bit chilly, but the people are solid. There are Christian Reformed churches everywhere. "Gentiles" (non-Dutch) will always be outsiders, but the people are friendly and ready to help in a crisis. They are farmers, especially dairy farmers. The schools are good—one of the few towns in America where the private school enrollment is larger than the government school enrollment.

Now, I'd like to talk about Paradise. Well, almost Paradise. There is one area of the U. S. that is still relatively inexpensive, lovely, and has a very fine climate. It's a freak of nature. More precisely, they are freaks of nature. They are the *San Juan Islands,* off the coast of northern Washington. It rains far less, the islands are a separate county, and potential rioters will have to stand in line to catch a ferry to get to the islands. Orcas is beautiful. If you want a marvelous vacation, spend a week at the Rosario Inn on Orcas. But there is one aspect of any island paradise that must be considered: in a true social collapse, goods will not flow in, and pirates might. Piracy is no joke. It is on the rise on the east coast. Killers will pull up beside power boats, dressed like amateur boat people, ask to get on board, and then murder those on board. Then they steal the boat and use it for drug running. But I still regard the San Juans as the finest place in America for a retirement home if you're willing to put up with a slow pace of life. For a summer place, it's gorgeous geography. (I've held off telling people about the San Juans for 5 years. I didn't want to spoil a potential paradise by raising prices when I lived in the West. But I'm convinced that few people will ever go there permanently, so I decided to write the islands up in this chapter.)

Of all places in the U. S., southwestern Oregon is probably the safest from the fallout. A town like Cave Junction, in the Illinois Valley, would be fairly safe. For more specific recommendations, you might consult Joel Skousen's firm, Survival Homes: (see p. 237). Most survivalists recommend Oregon because of its climate. Warning: it is a very bureaucratic state.

Big Sky Country

The intermountain range in the Rockies offers a lot of advantages, most notably, a low population density. The cold climate of Wyoming scares away lots of people, but the energy boom is filling up places like Gillette (perhaps the ugliest city west of Newark). Northwest Wyoming is a good area. There is no state income tax in Wyoming (as is also the case in Washington state and Texas).

Montana is another good area, but they have a 10% state income tax. The one area I know something about is the *Kalispell-Whitefish* area. The Cross Currents Christian School is located in Whitefish. You can get a brochure on the school by writing to 625 Park Ave., Whitefish, MT 59937. A real estate contact is Jeanie Thallman, at Thallman Co., 6th & Spokane Ave., Whitefish. A weakness of the area is the lack of churches that speak to the issues of the day. In a nuclear war, there would be little fallout here.

Other areas are good from the point of view of geography, though I am unable to recommend people to contact. These areas are: Hamilton (south of Missoula) and Dillon (south of Butte).

Midwest

Northern North Dakota and Northern Minnesota are good, assuming you can stand the winters. The reason for putting up with the weather is simple: not many people will.

Northwest Arkansas is good. One survival expert who has headed to *Harrison* is Kurt Saxon. Saxon has relatives there, however. This helps. If you go into northern Arkansas, you had better be nice, friendly, and inconspicuous; these people have no particular need for outsiders. You will do things their way. Saxon's books, *The Survivor,* Vols. 1-4, are among the most comprehensive in the field. If you are serious about exploring the possibilities of self-sufficiency, I suggest that you order this set for $35. For maximum privacy, order from Privacy Publications, Box 338, Bullard, TX 75757.

The Ozarks in general provide a lot of safety for your money. They are rivaled, in my opinion, only by the Great Smoky Mountains in western North Carolina and eastern Tennessee.

Texas has one area that is ideal, the hill country, which is northwest of San Antonio. *Kerrville* has become a popular retirement center. Another nice town is *Mason.* The heat is far less in the summer, and there are rolling hills.

East Texas has water. This may come as a shock to many readers. East of Dallas there is a remarkable climatic shift. The winters get warmer, snow is not a problem, but predictably the summers are humid. Several of my subscribers and reference people have congregated in *Tyler,* the "rose capital of the world." There is a Christian school that offers Greek to kindergarteners, Hebrew to first graders, and continues upward giving first-rate academic training: the Geneva School. It is a private, profit-seeking school, but it is housed in the Westminster Presbyterian Church, 708 Hamvassy, and the pastor is Rev. Ray Sutton. Other nearby towns that are small and attractive are *Palestine* and *Rusk.* There are several large Christian organizations operating in *Lindale,* including the Agape Fellowship and Youth With a Mission. One aspect of the east Texas area around Tyler and Longview is oil: there is virtually a recession-proof economy. Even in the 1930's, the area was booming.

Texas has very low taxes, a booming economy, and a lot of energy sources. Some properties even come with natural gas rights for the homestead: you can hook up a butane power generator and be completely independent of the power companies. Gun shows are plentiful. Guns bought at a Texas gun show are not registered—a very interesting prospect.

Smoky Mountains

The border states—North Carolina, Tennessee, Georgia—offer good weather, low taxes, minimal bureaucracy, lovely scenery, low land prices, and independent neighbors. I am partial to western North Carolina and eastern Tennessee. Western North Carolina is as beautiful a region as we have in this country. The town of *Murphy* impresses me. I am aware of several families on my mailing list who have moved there. After investigating the region, I can offer it almost without reservations from the standpoint of geography. Western North Carolina is a long way from the state capital, Raleigh. *Hendersonville* is the headquarters of *Mother Earth News.* Actually, I have neglected western South Carolina, which is also fine. The tiny town (2,000) of *Cullowhee,* NC, is home of Western Carolina University, which meets the specifications of small town, safe region, and at least some college-town social events that help keep newcomers from getting the rural bends.

Jonesboro, Tennessee, is another nice town. It has a conservative Presbyterian Church pastored by Rev. Ken Gentry: Midway

Presbyterian Church, Rt. 11, Box 296, Jonesboro 37659. A major
defect is the absence of a good private school, although families in
Bristol, TN are talking about starting one. The tri-city area of *Bristol-
Johnson City-Kingsport* is an appealing one. Kodak has its chemical
operation in Kingsport, and employment opportunities seem good, at
least so far. Tennessee's taxes are lower than the surrounding states.
There is no state income tax on "earned" income, although there is a
tax on interest and dividends.

Northeast

Bad as it appears to be in this region, there are still places to go.
Central Pennsylvania still looks good to me. The towns north of
highway 80—places like *Troy* or *Wellsboro*—are far enough off the
beaten path to offer safety. In the spring and fall months, this region
is beautiful. There is a solid agricultural base, so people are not going
to go hungry. Somewhat farther south is *Lock Haven,* which interests
me because of a unique educational program that is beginning there, a
private Christian apprenticeship school, Walk-Way, operated by Dr.
Robert Barr (zip: 17745). I am convinced that without a revival of the
apprenticeship system, many craft skills are going to be lost, but those
few people who possess them will be in very high demand. (Any information you have about craft training programs of any kind,
anywhere, should be sent to me. I may even finance such a program
myself. I am very serious about this.)

The *Grove City* area is still a possibility. There is a good private
school run by Dr. Leonard Coppes, pastor of the Calvary Orthodox
Presbyterian Church of *Harrisville,* PA. He has written a chapter in
the book, *The Purpose of a Christ-Centered Education,* which is sold
by Fairfax Christian Books, 11121 Pope's Head Rd., Fairfax, VA
22030: $4.50. You can check out his perspective in that book, if you're
interested in the school. The problem with this region is the declining
economy. Land and homes are inexpensive, compared to other
regions of the country, but opportunities are limited. Also, Pittsburgh
is only 60 miles away, which could produce a problem in a major
crisis. I think that north central and central Pennsylvania are better,
geographically speaking.

Preparation

One of the best ways to find out about an area is to subscribe for a
few months to the local newspaper, especially the Sunday issue (if it's
a daily). This lets you get a feel for the region, especially prices. If
you're trying to find the name, address, etc. of the paper in some
boondock town, and you can't get the telephone information lady to

give you the name, you can get it out of the *Editor & Publisher International Yearbook,* published by Editor & Publisher, 575 Lexington Ave., New York, NY 10022. You can probably find a copy in your public library, or at least at your local newspaper office.

Anyone who is serious about the possibility of locating in a safer region should buy several books and booklets, and get on some mailing lists, so that he can find out what he needs to know.

Two books by Joel Skousen are important. One is super cheap, a little booklet that will be very useful to you, *Ten Packs for Survival* ($3.00). The other is the *Survival Home Manual* ($25). For $27, you can get both books. Skousen also sells the national survival map ($45), for those interested not in the danger areas, but in the safe areas. You can order from

> Survival Homes
> 4270 Westcliff Dr.
> Hood River, OR 97031

Skousen also offers customized survival counselling at $500 per day, plus expenses.

Two other books to consider are Les Scher's *Finding and Buying Your Place in the Country,* published by Collier Books as a large paperback. It's a guide to what kinds of questions to ask, what to look for, and where you get ruined by sellers. The second is not so well known, but is important for you if you're thinking of building an underground home (which I am doing). It's called *Earth Sheltered Housing Design,* published by Van Nostrand Reinhold ($10). Order both at your local bookstore. (If you're not aware of it, there is a series of books published by Bowker Co., *Books in Print,* which your local library or book store will have. You can look up books by author, title, or subject. It gives you the addresses of most publishers, too. Always start with this guide before you give up on locating a book you want to buy.)

The question of books brings up another touchy point. There are certain companies that sell some remarkable survival books. Unfortunately, they also sell some other books that are, figuratively and litterally, inflammatory. I have never recommended that my readers buy these books directly from the companies (the mailing list problem), yet there are books that people ought to have. *These books are not about to show up in supermarket racks,* I assure you. But who wants to get himself identified as a buyer when Feds come snooping?

I have worked out a solution to this problem—not perfect, but better than anything else I could arrange. The Texas firm, Privacy Publications, has agreed to provide the following service. It will publish an annotated bibliography of the best of the self-sufficiency books. It will stock these books. My readers will be able to order them from the intermediary firm. Each name will be coded. The master code will be kept separate from the mailing list. Only officers of the company will have access to both the master code and the list. The list will never be rented. The company, being small, will not attract attention, since it doesn't actually print the books. The specialists who have set up the company will screen the books carefully, but the buyers will not be buying directly from the publishers—firms that may be subject to Federal scrutiny. The IRS will be able to get access only to raw dollar figures during an audit—not the names and addresses of the buyers. Sales records will be separate from the membership list.

All this privacy may not appeal to you or seem necessary to you. That's fine; you can pretend that it doesn't exist when you order your books. But others will see the usefulness of the screening process they have devised. Membership costs $5. For this you will receive an annotated catalogue plus periodic updates. The fee is an annual fee, but anyone buying $25 worth of books in any calendar year will have his fee waived the following year. *You're buying privacy for $5.* Books are sold at retail, except when the firm offers special package deals. It's the *only* way to buy these items!

Privacy Publications
P. O. Box 338
Bullard, TX 75757

Chapter 29

POLITICAL SELF-DEFENSE

There are a lot of economic newsletters around, several thousand of them. They service the needs and desires of relatively small audiences, except for the really large ones like the *Kiplinger Letter*. A few of them are of the "doom and gloom" variety, and these have grown in number since the mid-1960's. Harry Schultz and James Dines were the leading newsletter writers in the goldfields, back in the days when everyone knew that the dollar would never be devalued, gold would forever remain at $35/oz., etc., etc. These men who stuck their necks out then deserve a lot of credit; they subjected themselves to a considerable amount of ridicule for the stand they took. On gold, at least, they were correct. The 1975 and 1980 drops in gold, however, took most gold advocates by surprise, myself included (not that it dropped, but the magnitude of the drop). By equating a rise in the price of gold with the collapse of Western civilization, the gold newsletters can find themselves in a bind: With gold down, doesn't this mean that things really aren't so bad? Can't the increasingly harsh warnings of the doom and gloomers be discounted, or even ignored? Isn't business running as usual? The bears and bulls are at war, as always, but isn't the system proving its strength?

Well, as they say, yes and no. The *strength of the American economy* is enormous. It should continue to be strong for as long as entrepreneurs have even a minimal degree of freedom to forecast and allocate resources in terms of their forecasts. He who underestimates the productive capacity of a free market is making a serious error. Our markets are still basically free, and businessmen still have room to maneuver. Furthermore, social change is not normally discontinuous. Habits are slow to change, and people muddle through. Take a look at Northern Ireland. We Americans can hardly imagine why or how anyone lives in Belfast, yet they do. Men have an incredible capacity to adjust to external conditions. Even the violent demonstrators of 1968 hold jobs in the Establishment today.

Let us not forget, however, that most men had jobs and went to work at the end of the German inflation of 1923. The same was true of the repressed (price controlled) inflation of 1945-48. The whole

239

German nation did not come to a grinding halt. Yet it was still disastrously crippled. Its normally productive people were staggering. And the standard of living was dreadful. So the mere existence of statistical stability is not proof that men are not increasingly hard-pressed.

So I will say it: *Western civilization is in danger*. It is in danger because the inherited religious and philosophical outlook that undergirded the rise of the West and promoted its expansion is now under fire in every major Western nation. We are being engulfed by the *ethics of redistribution,* and its means of expansion is the *politics of envy*. Whether gold fluctuates more than anyone had expected, or whether the balance of payments is in surplus, are interesting and important facts for short-run speculators. Whether men will permit their neighbors and themselves to be engulfed by today's *rising tide of bureaucracy and taxation* is a question of far greater importance over the next decade. Whether they will accept and even cheer on those who would impose price and wage controls is crucially important for both the short and long runs. We cannot expect to see the flourishing of our economic system in the face of legislation which is the product of ideas that would never have permitted the growth of Western culture had they been shared by the bulk of the population four centuries ago. Economic growth is not a one-way street. Inventiveness, apart from capital to finance the devices of the mind, will not continue to revolutionize production and consumption. And it is capital which is threatened, including the most important capital resource of all: *freedom*.

Leonard Read, the President of the Foundation for Economic Education, once remarked that he is glad that socialism does not and cannot work to improve men's economic lives, for if it did, we would be living in a perverse universe. It would be a world in which fundamentally immoral actions could produce beneficial results. Read's point is well-taken. But at the same time, it stands as a warning, for the idea of the omnicompetent State, while disbelieved by those who may live under socialism, is triumphing steadily all over the earth. The ideas of limited civil government and a truly free and unregulated market, are disbelieved even more than the idea of the omnicompetent State. Men are well aware of the incompetence of the State, but they cannot believe their eyes when they look at the fruits of freedom. Thus, the setbacks that the State has been having—in Australia, in British Columbia, in local bond elections—should not be taken too seriously. The populist trend is not undergirded by anything more than instinctive feelings that the bureaucrats should get off *my* back; but the socialist creed comes in the name of a higher morality—the "just" distribution of income—while it simultaneously appeals to one of mankind's basest and most destructive instincts: *envy*. To "pull down the rich to my level" is worth the price of forfeited freedom in the eyes of most voters today. The result is bureaucratic tyranny.

Our present economic troubles are merely a foretaste of worse things to come—a kind of down payment on disaster. What most men do not consider for a moment is that ideas *do* have consequences. It does make a difference how men view the world. The politics of envy is capable of stifling freedom, and all the computer chips, technological marvels, and innate American genius in the world cannot continue to produce efficiently in the face of this single idea, namely, that the productive rich do not have the right to enjoy the fruits of their labor. Economics will triumph over mere technology, and economics is the product of a fundamental moral position, whether socialist or capitalist. Gold is a barometer, silver is a thermometer, but *men's commitment to ideas determine the kind of world we live in.*

The Political Scene

We have entered a profoundly disturbing period of political confusion. Not since the days of the pre-Civil War period have we seen anything like it, not even in the days of the Great Depression. The political crisis is vastly more important than the economic crisis precisely because ours is a political age. Economic charts and graphs, if studied within a political vacuum, cannot tell us what is happening, for such intellectual tools operate in terms of the philosophy of "business as usual."

The Watergate crisis was real. Watergate was a watershed historically. Half a dozen nonentities invaded the offices of another nonentity, and the end result has been a wave of cynicism about political life that is, as far as I can determine, unique in American history. Why? I think it is because men were rudely forced to witness *the visible corruption of politics.* The lying, the maneuvering, the ugliness of it all simultaneously shocked men and forced them to ignore it. "Nixon got caught, but the rest of them did the same things." Quite true, and how long can men continue to put their faith in political salvation that necessarily corrupts its high priests? Anyone who discounts the moral crisis of Watergate is whistling in the dark. Men were forced by the media to look into the mirror of politics, and they saw the end product of two generations of political centralization. Bugging is bad enough, but the revelation that Nixon tried to use the IRS—one of the most feared and fearful bureaucracies in this nation—to harass his enemies did shock men. The IRS bureaucrats claimed that they refused, and it may be true, but other Presidents had used the IRS along these lines. "Oh, well, that's politics," men shrug, but men have been told by pundits and professors and priests and politicians for two generations that social salvation is to come by political manipulation. Americans lost their faith with Watergate. They lost their will in Vietnam. And they lost their money on Wall Street. They are angry, frustrated, and dangerous precisely because they no longer know who or what to believe. Discount a crisis of faith, and you have made a fatal error. There is no one around these days to give us fireside chats.

"Picking Up the Pieces"

Men who do not know what to believe or who to listen to are men ripe for tyranny, not freedom. Freedom is not moral anarchism. Freedom is the product of a basic moral commitment to let other men work out the peaceful implications of their lives without interference. *It takes moral restraint to withstand the lure of envy.* Most nations have not resisted, and most nations have stayed primitive. Men today are believers in the rightness of redistribution, despite the fact that they complain endlessly about "the bureaucrats."

The *key facts of economic life* are not technological; they are *moral* and *intellectual.* Men are left without internal moral restraints on their own passion for equality, and for this reason the modern State is running wild. There are no political vacuums, for there are no moral vacuums. *The State rushes in where the politics of envy rules.* The intellectuals and scribblers of our century have, by and large, been advocates of the efficacy of redistribution. They have helped to erode men's faith in inherited values of thrift, honesty, and self-help. Such values are "19th century" or "out of date"—in short, unworkable. The intellectuals of the salon culture of France in the 18th century performed a similar moral function, as did the intelligentsia of Russia in the late 19th century. They succeeded in calling into question the religious foundations of the culture, and then a revolution in each case captured the already swollen bureaucracies that were a part of the ancient regimes of both countries. *The bureaucrats picked up the pieces;* the faces at the top changed, but the bureaucrats and the bureaucratic culture triumphed. They knew what they believed in: institutional continuity. They had a faith. Ours do, too.

As was the case in earlier revolutionary periods, small groups of ideologically oriented men believed fervently that after the great conflagration, they would be able to "pick up the pieces." Their group's witness would convert men from out of the rubble. Their ideas would win out. In France, Napoleon won out. In Russia, it was Lenin and Stalin. The little groups disappeared from the pages of rewritten history. It was the *bureaucracy,* the *military,* the *control apparatus* which won out. Men will not live in philosophical anarchy, any more than they will live in political anarchy. They prefer power and stability. Men who believe in no ideals at all believe in stability, even imposed stability. The bureaucrats, as the agents of stability, are the survivors.

Remnant Review goes out to members of various groups that are tiny, ideologically or religiously oriented, and free market oriented. No doubt there are many like myself, who view the last four decades of political life and conclude that things can't get much worse, but if they do, they can't stay too bad for long. *Their* group will be able to pick up the pieces. Then freedom and productivity will flourish once more. It sounds wonderful. But I am a great believer in institutional stability. I believe in "business as usual," except that I think men can get used to almost anything except institutional chaos, and call it "as usual." To pick up the pieces takes leadership. It takes experience. It takes the ability to convince others of the rightness, or at least the necessity, of one's position. These attributes are what our little groups always lack, and we fall prey to the power-hunting criminals, revolutionaries, and above all, the entrenched bureaucrats.

Leisure and Localism

I am not politically motivated, and I do not pay much attention to national politics. But I do think *local* politics is vital, for many reasons. Local politics is where the bond issues are, and these are the soft underbelly of the present tax structure. In 1975, 93% of the dollar value of all bond elections went down to defeat—absolutely unprecedented in our time (First National City Bank's *Monthly Economic Letter,* Dec., 1975). Local politics is where power will count in the 1980's, for inflation will take its toll of the power and efficiency of the national bureaucracies. As the disruption of the market by price inflation and price controls forces men to rely on local services, and revenue sharing is exposed for what it really is—deficit sharing—the importance of local politics will become more obvious.

Now is the time for local groups to start gaining the experience necessary to take a position of leadership in a time of political turmoil or bureaucratic centralization. Setting up local private schools is a very important step in this process. Setting up committees to monitor the local budget and publicize it, in their own newsletters, if necessary, is another way. Each county meeting should be monitored by respectable citizens. These meetings should not be disrupted; they must be publicized. Good men should be encouraged to run for minor offices, the place where we gain the necessary experience for leadership. Forget the Senate for now; can someone in your midst win a post as a county commissioner? The bread and butter issues of our lives over the next quarter century will be made at the local level, once full-scale price controls are reimposed. Men must be available who can stand up and oppose the infusions of Federal money into a community, and local citizens must be convinced of the logic of their arguments. The glamour spots can go to those who are climbing up the political ladder. What good men need to do is to capture the less desirable posts.

How can we get good men to do it? How can men build up their own capital in a time of crisis, even to the extent of starting a second job, and serve at the same time? The only way I can see is for local groups to use the division of labor principle. Find those who can fill certain positions and then encourage them, both morally and financially, to go out and work. I think a local newsletter is a good way to start. This isn't as difficult as it sounds. Use a local print shop (like Postal Instant Press) to print up 1,000 or so. Use an IBM Selectric or its equivalent to type the original. Make it look readable. Do research on the bonded indebtedness of the local community. Nobody ever says to vote no on principle. No one ever has the facts and figures when he wants to vote no. Change this.

We can do very little to alter the drift into socialism. We can hardly convert 10 million college students and their tenured professors. We can barely get a voice for purely voluntary economics inside the Chambers of Commerce. We have to start where we are, and where we are is *local*. Find an issue that can be spoken to in terms of broader principles, and then capture the local forces on the right side of the issue. If busing is the burning issue—literally—use it to build up a private school. If welfare is the issue, battle to keep the budget in check. Find the hot issue and take it over.

The crime issue is another one. Organize a local group to go out on the week-ends and (with prior police support) offer to mark people's valuables with electronic markers. Or have them borrow the markers for an hour to mark their own (maintaining their privacy). Owners should use their driver's license number, not Social Security, since the Social Security bureaucrats refuse to cooperate with police to locate the owners of recovered goods. Then pass out a tract for the local group to stimulate interest. Or a campaign brochure. Help to set up a "neighborhood watch" organization to keep an eye open for each other's property and homes. Let people know your group is there to help.

Federal Tyranny and Local Resistance

In my speech at the National Committee for Monetary Reform meeting in New Orleans in November, 1980, I stressed the fact that the rise of single-interest voting blocs has driven the liberals crazy. Especially in Congress, the single-issue voters have flattened the traditional politicians. They can no longer hide. They have to face the grim reality (for them) of voting groups that cannot be placated if you vote against them. Too often for comfort, they seem to be equally well organized. The anti-ERA forces and the pro-ERA forces are equally noisy, as far as a Senator is concerned. Congress can't hide any more—a true political revolution. So they are trapped. They prefer to defer; specifically, they prefer to defer to the Executive or the Judicial branches. "It's out of our jurisdiction," they imply, which isn't true, according to the Constitution, but there is no issue of less interest to most Congressmen and Senators than Constitutionalism.

Congress has become paralyzed by the threat of retaliation from determined and well-organized single-interest voting blocs. This paralysis was evident when I was on a Congressional staff back in 1976, but it has now bloomed remarkably. In discussing my thesis with Dr. John Robbins, who serves on Congressman Ron Paul's staff, and who had been on Capitol Hill for several years, I got confirmation. As the pressures intensify, Congress has a tendency to jump back into bed and turn the electric blanket up to nine.

Robbins expressed the hope that the conservatives will continue to exploit their advantage over the liberals in the direct-mail field. The pioneer work of Viguerie has placed a major political technique in the hands of the Right, and the Left is only now catching on to what happened to them, especially in the Senate races in 1980's rout, as a direct result of direct mail appeals. Yet we have to be reasonable. *If anything is mobile, it's technology.* No technique is likely to remain unexploited which is rolling up political victories. That's what direct mail is doing. The Right has perhaps, a 4-year lead, but the gap will probably be narrowed. I will state it more strongly: it *will* be narrowed. There are too many people who see profit, both political and economic, in selling computers, devising mailing programs, and so forth. The market will respond. It always does.

Conclusion: Congress will not simply remain paralyzed; it will become *catatonic*. Robbins has concluded exactly what I did in 1980: the winners will be the faceless, invisible, Civil-Service-protected bureaucrats in the Federal bureaucracy. We will see *decentralization within the Executive.* Power will be deferred from the Cabinet down to the lower levels of the great bureaucratic pyramids. This is not a pleasant thought. We are already being strangled to death by bureaucracy. Yet the 1980's will become the decade of the executive order and the "unleashed bureaucracy." *The bureaucracy is out of control.* Only one thing can stop it: reduced budgets. Nothing else will work. It is imperative that *budgets be rolled back*. But they won't be. Already Republican Congressmen have capitulated to the increase of the Federal budget ceiling—capitulating, in other words, to a massive Federal budget deficit. They will not challenge a Republican President. They are going to vote for the system, and the system will become entrenched as never before.

Yes, some sections may be cut back. In freight transportation, airlines, communications, and a few other areas where price *floors* have protected monopolistic industries and suppliers, there is hope. I don't want to come on as an "all is lost" prophet. We *are* having some victories. Ted Kennedy and the liberals have begun to figure out that regulatory agencies that encourage price floors are a liability economically, and to reduce their monopolistic power may not be a political liability any more. This attitude is all to the good. But with inflation roaring, I am more concerned about price *ceilings* than I am about price floors. Here we have a long battle ahead of us—a battle which I think we are going to lose before the new Administration gets to its second term.

It doesn't do any good to bewail the world situation. I am an activist. I think you start doing what is necessary to protect your immediate family. That goes without saying. But I'm also convinced that we can, sometimes, do more than this. If we can find ways to begin to affect the political process on a local level, without bankrupting ourselves, and without engaging in futile battles, then I'm for it. But I don't want to spend my time tilting at windmills. Time is too precious. If we fight, it should be to win.

The Battle for the Counties

Where can we get the most "bang for the buck"? Where can we exercise the political leverage that can pay off in actual economic benefits, that is, in freedom? It has to be the county. The county has been neglected by politicians for too long. City politicians are in the limelight a lot more. There's more glory there. State and Federal offices also attract the power-seekers. But the county is the neglected child in American political life.

This was not always so. One historian who has commented on this point is R. J. Rushdoony, whose book, *The Nature of the American System,* first published in 1965, has an analysis of the county in early American history. I cannot resist quoting from this book (Thoburn Press, 11121 Pope's Head Rd., Fairfax, VA 22030; $3):

> But it would be a serious error to assert that the alternative to federal sovereignty is State Rights. Important as the states are, they are not the basic unit of the American system. The basic unit is clearly and without question *the county:* significantly, one of the first steps towards independence was taken by Mecklenberg County,

North Carolina, May 31, 1775, in order to prevent a legal vacuum. . . .

First, the *property tax* remained in the hands of the county, which had early established its jurisdiction. The people of an area thus controlled their tax assessor and their county supervisors, so that the taxing power was not beyond their jurisdiction. When the power to tax leaves the county, tyranny will then begin in the United States. Socialism or communism will be only a step away. The people of a county will be helpless as their property is taxed to the point of expropriation by a distant state capital. . . .

Second, *criminal law* was and is county law in essence. This was an important safeguard against tyranny and against the political use of criminal law. Law enforcement officers, including judges, were and are officers of the county, in the main, or of its constituent units. As T. Robert Ingram has pointed out, not too many years ago executions were also held at the county seat. Police power and criminal law are thus matters of local jurisdiction in the American system. . . .

Third, *civil law* is also county law to a great degree, enforced by local courts and by locally elected officials. The American citizen is thus for the most part under county government rather than state and federal government. His basic instruments of civil government are local, residing in the county, and the county is his historic line of defense against the encroachments of state and federal governments. In early America, town and county elections were properly regarded as more important than state and federal elections, and property qualifications more strict on the local level.

When was the last time you heard anyone talk about these facts of American history? I was never taught this, or at least nobody ever emphasized it, in my academic training, and I had a pile of graduate level courses in U. S. history. It has simply been forgotten by today's scholars. It has also been neglected by the politicians.

There are signs that the liberals have begun to catch on. Let me be very specific. In Arlington, Virginia, and Montgomery County, Maryland, both of which border on Washington, D. C., there are new laws on the books making it illegal to buy and sell gold coins without using a check, and without having your name and address recorded by the seller. In one instance, it requires a week's wait to get paid off. Police are to be notified in the case of a retail store buying back coins. This is to "protect us from burglars" who will try to peddle our stolen coins. The Federal government has more or less neglected gold and silver coin sales since 1975, but politically liberal counties are catching on to what is going on in the "underground economy." It is *imperative* that defenders of the limited government philosophy understand where *the last line of political defense* is: the county. It is also imperative that they become alert to developments in their county government structure that will lead to a revocation of their personal rights.

Now, let's consider the advantages we enjoy, politically speaking, at the county level. Nobody seems to care much about it. It is less expensive to pick off county offices. We can more easily organize protests against undesirable political legislation at the county level. "Support your local sheriff" is no joke. Better yet: *elect* your local sheriff.

But how do you do it? How do amateurs get power locally? That's the question.

The Technological Breakthrough

Where there is a market, there will be profit opportunities for ingenious entrepreneurs. The technology is here: the computer. The thing that we needed was this: software (programs) geared to the needs of local politicians, local political action groups, and cheap enough to let amateurs give the incumbents a run for their money. We now have the software, and it's designed to fit the most accessible computer, the Radio Shack TRS-80 (Models I and III).

This program is good for a lot of things: political action, reports on donors, political (or any other) persuasion—up to 48 separate entries. It can sort according to zip code, precinct number, or any other category you want. It enables you to identify phone numbers, the first name of spouses, whether or not the person has volunteered in the past. It enables you to crank out thousands of labels for letters in a matter of hours. It eliminates the famous "addressing parties." It is suitable for churches in their efforts to canvass a neighborhood, or businessmen who are setting up "tickler files" for making sales. The thing has been designed for use by *absolute amateurs who know zero about a computer.*

Let me give an example of what one man did, without ever "blowing his cover," in 1980. Without getting on television (expensive) or attracting public attention from potential opponents, Virginia State Legislature Delegate Larry Pratt killed publicly financed abortions in Virginia. In the spring of 1980, the State Board of Health decided to hold hearings in September on the question of taxpayer-funded abortions in Virginia. Pratt believes that someone on the Board tipped off the pro-abortion forces concerning the date of the hearings. The pro-abortionists had four months to get a conventional letter-writing campaign going, and they alerted their people to be ready to come to Richmond to attend (stack) the hearings. Pratt, as a member of the House of Delegates, did not learn of the hearings until late August. He had about three weeks to organize the anti-abortion forces.

He went down into his basement and turned on his Radio Shack TRS-80 Model I. This is now an obsolete unit, but it was good enough in 1980. Pratt had been entering names, addresses, and identifying information into the computer files for about a year. At that time, he had about 9,000 entries. He told the machine to pull out the names of all identified anti-abortionists and print them on labels. Less than an hour later, he had 3,500 labels. He then took the labels to a letter-print shop, plus 3,500 more from the statewide Virginia Society for Human Life, and had the shop stick them on envelopes.

Inside each envelope were the following: 1) a cover letter explaining what the Board of Health was considering; 2) a petition with about 10 lines for names; 3) a reply envelope to the Virginia Society for Human Life; and 4) a contribution form for donations. Elapsed time: 48 hours, from start to mailing.

What were the results? Three weeks later, 150 anti-abortionists showed up at the hearing, to the pro-abortionists' 25 or so. About 9,000 names protesting the idea of publicly funded abortions were sent back to the Virginia Society for Human Life, which went into its computer (and Pratt's, eventually). Enough money from donations came in to pay for the original mailing. The Board was sent the 9,000 names, while the pro-abortionists could muster only half as many. The Board, which had been expected to vote 7 to 2 in favor, then voted 5 to 4 in favor. The Governor saw which way the wind appeared to be blowing, and he vetoed the Board of Health's decision.

Today, Pratt has over 20,000 names of anti-abortion people in his files. He has thousands of other voter-interest-identified names. He has a TRS-80 Model III, which is twice as powerful as the older Model I. Did the system cost him $50,000? Hardly. The computer, the special program for political mobilization (and mailing list maintenance), and the rapid-output printer can be purchased for under $7,000. For $11,000, you can buy the whole system with a letter-quality (typewriter appearance) printer, which pumps out 400 letters (seemingly personally typed) per hour. Over 10,000 labels per hour can be printed out by this combination; the less expensive system puts out 5,000 per hour.

The secret is the program that operates the Radio Shack microcomputer. The computer revolution is coming, but the weak link, so far, is the quality of the programs (software) that operate the computers. The hardware—the actual computer—is over powerful, but the programs are the equivalent of the "98-pound weakling" in the old Charles Atlas comic book advertisements: the 200-pound bully— $50,000 to $250,000 minicomputers—keeps kicking sand in his face. But the program Pratt uses is the equivalent of Atlas' "dynamic tension": it gets the weakling into shape, fast. It costs as much as the computer, but it makes the computer far more powerful—so powerful, in fact, that the computer can challenge systems that cost five times as much. This is not a promised technology; this is a present-day reality. You can buy it off the shelf. But you have to know where the shelf is; nothing generally available comes close, and your local Radio Shack dealer isn't aware of its existence. (Neither is your political opponent, unless he has read this book, or the limited-circulation computer magazine, *Desktop Computing,* in which I have told this story.)

It was designed by a man with over a decade of experience in political direct-mail operations. I agree with his claim: for local politics, there is no existing program available today which offers a faster pay-off in political leverage than this. It has potentially revolutionized local politics. Of course, it will have imitators. The technology for a whole new ball game is now available in cheap computers. But the "dead box" isn't enough. You need the program. For the moment—and this may be true for several years—this new program is the Cadillac. The company is selling it only to conservative organizations and politicians. The big-government people will have to design their own.

Now it becomes possible for local groups to gather names and addresses on a systematic basis, not to put into labor-intensive, inefficient card files, but to put into a home computer. It can't be stolen easily. It's private. It's quiet. Nobody needs to know who is mobilizing the troops. But as the file grows, the political effects will be noticeable.

I'll say it here: *without this system, or something comparable, you won't be able to compete politically by the end of this decade* (unless a nuclear war blows the technology out of existence). This is the wave of the future. The "quill and card" methods of political mobilization are dead. We just haven't buried the body.

This technology, for the moment at least, transfers *enormous political leverage* to underfunded, but ideologically dedicated, local groups. The cost of delivering an effective message to voters—targeted, screened voters—has been reduced in one huge leap. But few people know it yet. That's why I hope and pray that those of you who are plugged into the hard-money newsletter industry will take advantage of a technological gift that the opposition hasn't seen yet. They see what Viguerie has done with national mailing lists. They understand national elections. But we still have the advantage locally. County governments may be corrupt, but they are not so ideologically committed to the doctrine of salvation by legislation. We can live with local corruption; what we cannot live with is Federal salvation. We need to build a *political buffer* between us and the Federal bureaucrats, *before* the wave of bureaucratization hits this country.

The tax protest movement will pick up on this new technology very rapidly. But why not all other movements geared to rolling back Federal powers? I know that not every one of you can organize a political movement. I'm not suggesting that each of you has a moral obligation to drop everything and buy a computer. But what I am suggesting is that many of you know good men, or are members of local groups that can use this new technology. You can alert these people to a tremendous breakthrough for local, and even statewide, political action. Why don't you do it? This company sells *political power*.

The developers of this new software have sat down and produced a *cassette tape* describing what they have done, how the system has worked in actual situations, and what the potential is. *There is no* *reason why my readers shouldn't send them $2 and get that tape.* If nothing else, it will explain the nature of the technological revolution that toppled a dozen very unhappy U. S. Senators in 1980's rout. Not many conservatives know the story. This tape tells you how it was done. But it also tells how you, or people you influence, can do the same thing—and not just every four years, but on a regular basis, law by law, protest by protest. You can buy it and pass it along. If you think all this makes sense, write a check for $2, or put $2 in an envelope, and mail it to

Political Data Systems
5881 Leesburg Pike, Suite 204
Falls Church, VA 22041

Another important use for this program is the creation and maintenance of mailing lists for newsletters, direct-mail selling, and similar applications. Available programs in this field are not very powerful. Churches, study groups, small businesses, and others can put this computer system to good use. Businessmen could even write off its cost as a business expense, and then use it after hours, on a rental (or gift) basis, to help local political candidates.

The program can even be used for church evangelism. I have discussed this at length in my essay in *The Journal of Christian Reconstruction* (Winter, 1980-81): "Symposium on Evangelism." This is available for $5 from the Fairfax Christian Book Store, 11121 Pope's Head Rd., Fairfax, VA 22030.

Conclusion

Societies that are characterized by moral uncertainty and drift become the prey of the entrenched minorities, especially those that control the central bureaucratic posts (including the universities), for it is the vanguard of the political elite which seemingly controls the society. *But the character of the people determines the character of the elite which controls the seats of power and prestige.* This is why a man can be a prophet of gloom and doom, yet acknowledge the existence of a temporary economic boom. Men have chosen the politics of envy, and until they change their minds and remove their hands from their neighbors' wallets, all the griping about bureaucracy will amount to nothing more than a temporary slowdown in the size of the bureaucracy. The issues of the age are moral, not economic, and principled men are presently losing that battle. Are you prepared for a 20-year or 30-year political battle? This is what it will take.

The battle can be won. I think it will be won, but I don't expect to see it turned around in this century. Pragmatists respect external results, and until our pragmatic culture sees that bad principles produce ghastly consequences, the drift will continue. But we should do our best to swim upstream. If nothing else, the exercise will do us good.

Appendix A

RECOMMENDED SURVIVAL LISTS FOR
SELF-SUFFICIENCY PREPARATION

Joel M. Skousen*

The following recommended checklist contains essential and *convenient* supplies and equipment which *may not* be found in many homes. We have attempted to avoid listing common household items, except in the stockpiling lists which itemize products which would be difficult to manufacture in the home. The equipment list for workshops is a complete general listing due to the fact that many American homes do not have any shop facilities at all, and may wish to develop one. Explanatory notes and justifications are indicated by an asterisk next to the listing where the reason for an item's inclusion may not be understood commonly. Blank spaces to the left of each item is for the marking of quantities desired and already stocked. NOT LISTED IN PRIORITY.

Household Equipment

Quantity Desired	In Stock	
_____	_____	Manual Carpet Sweeper
_____	_____	Kerosene Lamps**
_____	_____	Propane Lanterns
_____	_____	White Gas Lanterns
_____	_____	Portable Rechargeable Battery Lights
_____	_____	50-hour Candles
_____	_____	Dish Drain
_____	_____	Rack
_____	_____	Portable Ice Chests
_____	_____	Catalytic Heater

*This appendix appears in *Survival Home Manual,* available from Survival Homes, 4270 Westcliff Dr., Hood River, OR 97031 ($10.95). Skousen provides personal survival counselling. I strongly recommend this book.
**Three types of lanterns listed are essential to make use of whatever fuel is available.   252

_____	_____	Heat Venting Fireplace
_____	_____	Fireplace Pokers
_____	_____	Tongs
_____	_____	Swinging Arm Pot Holder for Fireplace
_____	_____	Griddle and Grate for Use in Fireplace
_____	_____	Fan
_____	_____	Manual Typewriter
_____	_____	Manual Adding Machine, Calculator
_____	_____	59 Gallon Plastic Water Barrels (for water storage indoors, with pump attached)
_____	_____	Manual Clothes Washer Wringer
_____	_____	Scrub Board
_____	_____	Dual Stationary Tubs
_____	_____	Clothesline Pins
_____	_____	Soap
_____	_____	Candle Molds
_____	_____	Portable Chemical Toilet
_____	_____	Toilet Plunger and Flex-Cable Clean Out
_____	_____	Manual Treadle Sewing Machine (heavy duty commercial type)
_____	_____	Sewing Scissors
_____	_____	Utility Shears
_____	_____	Seam Ripper
_____	_____	Grommet Punch and Press
_____	_____	Conventional High Quality Sewing Machine (Have special pulley-machine to convert it to a treadle if necessary. We recommend ones of European manufacture only.)

Household Products to Be Stockpiled

_____	_____	Hand Soap
_____	_____	Liquid Detergent
_____	_____	All Purpose Cleaner
_____	_____	Cleanser
_____	_____	Laundry Detergent

_____	_____	Disinfectant
_____	_____	Rubbing Alcohol
_____	_____	Bleach
_____	_____	Oven Cleaner
_____	_____	Toothpaste
_____	_____	Baking Soda
_____	_____	Toothbrushes
_____	_____	Dental Floss (unwaxed)
_____	_____	Razor Blades or Straight Razor
_____	_____	Electric Razor Replacement Blades
_____	_____	Toilet Paper
_____	_____	Paper Towels
_____	_____	Seeds
_____	_____	Paraffin Wax (for sealing jams and preserves; for candles; and lubricant)
_____	_____	Cheesecloth (for sewing, cooking, cheesemaking, dehydrating)
_____	_____	Aluminum Foil
_____	_____	Waterproofing for Cloth
_____	_____	Silicone Leather Seal
_____	_____	Neatsfoot Oil (for keeping leather soft and pliable)
_____	_____	Absorbant Cotton Rags
_____	_____	Writing Paper
		Supplies
_____	_____	Pens
_____	_____	Ball Point
_____	_____	Felt-Tip
_____	_____	Fountain
_____	_____	Pencils
_____	_____	Inks
_____	_____	Eraser
_____	_____	Manual Pencil Sharpener
_____	_____	Drafting Equipment
_____	_____	Typewriter Ribbons
_____	_____	Glue
_____	_____	Steel Wool (all grades for scrubbing, cleaning, polishing)

———— ———— Brooms
———— ———— Scrub Brushes
———— ———— Mops
———— ———— Shoelaces

Home Appliance Repair Parts
———— ———— Belts
———— ———— Bags
———— ———— Cords
———— ———— Lights
———— ———— Switches
———— ———— Tubes
———— ———— Misc.

———— ———— String (various types and grades)
———— ———— Cord
———— ———— Rope
———— ————   Utility Hemp
———— ————   Polyester
———— ———— Household Oil
———— ———— Insect Repellant

Fire Extinguishers
———— ————   Chemical
———— ———— CO_2
———— ————   Water
———— ———— Matches
Tape
———— ————   Electrical
———— ————   Transparent
———— ————   Heat Duct
———— ————   Fiber Backed Packing Type

Sewing Supplies
Bolts of Cloth:
———— ————   Denim
———— ————   Flannel
———— ————   Nylon Rip Stop
———— ————   Light
———— ————   Medium
———— ————   Heavyweight
———— ————   Canvas Duck
———— ————   Wool
———— ————   Cotton Knit

_____   _____   Corduroy
_____   _____   Unbleached Muslin
_____   _____   Upholstery Material

_____   _____   Thread (Commercial sized spools)
_____   _____   Polyester
_____   _____   Nylon Polyester
_____   _____   Carpet, Button Cord
                      Needles
_____   _____   Machine
_____   _____   Hand-Type
_____   _____   Upholstery
_____   _____   Leather
_____   _____   Knitting
_____   _____   Crochet
_____   _____   Yarn
_____   _____   Patterns
_____   _____   Bobbins
_____   _____   Seam-Ripper
_____   _____   Zippers (all types and weights up to 48
                         inches)

_____   _____   Buttons
_____   _____   Snaps
_____   _____   Hooks, Eyes
_____   _____   Hand Sewing Awl

_____   _____   Tailor's Chalk
_____   _____   Hand Loom
_____   _____   Wool Cards (for carding wool)
_____   _____   Spinning Wheel for Yarn
_____   _____   Dyes
_____   _____   Polyester Batting (for quilts and window
                         lining)

Food Preparation Equipment

_____   _____   Wheat Grinder (Stone Mill)
_____   _____   Manual Corn/Wheat Mill
_____   _____   Dehydrator
_____   _____   Juice Extractor
_____   _____   Pressure Cooker Canner
_____   _____   Microwave Oven
_____   _____   Bread Mixer

_____	_____	Meat Slicer
_____	_____	Meat Grinder
_____	_____	Apple Peeler
_____	_____	Potato Peeler
_____	_____	Potato Ricer
_____	_____	Corn Cutter
_____	_____	Meat Saw
_____	_____	Manual Can-Opener (Wall-Mounted)
_____	_____	Hand-Held
_____	_____	Food Thermometer
_____	_____	Hand-Held Egg Beater
_____	_____	Flour Sifter
_____	_____	Strainers
_____	_____	Collander
_____	_____	Butcher Knife
_____	_____	Meat Cleaver
_____	_____	Serrated Knife
_____	_____	Paring Knife
_____	_____	Skinning Knife
_____	_____	Utility Knives
_____	_____	Ice Pick
_____	_____	Butter Churn
_____	_____	Molds
_____	_____	Press
_____	_____	Cream Separator
_____	_____	Cheese Press
_____	_____	Vegetable Slicer and Grater
_____	_____	Rotary
_____	_____	Hand-Held
_____	_____	Blender
_____	_____	Cast Iron Cookware
_____	_____	Skillet
_____	_____	Pots
_____	_____	Griddles
_____	_____	Grills
_____	_____	Canning Jars
_____	_____	Lids

		Rings
————	————	Bread Pans
————	————	Oversized Bowls (for kneading by hand)
————	————	Yogurt Maker
————	————	Sour-Dough Starter Unit
————	————	Hand Crank Ice Cream Freezer
————	————	Dutch Oven
————	————	Wooden Cooking Utensils
————	————	Monarch Combination Wood/Electric Stove
————	————	Kerosene Stove (Portable)
————	————	Gas Grill

Clothing and Apparel Stockpile List

		Shoes
————	————	Extra Soles and Heels
————	————	Athletic Shoes
————	————	Boots
————	————	Rubber Knee
————	————	Leather High Tops
————	————	Foam Insulated High Tops
————	————	Low Top Hiking
————	————	Steel Toe Working
————	————	Climbing Boot
————	————	Cross Country Ski Boots
————	————	Socks
————	————	Wool
————	————	Cotton
————	————	Polyester
————	————	Underwear
————	————	Cotton
————	————	Thermal
————	————	Wet Suit
————	————	Trousers
————	————	Denim
————	————	Polyester
————	————	Cotton
————	————	Wool
————	————	Shirts
————	————	Wool
————	————	Cotton
————	————	Polyester

_____	_____	Sweaters
_____	_____	Hats
_____	_____	Knit
_____	_____	Felt
_____	_____	Cotton
_____	_____	Gloves
_____	_____	Knit
_____	_____	Leather Insulated
_____	_____	Cotton Work
_____	_____	Leather Welding
_____	_____	Leather Work
_____	_____	Coats
_____	_____	Nylon-Down (Goose Prime, Cotton if Subject to Abrasion)
_____	_____	Cotton Duct (outer shell dacron insulated for work)
_____	_____	Camouflage
_____	_____	Nylon, Waterproof
_____	_____	Nylon Windbreaker
_____	_____	Towels
_____	_____	Sheets
_____	_____	Twin
_____	_____	Full
_____	_____	Queen
_____	_____	King
_____	_____	Pillow Cases
_____	_____	Wash Cloths
_____	_____	Hand Towels
_____	_____	Blankets
_____	_____	Wool
_____	_____	Quilts
_____	_____	Cotton
_____	_____	Pillows
_____	_____	Extra Mattresses
_____	_____	Belts
_____	_____	Leather
_____	_____	Woven

Medical Supplies and Equipment

_____	_____	Stretcher
_____	_____	Sphygmomanometer (to take blood pressure)

_____	_____	Stethoscope
_____	_____	Curved Scissors
_____	_____	Bandage Scissors
_____	_____	Long Tweezers
_____	_____	Straight Locking Forceps
_____	_____	Curved Locking Forceps
_____	_____	Pointed Scalpels
_____	_____	Curved Scalpels
		Thermometers
_____	_____	Oral
_____	_____	Rectal
_____	_____	Enema Equipment
_____	_____	Bed Pan
_____	_____	Water Bottle
_____	_____	Ice Pack
_____	_____	Splints
_____	_____	Sling Material
_____	_____	Bandages
_____	_____	Padded
_____	_____	Roll
_____	_____	Triangular
_____	_____	Elastic, Self Adhering
_____	_____	Disposable Gloves
_____	_____	Sutures
_____	_____	Gauze
_____	_____	Patch
_____	_____	Roll
_____	_____	Disposable Drapes
_____	_____	Surgical Tape
_____	_____	Athletic Tape
_____	_____	Ipecac Syrup (to induce vomiting)
_____	_____	Powdered Activated Charcoal
_____	_____	Baking Soda
_____	_____	Ammonia Capsules
_____	_____	Rubbing Alcohol
_____	_____	Antibotic Ointment
_____	_____	Aloe Vera Burn Ointments

_____	_____	Snake Bite Kit
_____	_____	Safety Pins
_____	_____	Tongue Depressors
_____	_____	Long Cotton Swabs
_____	_____	Tracheal Insertion Tube
_____	_____	Hypodermic Needles
_____	_____	Tourniquet
_____	_____	Surgical Mask
_____	_____	Antiseptic Soap
_____	_____	Catheter
_____	_____	Ear, Eye, Nose, and Throat
		Examination Light
_____	_____	Oxygen Respirator

Shops, Tools, Machinery, Equipment, Supplies

Metal Working Equipment

_____	_____	Portable Generator
_____	_____	Engine Lathe Plus Accessories
_____	_____	Milling Machine
_____	_____	Precision Grinder (for tool making)
_____	_____	Metal Cutting Band Saw
		Floor Model
_____	_____	Portable Saw
_____	_____	Drill Press
_____	_____	Sheet Metal Punch
_____	_____	Sheet Metal Bender
_____	_____	Sheet Metal Cutter
_____	_____	Anvil
_____	_____	Vise
_____	_____	Pipe Threader
_____	_____	Copper Pipe Cutter
_____	_____	Flaring Tools
_____	_____	Bender
_____	_____	Portable Drills
_____	_____	Portable Disc Grinder
_____	_____	Air Hammer
_____	_____	Chisel
_____	_____	Arc Welder
_____	_____	Gas Welder
_____	_____	Spot Welder (including band saw blade
		weld)

Automobile Machinery

_____	_____	Hydraulic Floor Jack
_____	_____	Jack Stands
_____	_____	Valve Grinder
_____	_____	Cylinder Hone
_____	_____	Electric Winch
_____	_____	Hydraulic Press

(Electronic Testing Equipment is listed Electronic Gear.)

Woodworking Machinery

_____	_____	Shopsmith Combination Machinery (lathe, drill press, table saw, jointer, etc.)
_____	_____	Table Saw (one horsepower minimum)
_____	_____	Radial Arm Saw (one horsepower, 12 inch blade)
_____	_____	6-Inch Jointer
_____	_____	Surfacing Planer (12 inches minimum)
_____	_____	Compressor (150 PSI minimum)
_____	_____	Tank
_____	_____	Spray Gun
_____	_____	Hose
_____	_____	Staple and Nail Guns
_____	_____	Chain Saw (Gasoline)
_____	_____	Circular Saw
_____	_____	Wood Vise
_____	_____	Belt Sander
_____	_____	Disc Sander
_____	_____	Vibrating Sander
_____	_____	Flex-O-Sander
_____	_____	Band Saw
_____	_____	Jig Saw
_____	_____	Shaper
_____	_____	Router
_____	_____	Power Plane
_____	_____	Reciprocating Saw (Commercial type)
_____	_____	Sabre or Scroll Saw

Hand Tools (Metal, Wood)

Hammers
  Ball Pein
  Brick Layer's
  16 oz. Straight Claw
  16 oz. Curved Claw
  20 oz. Long Handle
  Tack
  Sledgehammer
  Rubber Mallet
  Plastic Mallet
  Blacksmith Hammer

Saws
  Rip
  Crosscut
  Back Saw
  Coping
  Keyhold
  Hack
  Bow
  Pruning
  Two-Handled Crosscut Log Saw
  Hole Saws

Mechanic Tool Sets
  American
  Metric

Screwdrivers
  Phillips
  Flat
  Offset
  Flexible
  Screwdriver Bits for Electric Screw Drill

Pliers
  Locking
  Needle Nose
  Electrical
  Fencing
  Channel Lock
  Cutting
  Rod and Bolt Cutters

——————— ——————— Pop Riveter

——————— ——————— Chisels
——————— ———————   Cold Steel
——————— ———————   Wood
——————— ———————   Lathe Tools
——————— ——————— Nail Sets
——————— ——————— Allen Wrenches
——————— ——————— Forging Tongs
——————— ——————— Auger Brace and Bits

——————— ——————— Drills
——————— ———————   Twist
——————— ———————   Auger
——————— ———————   Carbide Tipped
——————— ———————   Speed Bits
——————— ———————   Expandable

——————— ——————— Tin Snips
——————— ——————— Grinding Wheel Dresser
——————— ——————— Slide Hammer, Dollies (auto body repair)
——————— ——————— Ear and Eye Protectors
——————— ——————— Pipe Wrenches
——————— ——————— Dial Indicator, Holding Apparatus
——————— ——————— Calipers
——————— ——————— Dividers
——————— ——————— Metal Straight Edes
——————— ——————— Scrapers
——————— ——————— Bearing Pullers

——————— ——————— Steering and Knuckle Separator
——————— ——————— Hand Planes
——————— ——————— Spark Lighter
——————— ——————— Floor Jack, Scissors
——————— ——————— Feeler Gauges
——————— ——————— Manual Winch
——————— ——————— Micrometers

——————— ——————— Wire Gauges
——————— ——————— Thread Gauges
——————— ——————— Tap and Die Sets
——————— ———————   Natural Fine
——————— ———————   Course
——————— ———————   Metric

_____	_____	Tire Pressure Gauge
_____	_____	Valve Spring Compressor
_____	_____	Tail Pipe Expander
_____	_____	Hand Truck
_____	_____	Caster Platforms
_____	_____	Ladders
_____	_____	Step
_____	_____	Extension
_____	_____	Cement Trowels
_____	_____	Floats
_____	_____	Screeds
_____	_____	Mixer

Electronic Equipment

_____	_____	Three Pronged Plug Adapters
_____	_____	12 Volt Test Lamp
_____	_____	110 Volt Test Lamp
_____	_____	Line Cord Energizer
_____	_____	Volt-Ammeter (For Car)
_____	_____	Volt-OHM-Ammeter (Electronic Circuits)
_____	_____	Soldering Equipment
_____	_____	Portable Work Lights
_____	_____	Nicad Battery Recharger
_____	_____	Lead Acid Battery Recharger
_____	_____	DC/AC Inverters
_____	_____	Communications Equipment (Radios)
_____	_____	All Frequency Receiver-Scanner
_____	_____	CB
_____	_____	Short Wave SSB
_____	_____	Hand-Held Portable
_____	_____	Hand Crank Generator
_____	_____	Fire Alarms
_____	_____	Intrusion Alarms
_____	_____	Oscilloscope
_____	_____	Auto Diagnostic Unit
_____	_____	Timing Light
_____	_____	Tac-Dwell Meter
_____	_____	Scope

——————— ——————— Exhaust Gas Analyzer
——————— ——————— Variable Resisters

Transportation

——————— ——————— Two Cars (same model and year so that
                   parts are interchangeable)
——————— ——————— Van or Pick-Up Truck with Camper
——————— ——————— Four-Wheel Drive Vehicle
——————— ——————— Trail Type Motorcycle
——————— ——————— Manual Powered Boat (Portable)
——————— ——————— Sea-Going Boat (if on Seacoast)
——————— ——————— Trailer and Hitch

Vehicle Supplies

——————— ——————— Radial Tires, Valves
——————— ——————— Snow or Desert Tires
——————— ——————— Chains
——————— ——————— Fire Extinguishers
——————— ——————— Gas Cans
——————— ——————— Tow Chains
——————— ——————— Jumper Cables
——————— ——————— Oil
——————— ——————— Filters
——————— ———————   Oil
——————— ———————   Gas
——————— ———————   Air
——————— ——————— Anti-Freeze
——————— ——————— Brake Fluid
——————— ——————— Hydraulic Fluid
——————— ——————— Grease

——————— ——————— Fan Belts
——————— ——————— Fuses
——————— ——————— Water Pump
——————— ——————— Radiator
——————— ——————— Spark Plugs

——————— ——————— Points for Electronic Ignition
——————— ——————— Distributor
——————— ——————— Coil
——————— ——————— Lights
——————— ——————— Radiator Hoses

———	———	Brake Linings, Pads
———	———	Shocks
———	———	Bearings
———	———	Pistons, Rings, Valves, Bearing Inserts
———	———	Gaskets
———	———	Carburetor Kits
———	———	Locking Gas Cap
———	———	Wiper Blades
———	———	Spark Plug Wires
———	———	Voltage Regulator
———	———	Alternator
———	———	Battery (Charged and Stored Dry Liquid Separate)
———	———	Keys
———	———	Vulcanizing Repair Kits
———	———	Universal Joints
———	———	Steering Joints

Shop Supplies To Be Stockpiled

———	———	Metal Cutting Tools and Bits
———	———	Files
———	———	Single Cut
———	———	Double Cut
———	———	Rasps
———	———	Different Shapes
———	———	Saw Blades
———	———	Coping
———	———	Hack
———	———	Circular Saw Blades
———	———	Stone Cutting
———	———	Metal Cutting
———	———	Abrasive Blades
———	———	Saber Blades
———	———	Band Saw Blades
———	———	Jig Saw
———	———	Scraper Blades
———	———	Grinding Wheels
———	———	Sharpening Stones
———	———	Welding Rods
———	———	Solder, Brazing Material

_____ _____ Rolls of Plastic
_____ _____   Clear
_____ _____   Black
_____ _____ Butane Tanks
_____ _____ Circular Hose Clamps

_____ _____ Wire
_____ _____   Fencing
_____ _____   Electrical
_____ _____   Cable
_____ _____ Hinges
_____ _____ Latches
_____ _____ Padlocks
_____ _____ Transistors

_____ _____ Resistors
_____ _____ Diodes
_____ _____ Reostats
_____ _____ Switches
_____ _____ Relays

_____ _____ Vacuum Tubes
_____ _____ Repair Parts for Appliances
_____ _____ Metal Rods, All Types
_____ _____ Sheet Metal, Most Common Gauges
_____ _____ Plate Metal
_____ _____ Aluminum, Brass Solid Stock

_____ _____ Hardwoods
_____ _____ Softwood in Dimensional Construction
    Lumber
_____ _____ Plywood
_____ _____ Particle Board
_____ _____ Glues
_____ _____   Epoxy and Cloth
_____ _____   White
_____ _____   Powdered
_____ _____   Plastic
_____ _____ Sandpaper (nos. 80, 100, 120, 220, 400, 600)
_____ _____ Sanding Belts
_____ _____ Sanding Discs

_____	_____	Screws
_____	_____	Phillips
_____	_____	Machine
_____	_____	Bolts, Nuts (All Sizes)
_____	_____	Nails
_____	_____	Common
_____	_____	Box
_____	_____	Finish
_____	_____	Cement
_____	_____	Tacks
_____	_____	Brads
_____	_____	Roofing
_____	_____	Staples
_____	_____	Tape

OUTDOOR SURVIVAL EQUIPMENT

Emergency Survival Escape Kit

Large Military Duffel Bag (All supplies packed herein)
Two Quart Canteen Water (Sealed, Pre-Sterilized)
Food Pack
   Wheat
   Rice
   Flour
   Protein Powder, Pills
   Vitamins
   Bouillon Cubes
   Dried Jerky Meat
   Peanut Butter
   Honey
   Dehydrated Fruit
   Freeze-Dried Casserole
   Dried Beans
   Powdered Milk
   Powdered Eggs

Collapsible 5 Gallon Water Container (Plastic)
Lightweight Cook Kit
Utensils (Plastic)

Cooking Utensils (Metal)
    Spoon (Large)
    Utility Knife
    Fork
    Spatula
Fire Starter Tinder Package

Solar Water Distiller including 4 Ft. Sq. Sheet Plastic, Drinking
    Tube, and Collection Cup and Dish
Large Plasticized Nylon Tarp
Lightweight Backpacking Tent With Rainfly
Goose Down Sleeping Bag
Goose Down Coat
Poncho (Nylon)
Waterproof Matches
Compass
Maps

Straightedge
Pencil
Paper
Whistle
Mirror, Signal
Swiss Army Knife
Large Bowie Knife (by Western Cutlery, the best all-around knife.
    Serves as hatchet, machete, and fire knife)

Toilet Paper
Fishing Line (25 lb. test)
Lures (depending on local area)
    Hooks
    Sinkers
    Spinners
    Flies
Snare Wire
Animal Trap

First Aid Kit
    Athletic Tape (must be Cotton-Backed, Perforated, to stick to
    all skin conditions)
    Gauze
    Clean Rags
    Soap (Liquid)

Tweezers
Scalpel
Padded Bandages (Large and Small)
Small Scissors
Small Lock Forceps
Disinfectant
Aloe Vera Burn Ointment
Antibacteria Antiseptic
Dissolving Sutures
Snake Bite Kit
Tournequet
Cotton Swabs

Nicad Rechargable Flashlight
Space Blanket
Aluminum Foil
Water Purification Tablets
Magnifying Glass (High powered for starting fires)
Nylon Shroud Line
¼ Inch Diameter Goldline
Carabiner
.22 Caliber Pistol, or "Take Down Rifle," or High-Powered
    Pellet Gun
One Change of Underwear and Socks

Additional Snow or Mountain Gear

Boots, Winter Insulated
150 Foot Mammut or Goldline Rope
Carabiners and Breakbar
Pitons, Ice Screws
Binoculars
Ice Ax
Piton Hammer
Crampons
Mechanical Rope Ascenders
Pulleys
Sunglasses

Skin Sun-Shield Cream
Nylon Webbing
Snow Shoes
Cross Country Skies
Car Tire Chains

Ensolite Sleeping Pad
Portable Kerosene Stove
Small Fuel Container
Leggings

Additional Outdoor Equipment List

General Use

Aluminum Boat or Canoe with Oars/Paddles
Large Family Tent with Floor and Rainfly
Backpacking Tents
Aluminum Frame Cots (Stacking Types)
Portable Toilet
Camouflage Clothing
Pack Frame
Portable Stools

Canteens, Thermos
Portable Stoves
    White Gas
    Propane
    Kerosene
Day Pack
Portable Freezer
Poncho

Archery Equipment
    Smallest Possible Compound Bow
    Aluminum Hunting Arrows
    Fishing Arrow and Line Kit
    Practice Arrows
    Wrist, Finger Guards
    Quiver
    Extra Strings
    Arrow Making Kit
Guns
    .22 Caliber Survival Rifle, Take-Down
    .22 Pistol
    .45 Auto Pistol
    .270 or Higher Caliber Auto Rifle with Scope
    12 Gauge Shotgun
Bullet Molding Equipment

Reloading Equipment
Cleaning Equipment
Supplies:
    .22 Cartridges
    Powder
    Primers
    Brass
    Wadding
    Shells
    Bullets

Bicycles
    Tubes
    Tires
    Brake Pads
    Pump
    Spokes
    Extra Rims
    Carriers
    Generator/Lights

Folding Shovel
Hatchet
Ax
Bow Saw

Appendix B

RECOMMENDED PORTFOLIOS

The problem with trying to construct an "ideal portfolio" is that there are too many variables. Such differences as age, geographical location, present and future income streams, existing capital, occupation, skills, educational background, health, experience in the markets, goals, family size, and liquidity all vary, person to person. Yet all these factors, and many more, are important in determining what a person should do with his money. This is why people need professional economic and legal counsel. But since you expect information in print, I will attempt to set forth a few basic strategies that I think will do most readers considerable good. These should be considered only in terms of the overall economic framework that has been presented in the main chapters of this book. What I did not want to do was to write down these portfolio recommendations before I had set forth my basic premises concerning the nature of the modern political economy. You know them if you've read the book.

I want to begin with the fundamentals. These are steps that you need to take before you even consider the relevance of the portfolios I have drawn up. *Everyone* needs to consider the following steps, unless he has already taken care of them. If you have neglected any of them, get them taken care of immediately. You can go on to the subsequent plans once these are behind you.

Life Insurance

You need annual renewable term insurance. You need a lot of it. If you are under age 50, you need at least three times your annual income, plus enough to pay off your estate taxes. The older you get, the less you need in relation to your income, but the more you need for estate tax purposes.

Very important: your wife should own the policy. She should pay the premiums with funds drawn on her own personal, private, exclusive checking account. This gets the pay-off out of your half of the joint estate when you die. The policy should be renewable to age 70. It should also permit you to reduce the coverage as you grow older.

The full story on life insurance, and how the public suffers from

274

systematic misinformation provided by the insurance industry, is provided in a unique pair of audio cassettes produced by Lewis Bulkeley, a former insurance salesman. Anyone who has *any hesitation* about term insurance as the *only* kind of life insurance to pay for needs to order this set of tapes. Bulkeley has seen some people save over $3,000 in premiums the very first year of switching to term. You can order your set for $25. If you can't save *twice* the cost of the tapes in premium savings in the *first year,* just send back the tapes for a 100% refund. Ask for the tapes on life insurance. Mail your order to

Privacy Publications
107 W. 6th St.
Tyler, TX 75701

Companies that provide inexpensive term coverage include Old Line Life, United Investors Life, First Pyramid Life, Executive Life, Philadelphia Life, Empire Life.

If you have a closely held corporation, you should consider having the firm purchase term insurance to cover liabilities and taxes. You may need professional counselling. One source of such counselling is a lawyer, whom I recommend:

George Williams
Linscomb & Williams
5909 W. Loop South, Suite 500
Bellaire, TX 77401
(713) 661-5000

Will and Trust

You need to get your estate in order. I strongly recommend reading B. Ray Anderson's book, *How to Use Inflation to Beat the IRS* (Harper & Row, 1981). Then take the book to your accountant and your lawyer. Make sure each of them reads it—on *his own time,* of course—and then get back to him to get your estate in order. I recommend that the person who sets up your trust—and you probably need at least one trust, no matter how poor you are—*not* be named the trustee or executor of your estate. Read Norman F. Dacey's book, *How to Avoid Probate* before you sign on any dotted line written by a lawyer. It won't take very long to read Dacey's book, and it could save you a lot of grief later. Be sure that your life insurance policy is owned by your heir(s), and that the proceeds go directly to the heir(s), and *not* to the estate.

I strongly recommend the use of trusts for the children. You and your wife can give jointly up to $6,000 a year to each trust without paying a gift tax. The trust(s) can purchase term insurance on your life, with the proceeds going directly to the trust(s) at your death.

Your will, trust instruments, and burial instructions should be in your wife's safe deposit box, not yours. She should give you her will and instructions to put in your safe deposit box. *Never use a common box.*

You should review your will and trust(s) at least once every five years, just to make certain that they are up to date. Tax laws are constantly changing. Be sure you know what will happen to your estate when you die.

It seems hard to believe, but if you take care of your estate, and you buy the proper amount of annual renewable term life insurance (not deposit term, or whole life, or ordinary life, or paid-up life insurance), you will have done more for your family's financial future than any other two comparably simple steps you can take. Most people die intestate (without a will), and most heirs are left with less than three year's income. Take care of these two items, and the risks to your family will drop sharply. Do this, and this book has paid for itself.

Food Storage

This is expensive, since it involves a cash purchase a year in advance. Most of us are not used to buying a year's supply of food in one transaction. We are certainly not used to buying a year's supply for every member of the family. Yet this is as important a step as you can take. It will scare most people off. They will not do it even if they can afford it. Why not? Because it involves admitting to oneself that the basic supply lines in this nation could be temporarily disrupted. This casts a doubt on everyone's future. Therefore, most people will recoil from this suggestion.

For those of you who have taken the mental step of questioning the envy-burdened delivery system, a food storage program makes sense. The cheapest way to buy a pile of food is to buy wheat from Walton's in Montpelier, Idaho. Then you buy a regular dehydrated food storage program from Arrowhead Mills (Simpler Life Foods) in Hereford, TX, or from one of the other firms. Make sure you stock up on fruits, vegetables, peanut butter, cheese, and other tasty items, since *food aversion* is a major problem. You will also need vitamins to compensate for what your body will burn up under stress. Your system may reject a diet of 100% dehydrated food, so be sure to have canned goods, especially water-packed fruits, to help make the transition easier. Rotate these canned goods, replacing them as you eat them.

A supply of *non-hybrid seeds* is important. This frees you from having to return to the seed companies to buy hybrid seeds (which do not reproduce in your garden). You can buy them from Burpees or other seed companies. You can also buy cans of mostly non-hybrid seeds from SI, P.O. Box 4727, Carson, CA 90479, or call, toll-free, at (800) 421-2179. Non-hybrid seeds are also available in sealed plastic jars. For information, write to Privacy Publications, 107 W. 6th St., Tyler, TX 75701.

First Aid Kit

A good first aid kit is difficult to locate. They can be very expensive if suitable for institutional use. I recommend that every family have a high quality emergency first aid kit, and you should be willing to spend $400 to $500 on one. In a major crisis, this investment could save lives. Even in a crisis more conventional than those surveyed in this book, a good first aid kit is vital. Every business should own one. The best mid-priced kit I have seen commercially available is the unit sold by Privacy Publications. You should write for complete information. It sells for $420.

Privacy Publications
107 W. 6th St.
Tyler, TX 75701

This is the kind of item that nobody buys because everybody wants to think about less disconcerting subjects. I recommend buying precisely those items that everyone takes for granted in "normal" times, but which are literally life-and-death items in periods of crisis.

Arson and Burglary

Owning several fire extinguishers is important. Obviously, every home should have several battery-operated smoke alarms. You would think that every home does. Does yours?

Every home needs deadbolt locks on the doors to the outside. Every home needs windows that can be locked from the inside, to make it difficult for burglars. No home needs bars; any home in a neighborhood so dangerous that bars are necessary on the windows is too dangerous a neighborhood to live in. People get trapped inside homes that are on fire; then bars are a disaster.

A very good source of information on home protection devices is Joel Skousen's book, *Survival Home Manual*. Order for $25 from

Survival Homes
4270 Westcliff Dr.
Hood River, OR 97031

Geography

This is the toughest recommendation of all. You probably need a safer residence. You need a place with its own independent water system, preferably with a fast-flowing creek. You need at least two 500-gallon fuel tanks in the ground, both filled with diesel or gasoline. You need at least a 3,500 watt power generator, preferably diesel, preferably one that operates at 1,800 rpm (not higher). You need invisibility from the highway. You need sufficient natural water to grow a garden. You need to be out of the clutches of municipal unions. You may need a bomb and radiation shelter, depending on where you live. You need to be at least 70 miles upwind from any missile site or Strategic Air Command base. And in all likelihood, you will need a job.

That is the main problem: a job in a safe place. But there are other problems: distance from relatives, distance from cultural centers, distance from visible neighbors, distance from schools for the children. Nevertheless, the single most important thing to search for in a time of rampant envy is a safer location outside the city limits of any major metropolitan area—preferably at least a 40-minute drive outside. Commute, if necessary, but make the move.

I have covered this topic earlier in the book, but I wanted to reaffirm my commitment to geography as a primary topic. Crimes against property are on the increase everywhere, including rural areas, but violent crimes are far more common, per capita, in the major urban centers.

You need, at the very least, a few acres to get away to, possibly with an older 12 by 70 foot mobile home on it, with a well and fuel tanks. Maybe you can buy land from a relative or friend in a rural area. But you ought to make the investment now, before all his friends and other relatives make a mad dash to his farm.

Portfolios

Age: 25-35

You're starting out, you have a growing family, you're getting used to your job, you don't have much money to invest, and what money you have should probably go into buying a home and starting a weekend family business. Your investments should be confined primarily to a food storage program, a minimal medical kit, tools, and a few gold and silver coins. At this stage of your career, your chief assets are youth, health, enthusiasm, and a willingness to innovate. You have income from your job, which must be regarded as a source of basic necessities. Your "free time" is never free at this stage. It must be converted into future assets or spent with the family in doing something other than watching T. V. The T. V. could cost you your future if you become addicted to it. If necessary, pull the plug.

Rather than stressing the familiar "survival" investments, let me focus on real estate, since buying a home and possibly a rental property or two should be the key investments, mainly because they can often be purchased with little or no money down. Read the book by Robert Allen, *No Money Down,* or Al Lowry's *How to Become Financially Independent by Investing in Real Estate.* Even more important, become fully familiar with the master in the field, A. D. Kessler, whose new book, *A Fortune at Your Feet* (Harcourt, Brace, Jovanovich, 1981; $10.95), unquestionably is the premier introductory study. Subscribe to his monthly magazine, *Creative Real Estate,* Box 2446, Leucadia, CA 92024 ($33/yr; 12 issues).

For the small investor, a very useful book is Mark Skousen's *High Finance on a Low Budget* (P. O. Box 611, Merrifield, VA 22116: $10), now available as a Bantam paperback.

What I am most concerned about is that young families have decent housing in safe communities, plus food storage and medical equipment. They need friends and good neighbors, too. Cultivating reliable friends is as important as cultivating a garden. Both are part of a long-range program for evading the effects of envy.

Having said this, what about any remaining assets? First, and most important, try not to get involved in a corporate retirement or profit-sharing program. Better to be self-employed, and start a personally managed Keogh retirement program. Second, if you are already in such a corporate program, minimize your contribution as much as possible. If your company gets into trouble, you could lose your job and your retirement fund. You could get hit with a double whammy. Also, don't trust third-party investors to manage your financial future. You have the greatest incentive to do well with your own funds. You are responsible for preparing for your own future, not some committee.

What should you do with your money, *after* you are in a decent home, *after* you have moved to a safer area, and *after* you have purchased a food storage program? Here is my recommended portfolio:

$10,000	*$20,000*
20% in silver dimes (pre-1965)	20% in silver dimes
20% in small Krugerrands (1/10 & 1/4 ounce)	20% in small Krugerrands
10% in rare (numismatic) coins	10% in rare coins
$100 in copper pennies	$200 in copper pennies
25% in a money-market fund	10% in money-market fund
remainder in tools, library, and education	10% in switch fund
	remainder in tools, library, and education

Should you have more assets than these (doubtful), then concentrate on real estate or your secondary occupation. Your investment portfolio at this stage should focus on *yourself:* capital that increases in value because of your *active management.* The above portfolios are essentially "buy and hold" portfolios, but in the early years of your career, you should put the bulk of your assets in your skills and personally managed assets. You invest where your strengths are. *Take more risks,* since you are young enough to recover from errors, and also because any successes will multiply over time as you build up skill and self-confidence in your abilities. *Self-confidence* is crucial to anyone who wants to build a financial future for himself.

Age: 36-45

At this stage of life, you should be pretty well secure in your job. You know your own skills and earning power in your company. You should be using your higher income to establish a smoothly operating business for yourself.

If you had read and followed the advice in the preceding section over the last ten years, you would be well on the way to total financial independence. But, then again, you probably wouldn't have bought this book. You would already have known the strategy of success. So I am writing from the assumption that you are just discovering that there are alternatives to your present way of life.

Your first step is to reduce your personal, consumer debt load to an absolute minimum, preferably zero (assuming you have a good credit record, which is a kind of reserve asset for a crisis). You need to cut your expenses by 10% or 20%, in order to increase your investing. You must forego luxuries, even though your friends may be more comfortable. This is imperative. If you can afford to move into a nicer neighborhood, don't. Take the money and buy an income-producing rental property instead. This is extremely important at your age: resist the signs, costs, and personal debt load of upward mobility. Postpone upward mobility for another ten years, when your wealth will enable you to make a debt-free upward leap in comfort. All debt at this stage must be either survival debt or investment debt. The only exception is your home. Buy older cars that have depreciated. Don't buy the best gadgets available. The secret of success at this stage: *deferred gratification.*

You need to work at least 60 hours a week. The 40-hour work week is for 9-5 wage earners who are going to die broke, or even worse, try to survive in a crisis when broke. You cannot afford to adopt the mentality of the 40-hour week worker. Those extra hours will become the foundation of your future financial success.

The earlier you begin this program, the better. I suggest small town real estate: 3-bedroom, bath-and-a-half homes. This is almost always the best way to invest in real estate. There will always be families needing homes. These homes are liquid. You can always sell them to the existing renters if the government imposes rent controls.

You should regard your present job as a source of income that offers you some security while you spend time creating a new family business. It lets you eat, takes your mind off your income problems, and frees up time for entrepreneurship. Work in a 40-hour a week job, so that you can devote 20 more to self-employment. Don't let your main job squeeze time out of you. You need extra time for future financial survival. Only if they'll let you transfer to a small town should you give your employers over 40 yours a week.

If you are in a big city, start looking for a way out. Sell your nicely appreciated home, get a smaller or less expensive one 40 minutes outside the city. Sink a well, buy a diesel generator, get some fuel tanks in the ground, and start making preparations for the crises. Use extra money on the sale of the city home to buy the equipment—home-supporting equipment—in the rural area.

If necessary, take a cut in pay and transfer within your company to a safer area. If this isn't possible, work like crazy to find suitable employment elsewhere, or to build up your family business fast enough to let you get out.

Do whatever you can to get out of your corporate pension or retirement fund. Make a deal: quit, get rehired as an independent contractor, and get your money. You need that depreciating capital. Don't let the company tie it up for 20 more years, or even 30. You need that money now, while there is still some purchasing power left in it.

All of the specific advice to younger men applies to you, except that you should have more capital in reserve, to compensate for the lost years. You must reduce your personal indebtedness, unless you are using the money to buy a food storage program. Downgrade your visible prosperity. Let the Smiths try to keep up with the Joneses. Get out of that rat race.

You need to decide where you will go in a crisis. Then start buying up small town real estate in that area, so that you will have a source of income if the roof caves in on the cities. In any case, this type of property should appreciate well, though perhaps not so fast as urban real estate does—until the crisis, anyway.

Be out of debt. I cannot stress this strongly enough. Debt ties you to existing patterns, existing jobs. It reduces your personal flexibility. *Debt ties you to the status quo.* Your only debt should be on your home and your real estate property, and this, in turn, should be located in the area to which you intend to travel within the next few years. *Debt makes you too cautious. You need to be innovative now, as never before.* The older you are, the less debt you should have.

You need liquid assets for any major change in your career or geographical location, but your goal should be to reduce that liquidity as soon as possible, either by purchasing "hard" assets, or by plunging capital into your family business. *Liquid assets are temporary;* either you spend them, or they depreciate with the inflation.

Here is my recommended portfolio for people in this age bracket:

$20,000	*$40,000*
20% in silver dimes	20% in silver dimes
20% in small Krugerrands	20% in small Krugerrands
10% in rare coins	10% in rare coins
$250 in copper pennies	$250 in copper pennies
20% in a money-market fund	15% in a money-market fund
10% in switch fund	15% in switch fund
remainder in tools, library, and education	15% in "penny" gold mining shares
	remainder in tools, library

Remember, these are semi-passive investments. I am not including your real estate investments, or food storage. If you have a closely-held corporate retirement program, remove the rare coins from the list, and put the coins in the retirement portfolio. Add a no-load mutual fund, or energy and resource stocks, to the regular portfolio. The stock market is for people with liquid assets of $40,000 or more, except possibly for high-risk, but potentially high-profit stocks. The best stocks for crap shooting are the North American "penny" gold and silver mining shares. The possibility of 4-to-one or even ten-to-one returns in three years is there, if gold doubles (as of 1981).

Age: 46-65

At this stage, it is imperative that you make plans for building an independent business. You are approaching your years of highest productivity. You must invest in yourself, so that your strength is not dissipated in working for somebody else.

The same principles of investing apply to this age group as apply to younger ones, except that there is less time remaining to build up capital. Presumably, those in this age group do have capital to draw upon. If not, then go to the capital bracket of the immediately preceding age bracket, and duplicate the recommended program. The portfolios for ages 36-45 are applicable, if you have under $50,000.

The primary focus has to be retirement. A person has to be ready to switch out of his present occupation, if it is a standard, salaried job. If necessary, sell the home, pay the capital gains taxes, buy a smaller home in a safer town, and put the extra money into the recommended portfolio. Don't have too much capital tied up into your own bricks and mortar. Another possibility: move out of your present home, rent it (thereby establishing it as an income-producing property), and then swap it for two less expensive properties, thereby deferring the capital gains taxes (Section 1031 of the Internal Revenue Code). Then buy a modest home in the small town. At age 55, you can sell your existing home, and take up to $100,000 of profit without having to pay any tax. This is a major source of investment capital. Or, finally, borrow on your existing home and use the money to invest (illegal in Texas, unfortunately). This is a last-resort measure.

Psychologically, it is difficult for anyone to make major changes in his life style, income level, occupation, and geography. Obviously, it is difficult for people who have established roots in a community. The older you are, the more you can afford to move (since your debt level should be dropping steadily), yet it is more difficult psychologically. Unquestionably, you will have great pressure put on you by friends and relatives to "stay put," to go on about your life as if the ravages of envy were not eating away the foundations of the free market economy. Nevertheless, if you make the move to a safer area, especially a rural area, you may find that you will be a lifesaver for your relatives. Your property could become a haven in a crisis.

Ask yourself this question: If the cities erupt in violence, including paralyzing strikes by municipal workers, where would I try to flee? Wouldn't you try to locate a friend or relative in a safe part of the country? Isn't it easier to go where you're known, rather than to drive randomly into a rural area, where you have no contacts to ease the transition? This is why someone in your family had better make the move before fear strikes at the stomachs of the public. What you can afford to do today may be impractical, or too expensive, or even illegal later on.

Safe real estate, preferably out of debt, for a homesite and guest facilities, is the premier investment avenue for any age group, but especially for those whose age makes them less resilient. As you get older, you generally lose resilience as you gain in experience and capital. It is best to move while moving is relatively simple. Set up a haven for those close to you. A simpler life style is preferable, once you have passed the years of highest productivity. Make the move before you pass through those high-productivity years.

The same basic strategy holds: safe homesite, debt-free (because you can afford to be out of debt at your age), plus some income-producing rental units (debt-free, if you can afford it), plus semi-passive investments that appreciate with the inflation.

$50,000	*$100,000*
20% in silver dimes	20% in silver dimes
20% in small Krugerrands	20% in small Krugerrands
10% in rare coins	$500 in copper pennies
$500 in copper pennies	15% in rare coins
15% in switch fund	15% in "penny" gold mining shares
15% in "penny" gold mining shares	10% in money-market fund
15% in money-market fund	10% in growth mutual fund (no-load)
remainder in tools, library	5% in oil & gas shelters
	remainder in tools, library

As you grow wealthier, a larger percentage of your assets can be risked in the stock market. The reason is simple: you have taken care of the major threats to your capital: inflation, social unrest, and war. This frees up other capital for somewhat more conventional investing. The stock market is only for rich people, since they can afford to lose their shirts. The poor man cannot afford to be in the market, as the performance of the market, 1966-80, should have taught everyone. The Dow Jones Industrial Average, adjusted for losses in purchasing power, is down (April, 1981) well over 60% since early 1966, whereas gold and silver coin investments are up more than ten to one. The "experts" told the little guy to avoid "speculative" gold and silver coins. The experts lost their shirts and their customers' shirts. Those who ignored the "wisdom" of the experts made very good profits.

Age: 66-?

Your main enemy at this stage is your body. Health crises destroy the capital of the aged. This is when you have to watch your diet carefully—if you haven't done so for years—avoiding the obvious killers like heavy drinking and smoking. Adopt a program of exercise. Your mental health is also crucial. At this point, you have made it or you haven't. If you're retired, and you are dependent on passive income, *the crisis is now.* You must get active again. You must not depend on passive income to support you. You cannot afford to be sick. That's the horror of the envy-dominated world of inflation which your generation voted for. The bills are coming due, and you are in no condition to pay.

It does little good for me to list what you should buy with your $150,000 life savings. Most people will not have this kind of capital at this stage in their careers. The middle class, when it retires, is unable to defend itself unless it goes back to work. This is the critical issue: *employment*. Don't worry about your capital until you are again gainfully employed. If you aren't working, you had better be a master investor-speculator, since your capital is unlikely to sustain you throughout your old age.

One very important decision which must be made in advance is this: When should you have the physicians send you home from the hospital? The final illness in the final year of life absorbs whole lifetimes of savings. Can you decide when to insist on going home? If you are incoherent, your heirs, probably guilt-ridden, will squander your life's savings to keep you alive. The most important single thrift decision that any older man can make is this one: to decide to die at home in his bed, cheaply. Your heirs had better know your feelings about this. If your goal is the preservation of family capital, you will have to decide when the physicians have done all they can for you (and to you), and it is time to go home.

Once you cannot earn a living, the most important decision you can make is *to abandon money*. Take your assets, convert a substantial proportion of them to durable consumer goods, meaning household goods, repair parts, a stocked freezer, and all those items you know you will use daily. Buy them now (preferably in bulk to get the discount), store them in several places (safety against theft), and put everything else you own into gold, silver, rare coins, and a money-market fund for emergencies. Be ready to spend money on items you know you will use in the future. The idea is to escape the ravages of inflation. You have to reduce your dependence on money income as never before. You need goods, not paper money income.

You have got to get younger people around you. Get them to live near you, if possible, or move to their area if they are in a safe location. You can swap: they help do physical labor you can no longer do, and you help support them by paying them in gold or silver coins. It's a good way to transfer wealth between generations. Each side gets something, so neither side is resentful. Neither envy nor guilt should be allowed to dominate such exchanges. Try to fit yourself into their productive system by doing minimal labor, or have them fit into yours, if you have the capital to finance their employment. It depends on which side is better able to afford to hire the other. But the idea is to become mutually beneficial.

Bet on youth. It's what you don't have any more. Unless you're a financial or industrial titan, you're going to have to face reality: *you are about to be replaced*. In fact, even the giants are about to be replaced, though they don't have to admit it to themselves. Aging bull elephants eventually wind up in the elephant burial grounds. They can go out gracefully, or they can be driven out by younger, stronger, more innovative bulls. Those who have dominated others all their lives find it difficult to sit down, shut up, and take orders from younger people. But they have no choice: they are about to depart anyway, and they might as well get used to it. You have been replaced. You can face up to this and make the best of it, or else you can dissipate your capital and your future by pretending that you are still in the driver's seat. You're not in the driver's seat any more. If you have built an empire, it is going to be inherited by others. If you have built a reputation, it is going to be interpreted by others. You are no longer in power, and you had better grow old gracefully.

If you built your personal fortune or empire on assertiveness, bowling over the opposition, dominating others, manipulating others, and always getting your own way, you have a lot of enemies. You also have a lot of bad habits. If you are really wealthy, you may get away with such behavior in old age, but your heirs will strip your inheritance clean—the way that vultures strip a carcass. If you have spent your life throwing tantrums, you are now at the mercy of those who have put up with your arrogance, insolence, and childish behavior. You have dished out arrogance; you are now sustained by mercy. It is not a pleasant end for the arrogant leader who failed to recognize his own mortality. Now, at best, he finds himself tolerated, or even patronized, by those who he thinks are his inferiors. But they are not his inferiors; they, being merciful, are his moral superiors, and age has brought this out plainly. This is why personal habits have got to be mastered early, before they become virtually impossible to overcome. Younger men will replace you eventually; get ready to go out gracefully now, while you still have your wits about you.

These are hard words, but they are truthful words. Facing the reality of age is not pleasant, but that's life. You must ally yourself with younger, stronger, more innovative men, so that both you and they can make the most productive use of your respective talents. I am a great supporter of apprenticeship programs. Here is one way of passing on knowledge, and earning income at the same time. If you have productive skills worth learning, you have a major capital asset.

Co-operation is the source of strength for the aged. They must be mature. The behavior of the immature can no longer be profitable for them. This is why inter-generation co-operation is important to cultivate early.

My recommended investment portfolo is colored by my concern about people's health and age. A healthy man who is still physically active can follow the guidelines for the man who is 46-65. Others should trim their financial sails accordingly.

$100,000	$200,000
35% in durable consumer goods	25% in durable consumer goods
35% in silver & gold coins	35% in silver & gold coins
10% in rare coins	15% in rare coins
10% in a money-market fund	10% in "penny" gold mining shares
$500 in copper pennies	10% in a money-market fund
remainder in tools, library	$500 in copper pennies
	remainder in tools, library

Conclusions

For the long haul, the best investments are as follows: a second occupation, and income-producing real estate, primarily single-family homes, but also small farms (sharecropped for 30% of the crop during crisis times). Also, a safe homesite that has independent water, power, and honest neighbors is worth more than any standard investment. Food and tools are crucially important. Beyond this basic "portfolio"—which is more than most people can afford, debt-free, in any case—we come to the semi-passive investments: gold bullion coins, silver bullion coins, rare coins, "penny" gold and silver mining shares in North America, money-market funds, no-load mutual funds, and so forth. It is my strongly held opinion that *most people cannot afford to be in "investment"markets unless they have covered the "survival" markets with the bulk of their assets.* Gold and silver coins are a kind of substitute survival asset, which presumably can be converted into survival products on demand. But in a real crisis, as the Germans found out in 1923, gold and silver are very poor survival substitutes. The actual life-giving products are what count during a true crisis. There is no effective substitute for the actual survival assets.

Readers may have noted that I am not fond of foreign bank accounts. I see them as useful for people who trade commodities in foreign nations, or who have sufficient capital to invest enough in gold and silver so that they could live for at least ten years outside the U. S. on money telexed to them in their foreign haven. Not many people can afford this sort of foreign investment. Also, if a nuclear war hits Europe, there is no guarantee that people will be able to gain access to their Swiss bank accounts. Someone living close to Canada, and who also owns Canadian land and a retreat property, or who has close relatives in Canada, might consider putting half his bullion coin investments in Canadian maple leaf gold coins, storing them in Canada. This is just about the only exception I would make to my lack of interest in foreign banks.

You are going to have to rethink your first principles of investing. I have devoted only this appendix to the details of an investment portfolio. I have put it at the end of the book. The important aspects of this book relate to the *overall investment strategy,* not to the specific portfolios. The portfolios are only for general guidelines. Some people may be able to design far more useful portfolios for themselves once they have mastered the general strategy of envy-avoiding, envy-escaping investing. People like model portfolios, not because they actually follow them to the letter (or number), but because they provide concrete examples of the possible applications of general investment strategies. The specific portfolios provide a glimpse of an ideal series of investment tactics—none of which may fit any one person's actual needs. Model portfolios are made to be tinkered with.

You must make up your mind first. Then you must *act* in terms of what you have decided concerning the drift of American society. *You must act before your stomach tells you that you must act.* When your stomach catches up with what you have learned in this book, a lot of other stomachs will also have caught up. This means that the price of taking action will be far, far higher. In a perceived crisis, people will begin to pay attention to survival information. There is a lot of such information around. Best-sellers have dealt with many of the issues raised in this book. Howard Ruff, Doug Casey, and Jerry Smith have all had best-sellers forecasting a series of inflationary and economic crises. People have read these books. Millions of copies have been sold. *People have not yet taken action in terms of what they suspect may be true concerning the U. S. and world economies.* When they perceive that crises are here, they will rush out to do what millions of other Americans have also read about. When they do, it will be too late for buying in at today's prices.

In 1973, price controls on meat created a shortage. Bill Pier, who owns SI, the survival center, ordered dehydrated food from a major supplier. He received delivery the following week. He ordered again the next week. He was informed that he could expect delivery in six months. The supplier had been deluged in one week. There was no war, no true shortage. There was a shortage of meat at the artificially suppressed official, legal prices. There was a perceived shortage on the part of those who knew about dehydrated food storage—a tiny minority in 1973. Yet when their fear drove them to do what they had known that they probably should have done beforehand, it became impossible for all of them to get delivery of the food they had ordered. I am predicting here and now: there will be other perceived crises, and other crisis-generated shortages. When those moments of fear hit, you would be wise to be out of those markets. Be out of them because you are willing to take your capital and act in terms of what you know today. *Buy now, sleep later.*

Appendix C

SUPPLIERS

You need to know which firms can help you in developing your own personal strategy for evading the economic effects of envy. There are a growing number of firms that are "hard money" oriented. I decided to list the firms I believe are reputable in an appendix to my book, *How You Can Profit from the Coming Price Controls* (1977 editions forward). I encouraged Howard Ruff to do the same in his book, *How to Prosper During the Coming Bad Years*. (I did personal telephone consulting for the *Ruff Times* as an independent consultant from early 1977 until the fall of 1979.) Without at least a preliminary list to consult, the "newly initiated" reader may not know where to begin.

I recommend one firm as the best available "one-stop shopping" organization for personal financial guidance. You can get your estate planning work, annual renewable term life insurance (if you ask for it), numismatic coins, and very good prices on investment-grade diamonds. Other firms are good, but if you want to talk with only one outfit, this is the one I suggest:

Financial Alternatives, Inc.
174 Currie-Hall Parkway, Suite 1
Kent, OH 44240
(216) 678-3791

The president, Lyle Loughery, is a fine Christian man, and his integrity has convinced Jewish diamond wholesalers in New York City that he can be trusted. He gets very good prices for his clients as a result of this personal relationship. He has assembled a team of lawyers and accountants to service clients all over the country. So for diamonds, colored stones, estate planning, and rare coins, this firm can get you squared away. The sooner you act, the better.

I am absolutely adamant about the importance of gold and silver coins. They must be in anyone's portfolio. Small investors have a problem, however: How to buy coins in small quantities? For individual coins, there are local coin stores and pawn shops, but these usually have high commissions (premiums) over bullion value. There are two firms that encourage the small investor, and beginners should consider using their services:

C. Rhyne & Associates
110 Cherry St., #202
Seattle, WA 98104
(800) 426-7835
(800) 542-0824 (Wash)

Auric United Corp.
15748 Interstate Highway
San Antonio, TX 78229
(800) 531-5777
(512) 696-1234 (Texas, collect)

Another item that I recommend is an investment manual, *Secrets of Diamond Dealing*. Only people in the "hard money" industry have heard of it. In fact, only a handful of people outside of my subscribers have learned of its existence. It is one of the most ingenious strategies to buying and selling diamonds that I've seen — the first and only book for the small investor. The secret is the jewelry-grade diamond. It is overpriced by at least 100% in any local jewelry store. This manual shows you how to buy at 25% of retail, sell at 50% of retail, and pocket 100% on your investment, time after time. Minimum investment to begin in this business? Under $200, plus a copy of the manual. Interested? Order from:

Vanguard International
106 W. 7th St.
Tyler, TX 75701
($75)

I have no financial relationship with any of these firms, except (in certain instances) as a customer.

Coins (bullion)

Camino Coin Co.
Box 4292
Burlingame, CA 94010
(415) 348-3000

Deak & Co. (many cities)
1800 K St., N.W.
Washington, D.C. 20006
(800) 424-1186

Joel D. Coen
39 W. 55th St.
New York, NY 10019
(800) 233-0868

Coins (rare)

Numisco
1423 W. Fullerton Ave.
Chicago, IL 60614
(800) 621-1339

Financial Alternatives, Inc.
174 Currie-Hall Parkway, Suite 1
Kent, OH 44240
(216) 678-3791

Camino Coin Co.
Box 4292
Burlingame, CA 94010
(415) 348-3000

Manfra, Tordella & Brooks
59 W. 49th St.
New York, NY 10112
(800)223-5818

Food Storage

Arrowhead Mills
P.O. Box 671
Hereford, TX 79045
(806) 364-0730

Walton Feed (bulk wheat)
P.O. Box 307
Montpelier, ID 83254
(208) 847-0465

Survival Products

SI Outdoor Food
& Equipment
P.O. Box 4727
Carson, CA 90749
(800) 421-2179

Survival Center
5555 Newton Falls Rd.
Ravenna, OH 44266
(800) 321-2900

Survival Publications

Josef's Storhaus
800 N. Devine Rd.
Suite 101
Vancouver, WA 98661

"Penny" Mining Shares

Jerry Pogue
National Securities Corp.
500 Union St.
Seattle, WA 98101
(800) 426-1608 (toll-free)
(5,000 minimum to begin)

Mutual Fund (energy & minerals)

Financial Industrial Income Fund
Financial Programs, Inc.
P.O. Box 2040
Denver, CO 80201
(800) 525-9831

Mutual Funds (gold mining)

Golconda Investors, Ltd.
11 Hanover Square
New York, NY 10005
(800) 431-6060

United Service Gold Shares
15748 Interstate Highway
San Antonio, TX 78229
(800) 531-5777

Mutual Funds (telephone switch)

Dreyfus Third Century
(Dreyfus #9: growth fund)
600 Madison Ave.
New York, NY 10022
(800) 223-5525

Energy Fund
522 Fifth Ave.
New York, NY 10036
(212) 790-9800

Pennsylvania Mutual Fund
127 John St.
New York, NY 10038
(800) 221-4268

Guardian Mutual Fund
522 Fifth Ave.
New York, NY 10036
(212) 790-9800

Mutual Funds (no-load directories)

Directory of No-Load
Mutual Funds
No-Load Mutual Fund
Association
Valley Forge, PA 19481
(215) 783-7600
($1.00)

No-Load Mutual Funds
Membership List
Investment Company Institute
1775 K St., NW
Washington, D.C. 20006
(202) 293-7700
(free)

Mutual Funds (no-load growth funds)

Guardian Mutual Fund
522 Fifth Ave.
New York, NY 10036
(212) 790-9800

Mutual Shares Corp.
170 Broadway
New York, NY 10038
(212) 267-4200

Money-Market Funds

Capital Preservation Fund
(T-Bills)
755 Page Mill Rd.
Pala Alto, CA 94304
(800) 227-8380 (USA)
(800) 982-5873 (Calif.)

American Liquid Trust
Box 2121
Boston, MA 02106
(800) 225-2618
(800) 343-2898 (Mass.)

Life Insurance

David Holmes
Life Insurance Truth Society
1 Miletus Way
Cross Plains, TX 76443
(817) 725-6635

David Phillips
1255 W. Baseline #160
Mesa, AZ 85202
(602) 897-6099

Towers & Associates
Heritage Bank Building
Suite 213
Tyler, TX 75711

George Williams
Linscomb & Williams
5909 W. Loop South, Suite 500
Bellaire, TX 77401
(713) 661-5000

Lawyers (trusts, estates)

Michael Ushijima
Law Offices
6300 River Rd., Suite 100
Rosemont, IL 60018
(312) 696-3466

Les Powers
Powers & Therrien, P.S.
811 Summitview, Suite 4
Yakima, WA 98902
(509) 453-8907

Peter Lind
2122—112th, N.E.
Bellevue, WA 98004
(206) 455-4240

B. Ray Anderson
Anderson & Reiser
1926 Tice Valley Blvd.
Walnut Creek, CA 94595
(415) 938-2500

INDEX

THE NEWSLETTER INDUSTRY

One of the most important sources of unconventional information today is the newsletter industry. There are several thousand independent newsletters on the market. What I have in mind, however, is the so-called hard-money newsletter industry. These newsletters are written by people who are convinced that the Federal Government cannot solve its problems, and will capitulate to short run political measures by tampering with the monetary system. Most of these authors think that mass inflation is coming, which will then be followed by deflation and depression. (I am in this camp.) A few others think that deflation is coming before mass inflation ever arrives (their numbers always decline during inflationary stages of the business cycle, e.g., 1971-74, 1977-80, and increase during the "disinflationary" stages, e.g., 1975, 1981).

There are many important advantages of a hard-money newsletter. First, you gain access to "alternative information" sources. Second, you get summaries of conventional information that gets buried on page 24 of the *New York Times*. Third, you get a perspective; "facts" have to be selected and analyzed in terms of their importance. This means you need to pick and choose from millions of facts in terms of criteria of relevance.

Newspapers and magazines are necessary in order to keep up with the overall picture. But the "overall picture" presented by conventional news sources is a painted picture. Sometimes the painters are blinded to important details because of their ignorance of economics, or their outright hostility to economics. (Try to find favorable stories on barter or hoarding during a period of price controls. See if *Newsweek* or *Time* identifies ways for you to participate successfully in the various "alternative markets.") Did they tell you to buy gold in 1971?

There is something else most readers never think about: conventional news sources make their money from advertisers, not readers. Readers are only the means to the end. The end is advertising revenue. Take a look at the advertisers who return again and again to the *Wall Street Journal* and other financial news magazines. If the editors depart too far from what big business regards as "true wisdom", the newspaper will encounter pressures. These pressures involve huge sums of advertising money. This is why you need information from a few other sources that comes to you because you and other subscribers pay for it. The newsletter industry makes most of its money from subscribers; some letters make all of their money from subscription fees. In short, newsletter editors must meet the needs of their subscribers.

The real money comes form renewals, not the initial subscription (which costs a lot to generate). If subscribers fail to renew, profits sag. Newsletters must satisfy subscribers, and only subscribers; advertisers have no clout with editors of independent newsletters.

Naturally, readers have to pay the freight to get truly independent news. A major newspaper may cost only a few cents per day. The cost per page is very inexpensive. Of course it's inexpensive; there are advertisements on every page. So when you "hire" an independent publisher meaning his staff, his research ability, his perspective, and his ability to dig into topics that aren't "respectable," you have to pay for it. I know of one newsletter that costs $15,000 a year. Only big businesses buy it. I know of others selling for $45 a year. It depends on what you want.

When you subscribe to a newsletter, most of your money isn't going for paper and ink to print the newsletter. It's going for research time, experience, and the advertising cost to the publisher of delivering the news about the opportunity of subscribing to his newsletter to potential subscribers. Problem: the average investor thinks in terms of cost per page, not his financial return on his newsletter subscription. This is why average investors make only average returns on their money: they treat information as an almost free good. After all, they think, "we can get news for free in the CBS Evening News." Sure they can! And it's worth twice what they're paying for it: nothing.

Let me offer an example. I offer financial counselling to subscribers to my newsletter, *Remnant Review*. Today, I charge $200 per hour. Back before inflation got so bad, I charged $100 per hour. I once received a friendly letter from a subscriber who asked why I charged so much. He was a professional (radiation scientist, as I remember), and he wasn't paid $100 per hour, he said. Correct; but I am not guaranteed a salary. I am not guaranteed eight hours a day at $200 an hour. But that isn't the real issue. The question is: If I can make you or save you $1,000 or $10,000, are you willing to pay me $200 per hour, until I start running out of ideas that can help you?

This man saw no reason to pay me the money because he was not an entrepreneur, and he probably believed that he had no opportunities to make or save more money than my time was going to cost him. He thought my advice was too expensive because he had no confidence in his own investment opportunities. He did not think my advice could increase his net worth as a salaried man. He was probably correct; as long as he relied on a salary for his financial future, as long as he was unwilling to break out of his shell and start taking some risks to make some money, as long as he was content to be a "cared for" citizen rather than a man who could make his own way even if he lost his job, there was not much I could tell him that would have been worth the counsulting fee. And most people are a lot less innovative than he was; after all, he was a *Remnant Review* subscriber.

I once sat down with a young man who was a very successful speculator. He made $300,000 a year, he said, speculating in commodities. Maybe he did. I gave him one tip that would have saved him at least $15,000 a year, after taxes, for every year that he made $300,000. It was a very simple piece of advice. He should have thought of it, but he hadn't. I had. Let me assure you, he was happy to write me his fully tax-deductible check (since he was an investor who was buying investment advice) for $100.

The average man thinks the way the first man thought. The second man, who was much younger and far wealthier, understood just how valuable accurate information is. The greater your vision, the more you are willing to pay for accurate information. The newsletter industry is aimed at people who have this sort of vision. It is aimed at people who are willing to pay $100 a year to receive information that they value more than $100. They know that this world is not going to give them something for nothing. They are unlikely to make $1,000 or even $100 from news that they get from the CBS Evening News or *Newsweek*. But those who think they are never, ever going to make $100 or $1,000 from something they read about are unlikely to pay $100, tax-deductible, for a newsletter subscription. They are also not going to take any of the steps I have described in this book.

If someone came to you and told you that he had developed a formula for pumping oil out of abandoned wells at a cost of $5 a barrel, would you be willing to consider buying that formula? Assume that you have reason to believe he is honest. He doesn't have the money to develop the equipment needed to pump the wells, but he does have the formula. Would you ask him the following questions? "What kind of paper is the formula written on?" "Is the formula printed with a four-color process?" "What did it cost you to print it up?" "Will I get 200 pages of additional material, including 100 pages of advertisements, along with the formula?" Nutty questions, right? Yet these are the kinds of questions that people ask themselves when they first hear about newsletters. They paralyze themselves with stupid questions. These people would demand a four-color travel brochure and a discount coupon for a local Holiday Inn from someone who wanted to sell them a map to Captain Kidd's treasure. They never ask themselves the obvious question: "Will I get a greater return from the investment information than it costs me to buy and act upon the information?"

The typical investor never asks himself this question. He worries about irrelevant issues. He worries about packaging. If his information sources are not conventional looking, and are not priced to sell on a local newsstand, he just isn't interested. If his next-door neighbor isn't reading it, then he is too scared to take the first step. That's why you can beat the controls. The average guy — meaning your competition — is not going to act. He is not going to see this book. He is not going to buy it if he stumbles across it somewhere, or sees an ad for it. He is not going to do anything innovative or risk-oriented. He is going to go to work, earn his minimal salary, and hope that his employer knows how to make enough money to keep him on the payroll. The average guy is going to remain at the mercy of his employer and at the mercy of the government-regulated economy.

Don't be an average guy.

What newsletters do you need? First, you need letters that are aimed at your specific occupation. You should be upgrading your skills and information all the time. Second, you may need a letter that deals with a particular segment of the market in which you want to become a specialist. Maybe you want to invest in the stock market. Maybe you think it is time to start a small business. Find out what letters are available in each field. One way to do this is through the services of the Select Information Exchange, 2095 Broadway, New York City, NY; 10023. For a few dollars, you can sign up to receive samples and brief subscriptions to dozens of newsletters per field, and, there are several fields to choose from. Write for a free catalog which gives you more details about which newsletter categories are available and which newsletters participate in the program.

Bank newsletters can sometimes be useful, though don't expect to get forthright reports on the looming banking crisis. Morgan

Guarantee Trust and Citibank in New York City publish good letters.

Morgan Guarantee Survey	Monthly Economic Report
23 Wall Street	399 Park Avenue
New York, NY 10015	New York, NY 10022

All of the regional Federal Reserve Banks offer free newsletters. You can get the addresses of the regional banks by writing to the Office of Public Affairs, Federal Reserve Bank, Washington, D.C.; 20551. The best of the publications come from the Federal Reserve Bank of St. Louis: *U.S. Financial Data* (weekly), *National Economic Trends* (monthly), *International Economic Trends* (quarterly), and the *Review* (monthly). Write:

Federal Reserve Bank of St. Louis
P.O. Box 442
St. Louis, MO 63116

A very good source of overall news is the *Daily News Digest,* a privately published weekly newsletter. It gives eight pages of information each week drawn from numerous sources. There is no better single source of "alternative" news reporting. Address: P.O. Box 39850, Phoenix, AZ; 85069 ($147/52 issues). Other newsletters are listed in the appendix on Sources of Information.

Remnant Review

My own newsletter, *Remnant Review,* is different from most other letters. It usually covers one topic per issue. My philosophy of investing and action is that it is better to know why you are taking action; you should know the risks and benefits in advance. I am not in the "guru" business. I don't think you should spend your money just because some "trusted expert" says to do it. The "expert" needs to explain just exactly why you should do it.

Naturally, a newsletter can provide only an introductory survey of information. Only a few readers will follow through on any given recommendation, but anyone who wants to pursue a topic should know where to go. I also think it is best to sell information and only information; thus, I accept no kick-backs or commissions from those companies that I recommend. I make my money on renewals, not kick-backs. I also try to negotiate discounts on products that will save subscribers the cost of their subscription — after-tax money.

I believe that a newsletter should not promise miracles. It should give the readers their money's worth, but not continuous miracles. "Miracle workers" in the newsletter field eventually become desperate people; each issue has to be "hot"; the readers get used to sensationalism. My attitude in subscribing to a magazine or newspaper is this: if I get two or three good ideas per year, or two or three really good investment tips that are suitable for me, in my circumstances, then it has been worth the subscription fee. People who expect a bi-weekly miracle for $95 a year are going to be disappointed — and possibly bankrupted. Sadly, there are a lot of "miracle buyers" shopping around for a financial guru. They want miracles; they buy tragedies.

You have already seen what *Remnant Review* is all about. Many chapters in this book are similar to what was first published as shorter, preliminary reports in the newsletter in previous years. You have already read 29 "sample copies" of *Remnant Review.*

If you had taken the advice in this book when it was first published in *Remnant Review,* you would have bought gold for under $200 per ounce, silver for under $5 per ounce, and single-family homes for under $50,000, even in southern California. Now you will have to pay more. On the other hand, if my strategy is correct, you will be able to sell these items to late-comers for a lot more dollars than you will have to shell out today. Perhaps most important of all, if you do what this book suggests, and what I will write about in *Remnant Review* over the next two or three years, you may be able to "lock in" your position at prices you can afford now, but will not be able to afford if you wait.

If you would like to subscribe for one year, I will let you do it for $80 the first year. Normally, it costs $95, but we send out a free copy of this book to new subscribers. Since you have bought the book, I am willing to let you sign up at a discount, since I won't have to send you another copy of this book. Just clip the tear-off sheet on back of the dust jacket (or enclose the sales receipt for this book), make out a check to Remnant Review for $80 and you will be sent 22 issues over the next year plus a paperback copy of my new investment book, *The Last Train Out.* But you must identify yourself as a buyer of *Successful Investing In An Age Of Envy.* Because of price inflation and the threat of controls, this offer expires on December 31, 1983. We may extend it, but if you are reading this after the cut-off date, you will have to contact us to find out. That's why it pays to act immediately. Write:

Remnant Review
P.O. Box 8204
Fort Worth, TX 76112

You still may be saying to yourself, "But I just can't afford $80." All right, do this much for yourself. Take a look at your life insurance coverage. Then contact both the Life Insurance Truth Society (David Holmes) and David Phillips (for their addresses, just keep reading). See if these two insurance firms can sell you more life insurance coverage for less money than you are paying today. Just send them the following information on a sheet of paper or on a postcard:

> Your date of birth
> The name of your present insurance company
> Your present coverage (dollar amount)
> Your premium fee per year
> The cash value, if any, in the policy
> The interest rate at which you can borrow from it

You may not want to go to all the trouble of looking up this information. (If you don't know it off the top of your head, then you are almost certianly paying hundreds of dollars too much every year for your life insurance, since available rates have dropped sharply since 1981.) If you don't want to look it up, just send them: (1) your date of birth, (2) your present premium fee per year, and (3) the total amount of your coverage. They will send you back some low-cost alternatives. You will be amazed at the results. I predict that you will be able to buy the same amount of life insurance coverage for less money, and save enough to subscribe to *Remnant Review* for a year (tax deductible, if you are an investor), and still put after-tax money in your pocket. In fact, I think you will be able to double your life insurance coverage and still pay for a year of *Remnant Review*.

If I am correct, are you willing to subscribe for a year? After all, if this single tip saves you enough money to buy a year of *Remnant Review*, plus receive my two additional investment books, and still puts money in your pocket, then you can't legitimately use the argument that "you just can't afford to get into the big investment league and subscribe to an expensive newsletter." Remember: *Remnant Review* isn't expensive, if you can save or make more than the subscription fee. I think you can.

In a sense, this insurance deal is a two-way test. First, you can test me. Is my advice valid? Can it save you money? If it does, you will get an idea of how I can help you. If it doesn't, then you can take my advice with a grain of salt — or maybe a whole salt shaker full. Second, you can test yourself. Are you really trying to find ways to improve your financial position? Are you really ready to explore new ways of doing things? Are you willing to invest a stamp, an envelope, and five minutes of your time in filling out a card or piece of paper (not even typed) to save yourself up to several thousand dollars over the next few years in insurance premiums. (That's right: up to several thousand dollars, depending on your present coverage and type of policy.) This is such a sure thing — a "slam dunk" strategy, to use basketball terminology — that if you are unwilling to do this, then you have to ask yourself this question: What am I really trying to accomplish with my money?

Let me give you a specific case. I have to carry a lot of life insurance, to cover tax liabilities, estate taxes, and an estate for my family. (Every family with a husband under age 50 probably needs a minimum of $100,000, since few families in suburbia can be comfortable today on less than $18,000 a year, and inflation keeps rising.) The corporation which publishes *Remnant Review* also has to carry a lot of life insurance on my life to cover taxes and to insure that subscribers get their money back if I die, or access to a substitute newsletter. There is over a million dollars of life insurance coverage on my life. I previously dealt with a company which offered a highly competitive policy in 1980. One of the policies discovered in 1982 by the Life Insurance Truth Society can save me and the corporation about $9,000 in premiums over the next decade. Do you think that was worth a letter and a 20 cent stamp? I thought it was. Write:

Life Insurance Truth Society	David Phillips
P.O. Box 117	1255 W. Baseline, Suite #160
Cross Plains, TX 76443	Mesa, AZ 85202

Conclusion

You know it as well as I do: there are no free lunches. There are hidden costs of so-called free lunches.[1] You had better understand that a government which promises free lunches to one group of voters will get the money to pay for these lunches from somewhere. Usually, the people who pay are the very same people who think they are getting free lunches. My favorite example is the person who thinks he is getting a "free" education for his children, and who is being ruined by property taxes that finance the "free" schools. Another example is Social Security. Inflation is yet another example.

When the government promises you below-market prices for what you want to buy, get ready: you are about to get sheared. If you refuse to get ready, you will be sheared. If you start taking some of the steps I have outlined in this book, you may avoid the shearing.

---

[1] Gary North, "The Hidden Costs of Free Lunches," *The Freeman* (April, 1978).

Therefore, you must act. You must also read more. Then you must act again. You must get your own system of "positive feedback" going: read, act, learn from your mistakes; read, act, learn from your mistakes . . . You have to get moving. If you stand still, you will be a very easy target. If you do nothing, you will almost certainly become a loser. The illusion of Federal solvency will lead you into the same ditch that most voters are already headed for. It will take time and effort, and some capital, for you to get off the highway for economic lemmings which leads into the ditch.

This is a long-term program. I am not selling snake oil. There are no free lunches. What I have described may not be easy, but neither is surviving in an age of envy. If you close your eyes and ears, if you forget what you have now learned, if you walk away thinking, "Very interesting," and then do nothing about it, you will have no one to blame but yourself. Warning: you may turn out to be a very nasty self-critic when things go the way I have predicted, and you haven't followed any of my advice.

And when you begin your controls-beating program, don't forget my motto: "It is better to be rich and healthy than it is to be poor and sick."